T0171525

$$\int\!\mathbf{P}$$

Chasing Matisse

*A Year in France
Living My Dream*

James Morgan

Free Press
New York London Toronto Sydney

*f*P

A Division of Simon & Schuster, Inc.
1230 Avenue of the Americas
New York, NY 10020

FREE PRESS and colophon are trademarks of Simon & Schuster, Inc.

For information regarding special discounts for bulk purchases,
please contact Simon & Schuster Special Sales at 1-800-456-6798 or
business@simonandschuster.com

Book design by Ellen R. Sasahara

Manufactured in the United States of America

10 9 8 7 6 5 4 3 2 1

Library of Congress Cataloging-in-Publication Data

Morgan, James.
    Chasing Matisse : a year in France living my dream / James Morgan.
        p. cm.
    Includes bibliographical references and index.
    1. Matisse, Henri, 1869–1954. 2. Artists—France—Biography.
3. Morgan, James, 1944—Travel—France. 4. France—Description
and travel. I. Title.
N6853.M33M67   2005
759.4—dc22
                                                        2004061605

ISBN 978-1-4391-6724-3

For Beth,
muse, model, mate

And for Blair and Bret,
waifs for art

Nothing is more difficult for a true painter than to paint a rose,
since before he can do so, he has first
to forget all the roses that were ever painted.

—HENRI MATISSE

Contents

List of Illustrations

p. 45
In time, our cozy Paris courtyard turned claustrophobic, and I vowed to capture the feeling in paint.

p. 53
Self Portrait in a Paris winter—deep in existential reflection, or as Beth calls it, The Big Whine.

p. 62
As the stress of holidays and taxes encroached, I found myself missing the hideaway of my art studio back home.

p. 73
Too cold to sketch in cafes, I cheated with a scene from a book by Los Angeles photographer Iris Wolf. She snapped two dogs, but one fell off my page.

p. 83
Belle Île's rocky Port-Coton has been rendered by the likes of Monet, Matisse, John Peter Russell, and me.

p. 95
Once settled in Auray, I translated this sketch of our elegant room at Honfleur's Hôtel L'Écrin into a painting—complete with uneven table.

p. 107
In Corsica, Matisse first experienced the light from the scorching Mediterranean sun—here holding forth over Ajaccio's Îles Sanguinaires.

p. 116
In Little Rock, I studied Matisse's *Themes et Variations* to draw women who didn't look like unconvincing drag queens (convincing was okay).

Prologue

Learning to See

THE CREATIVE LIFE is a wonderful life, which is why it pays so poorly. That's the trade-off for getting to spend your days following your heart instead of the life-sapping dictates of some neurotic middling manager. Who among us needs to go elsewhere for neurosis?

My wife, Beth, and I are both writers. For many years before that I was a magazine editor, a period of my life I refer to as being on the solvent side of the desk. And yet I came to envy my writers their apparent freedom. Their idea of a meeting was a long walk in the woods with a dog. My conversion was inevitable: Friends who knew me in junior high school say I talked even then about becoming a writer. In college, in the home of Faulkner, I studied Hemingway. I admired his direct sentences and his pregnant omissions, and for a long time I didn't even mind his buffoonish posturing. I reveled in his doomed brilliance and wished that I'd been in Paris in the 1920s, sitting in a café on the Left Bank scribbling my own stories into notebooks with covers like swirled marble.

Very quickly, though, life got in my way: at twenty-one, marriage; at twenty-four, career; at twenty-five, fatherhood; at twenty-eight, homeownership. From there it's a short leap to believing that the perfect car, the perfect lawn, the perfect suit, the perfect portfolio are the balms your restless soul aches for.

At age forty-five I escaped the tyranny of the requisite celebrity profile and the numbing predictability of the annual football forecast. (Not so incidentally, I also "escaped" the salaried life.) Newly married, Beth and I moved with her two young daughters into a wonderful old Craftsman bungalow in Little Rock, Arkansas, our dream to live and *write* together. We soon found ourselves turning out celebrity profiles and other magazine pieces in order to pay for the time to fashion screenplays and plot book ideas.

In the meantime, our house became the outer manifestation of our internal life together. We nurtured it, fussed over it, embellished it according to the advice of Beth's late brother, Brent Arnold, who was then a decorator in New York. "Matisse colors, Vuillard patterns," he prescribed. Until then, I hadn't paid much attention to the vivid, decorative canvases of Henri Matisse—and none at all to Édouard Vuillard's soft renderings of highly textured interiors. My idea of an artist was the American Edward Hopper, whose edgy themes of light versus dark told ominous, and ominously recognizable, stories of alienation and domestic silence. But we took Brent's cue, painting our walls in shades of Mediterranean blue, sunflower yellow, ochre, terra-cotta, periwinkle, and our favorite of all, a color that reminded us of geraniums.

For thirteen years we lived and worked there together. Beth wrote a novel that earned her finalist distinction for a Bunting Fellowship at Radcliffe, and a screenplay that won her recognition as a semifinalist for the prestigious Nicholl Fellowship, presented by the Academy of Motion Picture Arts and Sciences. I wrote several books, one of which debuted on the cover of the *New York Times Book Review* and was named, along with another of mine, a "Notable Book of the Year" by the *Times*. All the while our girls were growing up and heading for college, and my own two sons were becoming men with degrees, careers, and wives.

For all the romance of it, however, our life wasn't easy. In any chronicle of the creative process, money and art are Siamese twins; usually, only one can survive. Trying to save both, we amassed a considerable amount of debt—not by buying things, but by buying time.

SOMEWHERE IN THERE I became disenchanted with my old hero, Hemingway. I still appreciated the cleanness of his prose, but the messy matter of the shotgun in the mouth began to supersede the solid sentence. By that time I had lain awake a lot of nights thinking about the creative life. I had vacillated between fearing that it might be the ultimate selfishness ("Get a real job!") to deciding that it was the ultimate generosity of spirit. You can be creative in any endeavor, but *to create* is something unto itself: It's contributing a piece of your soul to the world. It's struggling to find the exquisite beauty in the mystery of life. To pursue a life of creating is to follow the archetypal "hero's journey," a path of danger and hardship leading toward a beautiful goal. The closer I came to the age Hemingway was when he took his life, the more strongly I felt that it was wrong, even uncool, to off oneself just because of a little writer's block. Nor was this a merely intellectual epiphany. Cliché of clichés: Gloom and doom runs in my Mississippi family—along, thankfully, with a sense of humor that recognizes black as a primary color. My grandfather retired to his study and shot himself after lunch on a beautiful spring day in 1924, with the jonquils swaying just outside his window. Not much funny in that, unless you count the man who stopped his car for the fourteen-year-old girl who would become my mother. "Git in, Patti," he said. "Your daddy's done shot hisself."

Our heroes gain complexity as we gain maturity, and today, as I look around at age fifty-nine, my hero is Henri Matisse. This has been building for a number of years, beginning, undoubtedly, with Brent Arnold's admonition about "Matisse colors." I had drawn and painted when I was a child, copying the faces of the presidents from the encyclopedia, then moving on to cowboys, soldiers, and knights, with their guns and helmets and shields, and eventually spending many hours trying to capture the exact shape of Elvis Presley's sneering lips and the way his hair ducktailed just above his turned-up collar. In seventh grade, I often sat in class sketching various examples of the female breast—pointed, cylindrical, voluptuous, *pert*—on notebook paper hidden beneath my textbook. I took an art course in high school, achieving excellence mostly as class clown. Then I put away my pencils and brushes for the better part of the next quarter century.

A year after Beth and I moved into our Little Rock house, I felt an inexplicable urge to paint again. I signed up for a three-month course at the Arkansas Arts Center, my only formal art instruction other than that year in high school. It was good to smell the oils after so many years, but while I could create recognizable shapes I still had no idea what I was doing. I didn't know if I wanted to be a realist or an impressionist (impressionist looked easier). I didn't know if I wanted to paint landscapes, still lifes, or portraits. And even if I'd known my mind, I didn't know how to control the paints so that they would express what I wanted to say. The three-month course was way too short.

After it was over I didn't sign up for another. Instead, I plodded on, hit and miss, all by myself. I also began reading about Matisse and studying his work. But the more I painted, and the more I pored over Matisse's brilliant panels of shape and color, the more importance I attached to one thing the teacher had casually tossed out during one of his art lessons that summer: "Most people don't really see," he said. "They just look. If you're going to be an artist, you have to train yourself to *see*."

For the first time in my life I understood how Monet could continue to paint the same water lilies and Degas the same ballet dancers—and why Matisse inevitably returned to his pewter pitcher, his wrought-iron table, his goldfish bowl, his rocaille armchair. What I suddenly grasped was a concept as profound as it was simple: *It's not the scene, it's the seeing.*

In due time I ran across a galvanizing quote on the subject from Matisse himself: "Everything that we see in our daily life is more or less distorted by acquired habits," he said in 1953, "and this is perhaps more evident in an age like ours when cinema posters and magazines present us every day with a flood of ready-made images which are to the eye what prejudices are to the mind. The effort to see things without distortion demands a kind of courage; and this courage is essential to the artist, who has to look at everything as though he were seeing it for the first time: He has to look at life as he did when he was a child and, if he loses that faculty, he cannot express himself in an original, that is, a personal way."

When I read those sentences the hair stood up on my arms. Here was not only a manifesto for the creative life, but a guide to living itself. Most of society wants to fit us with blinders, and if we accept them, we proceed through the world narrowing, rather than expanding, our focus. Eventually, that view becomes the only recognized view. Even our self-images are beamed back with the sides lopped off.

Maybe that's what happened to Hemingway. His blinders permitted only his mythology to enter, and he was no longer the man in the myth. The day Hemingway committed suicide, I was parked in my high school girlfriend's driveway and heard a radio announcer report the great man's death. Much later I would understand that he gave up because he couldn't see himself with fresh eyes.

Matisse resisted the blinders every day of his long life, and his story is both literally and figuratively that of a journey from darkness to light. Born in the cold northern textile town of Le Cateau–Cambrésis and reared in nearby Bohain, he was a sickly, frail child. His father was a hardware and grain merchant, his mother a milliner. Not knowing what he wanted to do with his life, young Henri went to school and became a law clerk. He found no meaning in it. After taking early-morning drawing classes for a couple of years, he discovered his calling. Eventually he persuaded his parents to let him go to Paris and study art. "From the moment I held the box of colors in my hand, I knew this was my life," he said. "Like an animal that plunges headlong toward what it loves, I dived in. . . . It was a tremendous attraction, a sort of Paradise Found, in which I was completely free, alone, at peace."

But his studio was the only place he found peace. Matisse's art teacher at the Académie Julian told him he couldn't draw and would never learn—and furthermore that he had absolutely no understanding of perspective. For the next decade and a half Matisse struggled, fighting against the art establishment to do the work he felt called to do. He was jeered and ridiculed, and didn't sell a painting for years. At the lowest point of his artistic career, when he and his family were so broke that he was considering giving up painting, Matisse couldn't even persuade his younger brother, Auguste, to buy a canvas for one hundred francs. Auguste bought a bicycle instead, as Henri liked to remind him in later years.

But Matisse persevered. He boldly abandoned the art establishment palette of browns and grays and took up the exuberant and, in his day, dangerous cause of color. He also rejected the dictates of realistic representation, arguing that the way of the true artist was to express what he felt inside. Beyond his purely artistic struggles, he fought to establish the kind of life he knew in his bones that he had to live—a life conducive to making art. It was a life marked by enough leisure to think, enough isolation to act, and enough resources not to compromise.

My favorite Matisse paintings are his interiors, perhaps for the same harmonic reasons he chose to paint them. Many people look at his works and dismiss them as merely decorative, pretty paintings for pretty people. But there was in Matisse—as there is in even his most beautiful paintings—what some of his contemporaries described as "smouldering, sometimes barely contained fires." I was surprised to learn that he was tormented, a chronic insomniac beset by demons. Painting—which he attacked with relentless, seething intensity—was his way of bringing order and beauty to his own rocky universe.

Matisse's relentless need to create inspires me, and no doubt more today than if I had discovered him when I was thirty. Now I can appreciate the courage and commitment he showed, time and again, when circumstances threatened to snatch away his dream. Now I can understand what he meant about learning to see the world the way we did as children.

What I admire about Matisse's story, compared to that of Hemingway, is that Matisse went the distance—he kept finding ways to plumb the new, the creative, the life-affirming within himself. Hemingway quit at age sixty-two, just three years older than I am now. But at age eighty-five, when he could hardly even see to paint, Matisse sat in a wheelchair in the sun-drenched south of France struggling to express himself by cutting shapes of brightly painted paper and pinning them to his studio wall.

AN IDEA BEGAN taking shape one day four years ago when Beth and I were sitting in my upstairs office at home trying to figure out what project I should do next. By then, my easel had begun to vie with my writing desk for my affections. But even as I found solace in applying colors to canvas, I wondered about the very nature and purpose of painting. Writers write to describe, to interpret, to explain, to show how smart they are. Many painters probably paint for similar reasons. But at this stage of my life, which I hope can still squeak by as middle age, I found painting taking me back to someplace I hadn't been in a long time. Painting is pure expression—a preverbal language, the language of feeling we all started with. There's something profoundly therapeutic about mixing primary colors into a harmonious whole; there's also great therapy for viewers able to lose themselves in such harmonies. Exactly what, I wondered, accounted for the healing relationship between tubes of paint and the human heart?

Not that I was any more adept at the language of painting than I am at French. Making a painting is, on some level, the physical expression of living a life. Despite my loftier intentions, I tend to dash them off, usually without preliminary sketches. I don't clean my brushes well enough, even as I'm painting—instead, I might take the brush that was already dipped in viridian and swipe it through the ultramarine, which makes for a portentous sky. And I don't take time to mix the precise color I need. In other words, I'm an amateur painter with a reckless streak. But since when has that ever stopped someone from applying paint to canvas?

With Beth as my muse and model, I planned to spend a few months following in the geographic footsteps of Henri Matisse, setting out to see and paint the world he saw and painted—in the textile marts of his native Picardy; in bustling, romantic Paris; on windswept Belle-Île off the Brittany coast; in sunny Corsica, where he fell in love with the life-changing light of the South; in Collioure, near the Pyrenees, where color became an explosive in his hands; in exotic Morocco, where he found a culture built around a sumptuous inner life; and across the French Riviera to sybaritic Nice and spiritual Vence, where the mature Matisse created so many of his master-pieces.

The idea wasn't for me to try to become even the faintest shadow of the painter Matisse was—I'm guilty of much folly, but not that one. But I did want to concentrate on replacing my bent toward gloom and doom with Matisse's affirming spirit. Beth and I both hoped to draw renewed strength from his commitment to a life of creating. And we especially wanted to co-opt his fierce courage to see without distortion. Finally freeing my pictures of breasts from behind their textbook cover, I planned to sign up for life drawing classes. I even thought of staging a show of my work, hoping that my newfound ability to "see" would translate readily to my canvas.

The more I pondered the adventure, the clearer one thing became: Mere months weren't enough. This was a project worthy of a *life*, not just a quarter year. But even a few months was logistically daunting—what do you do with a teenage daughter at home? With the dog and the cat? With the yard and the flowers and the pollen on the porch? What about all the bills, which were hard enough to manage while we were at home and not running up other expenses? We kept putting off the trip, trying to thread it in between that teen daughter's high school graduation and her leaving for college in Virginia, and then between that and my son's wedding in California.

Sometime in that period, I began to see my own life with shocking clarity. We had lived at the house in Little Rock for a long time. My book about that house, *If These Walls Had Ears*, is the story of the twentieth century told through the struggles of the eight families who had lived in that one Craftsman bungalow in the heart of America. After researching the lives that had been played out within those walls, I wrote that I could walk into any room in the house and see it in multiple dimensions: *"This is where the Armours danced the fox-trot during the Roaring Twenties; this is where Ruth Murphree's heart was broken when she learned her sixteen-year-old daughter had eloped during Central High's lost year; this is where the roller-skating transvestite hippies glided in their giddy circle throughout the downstairs; this is the precise spot where the floor caved in and took the Landers' marriage with it . . ."*

The truth was, I wasn't seeing that way much anymore. So many views had become habit: When I saw the pink morning glow in the Geranium Room, I knew it was 8:30. When I spotted the square of sun on the guest room table, it was 10:30. When my pale yellow office/studio shimmered like a veil of Chinese silk, it was no doubt half past four.

When the decisive moment came, it was as clear as the stars on a winter night. There was almost alignment: Last daughter leaving for college . . . a commissioned book project taking us to France . . . a hint of freedom beckoning. If we really believed in creating as a way of life—if we really believed in Matisse's lifelong striving to see without distortion—how could we simply return to our old existence? On the other hand, we could sell our house, pay off our debts, and stay in Matisse's France as long as we could make it work. Maybe we could finally understand this compulsion that makes people like us do the things that we do.

So the daughter went off to college, the dog and the cat went to visit Beth's mother, and the bills went to our accountant friend Lloyd Cobb; my job was to keep enough money in the pipeline. For the month before we left, Beth and I listened religiously to our CDs of Michel Thomas teaching students how to think out the French language, not just to memorize it. "Je *vaaaiis*," he would say. "I'm on my *waayyyy*."

NOW, AS I write these words, we've been in France a little over two months. The book advance is long since spent; the house still hasn't sold; we've dropped the price sixty thousand dollars; the economy is tanking; war is looming; and our debts are rising like baguettes at dawn.

If I'm going to learn to see without distortion, I need to look clearly at this project. It's either the craziest, most self-destructive dream of the craziest dreamers the world has ever known.

Or it's the most important thing we've ever done.

Part I

LEADEN SKIES

Up in Charcoal Country

WHERE WE COME from is never just a place on a map. The red roads are drawn in the blood of our veins, the green hills in the faith of our earliest hopes and dreams, and sometimes the blue rivers in the wash of our tears. Topography is a fingerprint.

Beth and I left Paris for Matisse's Picardy on a cold blustery Saturday in December, our leased Peugeot 307 wagon loaded down like a gypsy's caravan. This wasn't the car she had wanted us to get. Convinced that a station wagon would be too small, she had pressed for a minivan. At the Arc de Triomphe, a circle of madness that felt like a metaphor, I steered the car around a swath of pavement half a football field wide jammed with cars, trucks, bicyclists, and even Rollerbladers all going as fast as they could, darting this way and that, peeling off inches in front of one another to turn at any number of the spokes that branch out sadistically from the center. All I had to do was glance in my rearview mirror to know that Beth had been right. In our car, there wasn't even a clear sight line to the back window. Instead, I saw shifting mounds of coats, hats, suitcases, book boxes, file folders, computer bags, art supplies, and even our income tax records (we are, hilariously, a corporation). We seemed to be trying to haul our own topography with us.

"We look like the Joads," I said.

"Jwahds," said Beth, correcting my French.

We traversed the usual pattern of modern office buildings, depressing apartment houses, giant discount stores, and factories. Then, in a surprisingly short time, the buildings were gone and cows were grazing. Soon we came upon a sign proclaiming *"Picardie: Terre Fertile."* I had long wondered what Matisse's boyhood world looked like, and now I was in it. Picardy approaching winter was a muddy palette, a somber and cheerless farm landscape as far as the eye could see. It didn't strike me as the celebratory sort of fertility you find in Provence. This looked like hard-work country.

Matisse was born, on December 31, 1869, in the little textile town of Le Cateau-Cambrésis. Eight days later, the family moved a few miles south to Bohain-en-Vermandois, where Monsieur Matisse was taking ownership of a general store. Madame Matisse made hats and created delicate paintings on dishes. Still, Henri and his brother grew up over the family business, which in Henri's years there gradually shifted its focus to seeds, fertilizer, and other supplies for the local beet farmers. In his father's sphere, the social fabric was knit with hard reality, not romance and dreaming. If it took cutting down every single tree in Bohain to keep sun on the beet fields, then you got out the saws.

The irony was that Bohain's most famous industry was luxury

and beauty. In the design and manufacture of fine velvets and silks, cashmeres and tweeds, gauzes and tulles, the weavers of Bohain had no peer. They served the highest end of the Paris and world markets. The House of Chanel sold their masterpieces. Members of European royalty ordered their finest fabrics from Bohain, whose diligent weavers took pride in their renowned ability to seemingly reinvent the definition of beauty with each new pattern. But the weavers' own lives were lived in dark, cramped rooms. Their bodies were bent and their faces pale and gaunt. Alcoholism was rampant.

It's a curious combination, this yoked team of aesthetic expression and unindulgent self-discipline. Beautiful textiles and the airy wider world they furnished would forever play a role in Matisse's work. But so would an extreme and punishing sense of duty.

The largest of the towns we wanted to visit was Saint-Quentin, population some fifty thousand. It was the area business hub where Matisse was educated, worked as a law clerk, and first took art lessons. Late on Saturday afternoon, Saint-Quentin's *centre ville* reminded me of Saturdays in rural Arkansas. The main square, called the Place de l'Hôtel de Ville, was milling with rough-edged farm families doing their weekend shopping and socializing, with townspeople running their pre-Sunday errands, with knots of supercharged teens just hanging out like teens everywhere.

We drove around looking for lodging. Beth had by then formulated her *Rule d'Hôtel*, which held that only inns with three stars or above would have phone plug-ins for her computer; at that point it was merely theory, but the truth of it would be demonstrated time and again in our travels. We also hoped to find a hotel with a gated courtyard. I didn't relish the thought of hauling everything inside every time we stopped.

On a side street a block from the main square, Beth spotted the Hôtel des Canonniers. She checked it out and soon motioned for me to pull the car into the courtyard. "You won't believe this place," she said.

"How much?"

"Sixty-five euros a night."

The hotel was old and beautifully restored, with a handsome

black-and-white stone floor and a sweeping staircase flanked in dizzying swirls of wrought iron. It had once been a home and still felt like one. In fact it was: The proprietor and her family lived there. They had restored this place themselves, through four grueling years. A chic middle-aged woman in a bouclé jacket, Madame Marie-Paule Michel, led us up another staircase to a top-floor landing anchored by a deep red Oriental rug. She inserted an old-fashioned key into a lock and gently pushed open the door to reveal a sprawling space with a slanted ceiling, heavy wood timbers, a refrigerator, stove, sink, dining table, cable TV, queen-size bed with great reading lights, and a sparkling bathroom with a huge deep tub. For a pair of nomads traveling without reservations, we had hit the jackpot. I could hardly wait to fill up the tub and warm my bones.

As we began settling in, Madame told us, in thankfully fluent English, that there was only one other guest in the hotel—a man who was to play accordion at a jazz concert in Saint-Quentin the following night. New to France, I couldn't shake the image of Myron Floren grooving on *Round Midnight,* and made a mental note to be otherwise engaged.

ON MONDAY, WE drove through Bohain to Le Cateau–Cambrésis to visit the newly reopened Musée Matisse. Bohain was about sixteen miles from Saint-Quentin, Le Cateau nineteen miles beyond that. Outside industrial Saint-Quentin, the road quickly settled into muted pasture land, mostly flat, not many trees. Critic and curator John Elderfield searingly described this place in his introduction to *Henri Matisse: A Retrospective:* "It is a cold, inhospitable region of gray skies above a flat landscape with distant horizons, punctuated by church steeples around which cluster villages of dull brick houses." He could have added that the atmosphere pressed down with the weight of solid lead, the impression I had from the view out our car window.

We snaked through Bohain, the main thoroughfare curving sharply twice, and soon we were in country a little more rolling than before. The colors were still earthy—grays, browns, and rusts, deep red weathered-brick barns, touches of matte-toned lichens on black slate roofs like scumbled paint. They evoked thoughts of Matisse's famous *Studio Under the Eaves,* a picture of a small, dark, spare, makeshift art room—but with a far window opening onto bright sunlight. He painted it in Bohain, in the attic of a house he was renting from his father, during the hard winter of 1902–03, when he and his family were forced by circumstances to come back home to regroup. The painting caused a stir when it was later exhibited in Paris, and Matisse himself always considered it one of his best. Most scholars and critics read it as a disturbing portrait of claustrophobia and scarcity, but for anyone who's ever found serenity being closed off in a room alone making art, there are other possible interpretations. The room could also be seen as cozy—protective, even. It must surely have felt that way to Matisse at the time he painted it. Beyond those tight walls his world was bleak. After ten years of art study and few sales, Henri had "given up trying to please anyone but himself," as Hilary Spurling says in her excellent biography, *The Unknown Matisse.* Now, in letters from Bohain, where even beautiful fabrics were primarily a matter of no-nonsense wage earning, he told friends he was thinking of quitting painting altogether. His humiliated father told him that everyone in town took him for an imbecile.

In *Studio Under the Eaves,* hope floats like motes on the light from that one small opening. I imagine Matisse standing at the actual window looking out over the next-door factory to the land where he had come of age. He had always been a dreamer, as a young boy playing knights with his brother and friends in the ruins of Bohain's medieval castle, or attending visiting circus shows and imagining himself performing for the crowds. He established his own toy theater, putting on spectacles—such as the eruption of Vesuvius, in sulfuric blue—for his friends. In time he began studying the violin, an instrument that would show up time and again in his paintings, and he later equated making pictures with performing—with grabbing an audience by the lapels and telling them stories. Had he remained in Picardy, his narrative would've been dark and deeply shadowed, a modulated tale of a measured life. From the beginning he knew he wanted more. "You have first of all to feel this light," he said, "to find it within yourself."

Approaching Le Cateau, we could see a church steeple, which proved to be that of Église Saint-Martin, where Matisse was baptized. The road took us almost through the village, then twisted back left and brought us out on a busy street that sloped downward from the church to the river Selle. To the right at the bottom of the hill was the Matisse Museum.

It was more impressive than we had expected, a former palace, in fact—the Palais Fénelon, once the home of an archbishop. The museum had originally opened in another building in 1952, the aged Matisse himself donating many paintings and drawings. Since then, the collection had wandered from location to location, and had reopened only months before with a grand fete attended by dignitaries from all over France, including Matisse's three grandchildren. This building was laid out in a large U, with a wide brick courtyard entered through an imposing gated arch. Unfortunately, the gate was locked. Ice on the bricks, a sign said.

We wandered around to the back, through an expansive garden, and found an open door. The lobby was full of elementary school kids, all giggly and picking at one another's shirts and hair while their teachers tried to impose decorum. We bought our tickets and began the tour. The special exhibit had been donated by Alice Tériade, widow of the influential editor of *Verve*, Efstratios Eleftheriades—known simply as Tériade—who had commissioned every important artist of the time to design covers and features for his magazine. In the first downstairs gallery were pictures by Picasso, Léger, Chagall, Bonnard, Giacometti, Miró, Gris, Villon, Rouault, and, of course, Matisse.

Upstairs, beginning with samples of delicate Picardy silks, jacquards, and cashmeres, hung Matisse paintings that ranged from his early dark palette, through his shocking Fauvist period, and on to the large, colorful, stunning canvases from his time in Nice. There were many paintings I had never seen before—paintings I didn't even know existed. In another large gallery, this one slightly darkened, his four huge bas-relief sculptures of backs were spaced out on a long wall, like pillars.

In the long upstairs side gallery, we found a class of students solemnly studying, at close range, Matisse's drawings of impressively endowed nudes, both male and female. "Can you imagine that happening at home?" Beth whispered. "Some religious nut would be calling the school and having that teacher's job." The gallery devoted to Matisse's cutouts had become an atelier for second-graders—they were sitting and lying on the floor, filling every square meter, cutting and pasting their own bright paper shapes onto big sheets of white stock. One boy was cutting up more than cutting out, and a stern-eyed guard had stationed himself nearby to make sure no one got truly reckless.

Later, while Beth shopped for books and posters—the latter to tape up around me for inspiration when I was writing—I was staring out the front window as the cutout class made its ragged exit across the courtyard. One of the last in line was the bad boy, who was gesturing in the direction of the upstairs gallery. I glanced over and saw the stern guard, dressed in Matisse blue, standing at the tinted window, watching. The bad boy had a museum directory in his hand, which he first wagged as a tail. The guard was not amused. Then the boy wagged his directory as a horn. The guard remained stoic. Finally, just as he passed through the gate, the boy placed his directory on his middle finger and wagged it back and forth, slowly, repeatedly, until he disappeared behind the wall.

Matisse would probably have liked that kid. A notorious schoolboy cutup himself, he had once spat on the top hat of his art teacher in Saint-Quentin as the man ascended the stairs to class. As a frustrated lawyer's clerk, he would take out his pea shooter and pop passersby with wads of paper. Defiance, for an artist, can be a powerful arm of the creative arsenal.

ON MONDAY AFTERNOON our hotel was filling up with out-of-town businesspeople, and we had to move downstairs to a smaller room. She had a lot of regulars, Marie-Paule said. One psychologist had come in from Paris every Monday night for years. She arrived at 9:30, went out for dinner, came back and turned off her light, and returned to Paris Tuesday afternoon after her work was done.

That evening before supper, I sat in a comfortable chair on the landing above the marble staircase working on my notes. Downstairs, Marie-Paule was preparing for a big family dinner. The occasion was the impending departure, on Wednesday, of her oldest son, Victor, who was moving to California to start management training at the Ritz-Carlton. Marie-Paule was feeling very motherly, a little weepy, and had asked us what Laguna Beach was like. She wondered if Victor would like it, and it him. She and her husband, Gilles, were already making plans to visit him in August. "It'll be the first time ever that we've closed the hotel," she said.

As I wrote, I could hear the clatter of pots and the occasional clink of fine china. Soon Victor's sister arrived with her daughter, whose squeals and laughter infused the house with the palpable feel of family. I strained to hear those same joyous sounds in the story of the family Matisse, but I couldn't make them come to life. Monsieur Matisse, Henri's father, had always expected his older son to take over the family seed business, but as Henri's schooling was drawing to an end the very thought of such a future made the young man physically ill. He collapsed into bed for weeks complaining of stomach problems. Finally, abandoning all thought of Henri's running the family firm, and hoping now just to steer him toward gainful employment, Monsieur Matisse secured his son a job working for a local lawyer.

Henri seemed to do well, and even suggested to his father that he go to Paris for a year and study law. Upon his return he began working for a lawyer in Saint-Quentin. That's when reality set in. He was miserable, and soon fell into bed with a relapse. Thoroughly disgusted, Monsieur Matisse gave up on him. While Henri was recuperating, a neighbor suggested he pass the time copying "chromos" of Swiss landscapes from a then-popular hobby painting kit. Matisse's first picture was *Swiss Chalet with Pine Trees,* and he was hooked. He asked his mother to buy him his own paints, which she promptly did. "From the moment I held that box of colors in my hand," Matisse later said, "I knew this would be my life."

Although he continued to work at the law office, he had found the way to the light. "Other people's quarrels interested me much less than painting," Matisse later recalled, and, without telling his father, he enrolled in an early-morning drawing class at the Maurice Quentin de La Tour Free Art School. Like the École des Beaux-Arts in Paris, to which all such regional schools hoped to be conduits, the de La Tour school stressed strict monochromatic copying of plaster casts. Under Director Jules Degrave, color and painting *en plein air* were prohibited. Matisse bridled under such restrictions.

Then, in the fall of 1890, a new young assistant director, Emmanuel Croize, persuaded Degrave to let him open an academy of painting in an attic above his apartment at 11, rue Thiers. In the buttoned-up, bureaucratic world of academic art, all hell ensued. Live models! Brilliant palettes! Quick color sketches of actual sunsets! Matisse described Croize's class as "an open door," but Degrave quickly slammed it shut, expelling Matisse for painting outdoors. It was the end for him in Picardy. Somehow persuading his father to stake him to study art in Paris, Matisse and a couple of Saint-Quentin classmates left Picardy in the fall of 1891, bound for the city of light.

We, too, had planned to head back to Paris the next day, but as I made my notes I realized that I hadn't seen Bohain and Le Cateau well enough, and Saint-Quentin hardly at all. David Bailin, my art teacher that summer at the Arkansas Arts Center, had told me a story before we left. He had been stumped by one particular large drawing he'd been working on, one in a series of biblical themes. "For years," he said, "I would drive down Cantrell Road in Little Rock and see people in their yards trimming, pruning, preparing for the summer. None of it had particular significance to me. Then when I was working on this piece—I had Abraham over here on the left, startled, and then I had Sarah and their son, Isaac, over here. Abraham was going to be working in a vineyard. But I couldn't figure out what to do with the rest of the picture. So I was driving down Cantrell and saw this man pruning his crepe myrtles *way back,* and I saw all these knobs. Wow! I thought. That's it! I went from having the vineyard lush and full to being all this dead stuff, like the sacrifice of Isaac. It wasn't that I hadn't seen extremely pruned bushes before; it was that now they had a significance within a structure that I was working with." From that story, I understood that it's sometimes *making* art that causes you to see like an artist, rather than the other way around. I needed to look at Picardy, alone, with a sketch pad in my hand.

THE NEXT MORNING, before I set off, I ran into Marie-Paule and told her we would stay another night. As she marked it down in her book, I asked how the dinner had gone the night before. I was surprised at her perturbed response. Both sets of grandparents, aunts and uncles, Victor's sister, her husband and daughter, Victor's younger brother—all had come, she said, and *not one of them had cried.*

On the road to Bohain, I thought about Marie-Paule and Victor. Rural places like this must see going-away dinners like that a lot, with or without tears. In any case, how do you know whom to cry for? Hilary Spurling quotes young Henri telling of waking from a nightmare during his first year studying art in Paris. He had dreamed he was back working in the lawyer's office at Saint-Quentin: " 'I said to myself: That's it, you've had it. I was in a cold sweat, I was terrified. Then my eyes opened. I saw the sky and the stars. I was saved.' " On the other hand, his brother, Auguste, had remained in Bohain and made a tremendous success of the family seed business. When Henri and his family had to come back to Bohain in 1902–03, Auguste was the fair-haired one. He had just gotten married, and Henri's allowance had been cut off so their father could pay Auguste's marriage settlement of fifteen thousand francs—the same amount Monsieur Matisse had expended on Henri's ten-year struggle to find success as an artist.

The topography around Bohain echoed the gentle rolls of Matisse's mother and the furrowed brow of his father. As I drove I found myself thinking about my own father, whose face I see in the land every time I'm in a certain part of Mississippi. He was like Monsieur Matisse. For fifteen of his last twenty years, he had worked for the state of Florida's division of vocational rehabilitation, much of that time heading up the South Florida region. It was a tough job in a tough place, full of office politics and probably more disappointing days than rewarding ones. He groused a lot at night, regularly referring to his boss as "the little bastard."

But having escaped a poor upbringing and gone on to achieve BA and MA degrees, my father felt great satisfaction in helping give marginalized people the tools to become self-sufficient. He had worked hard all his life, and he wanted others to have that privilege. He never played golf or tennis. He never took glamorous vacations. He had fished as a youngster, but gave it up after he moved to Florida, where fishing was a sport. He seemed to have no personal interests besides working in the yard and fixing things around the house. His closest stab at a hobby was a brief pass at upholstering, but what enthusiasm he brought to the pastime sprang from practicality rather than passion—he hated paying store prices for furniture.

Then, in 1971, he suffered a massive heart attack. He was sixty years old. His doctor ordered him to retire. "Get a hobby," the doctor said. Lifting chairs for upholstering was too strenuous now, so my father came up with another idea: He would start painting bottles. As far as his family knew, he had never shown any interest in art. But as soon as he was able, he began driving his yellow Ford wagon out to dumps and bringing home bags and baskets of empty liquor and wine bottles. Mateuse containers, with their wide flat surfaces, were a particular favorite. For larger works, he leaned toward gallon jugs of Paisano wine. We were dumbfounded, but soon the bottles had taken the place of broken chairs in his garage shop, and he had replaced his commercial sewing machine with containers of paint and cans full of brushes.

What happened next seemed less like art than mass production. That was, of course, the way he had always done everything—quickly, compulsively, impatiently. He began cranking out painted bottles, as many as fifteen or twenty a day. At first we didn't know what to make of his masterpieces. They generally fell into two categories: The geometric designs, with blocks of gold-painted solder separating the colors like leaded glass in a church window; and the representational paintings, scenes of ducks and geese, horses and cows, forests and oceans, magnificent sunsets. He rendered boats and palm trees and love birds facing each other nibbling on a shared worm. In only one case did he depict a human figure—a face staring wide-eyed from inside a window, like Boo Radley.

He was, of course, following in a venerable southern tradition, and if he had taken himself more seriously, he might've become another revered Naïve icon. But art for art's sake wasn't something my father understood, so once he had a trunkload of bottles ready, he took them to local flea markets and set up shop. His given name had been Ledger James Morgan, but he had long since taken the liberty of dropping the *d* from his first name. Now he embellished that name for his art: On the bottoms of many of his bottles, right next to his pasted-on price, he scrawled, usually in gold paint, the name "Leger"—with an acute accent over the second *e*. *Voilà, l'artiste.*

During those years following his first heart attack, I felt that I got to know him better than I ever had. Once when I was visiting Miami, Dad and I went for a walk. He told me that he had handled a lot of things wrong in his life—that he had been too rigid, too focused on the job, too driven. Then we came home and he went to his workshop and dashed off a picture of a bird perched on the branches of a dogwood tree.

He suffered a second, and final, heart attack five years after the first. As I grew older I came to admire his bottle paintings, seeing in them not only surprising technique but an attempt at autobiography—his Mississippi boyhood in the little farms, the rolling hills, the wildlife, the tender leaves of spring; his Florida adulthood among the swaying palm trees, the ocean whitecaps, the silver moons. But I was afraid—for him—that the most personal painting of all was that face at the window, the haunted visage of someone trapped in a life that didn't fulfill.

THE HOUSE WHERE Matisse grew up was just on the left past the first S-curve in Bohain, on the corner of the main street, rue du Château, and the smaller Peu d'Aise. I parked in front of an insurance company across the way and took out my sketch pad. Something about Picardy made me think of charcoals. Maybe the relative absence of color brought forward the power of shape and line, but I didn't feel the call of pen and ink. They are for crisp climes, where the sun makes sharp edges. Picardy required layered shadows and thicker bones.

The Matisse house was sturdy and square, a two-story structure with a florist's shop on the street floor and a home above, to judge by the plants in window boxes. Someone, sometime, had painted the dentil work and window trim bright blue. It wasn't his shade, but it was still a nice Matisse-like touch, a clear color that stood out in this subdued landscape.

After sketching, I got back in my car and headed toward Le Cateau. Just outside town, I passed a creek with an old stone house by the road on the right. Beyond that, up a steep hill, was a big *mas*, a French farm enclave made up of several buildings. Across the road was a little house practically hidden in trees. I was at the top of the hill before something told me to slam on my brakes, turn into a driveway, and go back. I parked at the bottom next to the creek bridge. It struck me as a good Picardy scene, old stone and black trees and rolling land with shadows in the crevasses. In the center, a gray country road stopped at the horizon. Charcoal was definitely the right medium.

In fact, I spent much of that afternoon searching for a whole tree of charcoal. Bohain's most famous landmark is the Chêne Brûlé, or blasted oak, a massive tree northeast of town that was burned and partially destroyed by Spanish marauders in the seventeenth century. As a boy, Matisse and his friends played beneath it. When he was back living in Bohain, he painted it. The Chêne Brûlé was the subject of old picture postcards. Even today, a picture of the blasted oak is one of the first things visitors to the Hôtel de Ville see when they walk through the door.

I had already driven around Le Cateau searching out the site of Matisse's birthplace, a two-room house (no longer standing) with a packed dirt floor in the curve of a narrow street hardly more than an alley. I had drawn the steeple of the church where he'd been baptized. Cows in a pasture, stripes of black hedgerows, a dingy trestle outside Bohain—these were the subjects I entered in my sketchbook. Then I walked into the Hôtel de Ville and remembered the Chêne Brûlé.

A pleasant-looking woman came out of an office. "Pardon, madame," I said. "Où est le Chêne Brûlé?"

Her face lit up like I had just sung the Marsaillaise. "Le Chêne Brûlé? Ah, oui!" She couldn't tell me how to get there, but motioned for me to follow her into another office. There I waited while she consulted with a man in a cubicle. A framed painting of the tree in question hung on the office wall.

The man soon appeared with a spring in his step. "Le Chêne Brûlé, oui, oui," he said, and took out a city map. "Le Chêne Brûlé *ici!*" He pointed to a spot near the top of the grid. I must've looked blank, because he then made a kind of pirouette so that he was facing the street in front. "À droite . . . ," he said, moving both hands as though he were directing traffic. Another pirouette, this one ninety degrees clockwise. "À droite . . . ," he said, directing traffic again right. I followed his hands to the end of their arc. À droite et . . . [he spun] "à *gauche!*" With that, his body and hands together swooped sharply left, as though he were about to attempt a corkscrew dive. He seemed very pleased with himself.

I backed out the car and drove slowly along rue Fagard, taking a right at the first street, rue Petreaux. Just at the corner, second building in at 24, rue Fagard, was where Matisse painted *Studio Under the Eaves*. As I drove by, I craned my neck to try to catch a glimpse of that hopeful rear window from the painting, but the brick wall was too high.

At the next street I made a right, then a left at the first turn. *Voilà!* I was actually on a street called rue du Chêne Brûlé. But instead of leading me to the tree, that road petered out at the top of a hill near a stadium with pasture land beyond. I drove right along rue du Pont du Roi, then made another circle, ending up in the same place. On my next lap, I saw a man walking his dog. I stopped and rolled down my window. "Pardon, Monsieur." He seemed startled to encounter an American in his neighborhood. "Où est le Chêne Brûlé?"

They were magic words. He brightened. "Ah, oui, le Chêne Brûlé!" He pointed in the direction I had already gone.

I circled around by a school, then found myself back on the rue du Chêne Brûlé. Still no tree. A couple of boys on motorcycles passed me on a curve. When I got to the bottom of the hill, on a narrow one-way street, they were parked in front of a garage. I called one of them over. He was probably fifteen, with pink cheeks and a touch of an attitude. "Le Chêne Brûlé?" he said, and dropped his pose. He pointed down the hill, then two lefts, and a right. That took me back by Matisse's studio under the eaves.

My next time around, I spotted a young woman studying something in the trunk of her car. When I asked the question, she became immediately friendly, coming over and propping her arm on my roof. "Le Chêne Brûlé, ah, oui." Then she said, in enough English so that I could understand, that she didn't know exactly where the tree was—maybe in a yard at the top of the hill. Something in her words made me wonder if the Chêne Brûlé was still with us.

One more loop. As I descended into the one-way street, the kids were still lounging around their motorbikes. Now a couple of girls were with them. I stopped, and they all came over. The attitude was back. The girls' eyes were dancing. "Oui?" the cheeky boy said.

"Le Chêne Brûlé," I began.

"Ah, le Chêne Brûlé," he said, and the rest of them started giggling.

"C'est ici maintenant?" I was trying to ask if it was still here, but I clearly wasn't communicating. I had found a picture of the blasted oak in a small book from the Musée Matisse. I opened it and pointed to the massive tree.

Their faces fell. "No no no," the boy said, wagging a finger. The others shook their heads. "Le Chêne Brûlé est . . . peu." The tree was small.

"Le Chêne Brûlé est . . . mort?"

"Ah, oui," they all said together, and one of them repeated my word: "Mort." The Chêne Brûlé was dead.

I heard them laughing as I drove away. "Bonne journée!" one of them shouted.

"Bonne année!" I called back, to even greater laughter. It was my first try at a French joke.

I was hungry after that and stopped at a *bar américain,* which is to say a roadhouse. Three *bon* old boys were throwing darts at some kind of electronic board. Whenever one hit the bull's-eye, the machine would burst into James Brown's "I Feel Good" (*da-da-da-da-da-da-daaaa*). It being after normal serving hours, one of the men—the proprietor, presumably—grudgingly broke from his game long enough to go into the back and fetch his wife, who graciously slathered butter on a full baguette and loaded it with ham, and brought me a beer to go with it.

As I sat writing my notes about the afternoon, I marveled at the power of a symbol that still lived in the hearts of these people long after it had ceased to live in the world. The massive, wounded oak tree, its core charred black, had roots still resolutely holding tight to *Picardie: Terre Fertile.* Henri Matisse was much the same. To the end of his life, he felt wounded by the lack of respect he'd been accorded as a struggling young artist by his more practical countrymen—especially his father. That was combined with personal guilt over his own willful disregard of his bewildered father's wishes. ("It was the equivalent of saying . . . 'Everything you do is pointless and leads nowhere,' " Matisse later lamented.) As if in both defiance and reparation, he dug deeply into himself and stood firm, forever managing the business of creating beauty and light with a single-mindedness that recalled the way practical Bohain weavers had turned out their fabulous fabrics, or the way a Picardy grain merchant had driven himself to make a success of selling seeds.

On Tuesday night, before we checked out the next morning, we gave Marie-Paule and Victor the names and phone numbers of our good friends Jerry and Stephanie Atchley in Laguna Beach. We shook Victor's hand and wished him well. Marie-Paule hugged us good-bye. They were leaving for the airport the next morning at 5 A.M.

In the predawn darkness I awoke to hear them scurrying around downstairs, and then the sound of the ancient door settling shut. As they cranked up the car and drove off, I said a prayer for Victor. Then I drifted back to sleep thinking of the grand adventure he had before him in the Southern California light.

2.

Looking for the Light

HOW WE THINK determines how we see. I didn't always know
that. I used to believe that any of us could look at the same scene—
the early-morning skyline of Paris in December, say, viewed from a
leased Peugeot wagon weighted down to the rocker panels with an
obscene amount of baggage—and see the very same thing. But that's
not true. Before we left Arkansas, I interviewed an ophthalmologist
about the actual process of seeing. "We don't see with the eye," he

said. "We see with the brain. The eye is just a camera, like on a security system. You know, when you knock on someone's door and that little camera is looking at you? That's the eye. Vision is back in the back where the TV monitor is, with the security guard looking at the monitor. And that's the brain."

All of which explained how Beth could gaze giddily through the drizzle and see a Paris of magic and beauty while I was confronted with a gray, impersonal fortress. I, too, wanted to be in France, but even though we lived together, we had arrived in Paris from vastly different places. Both our views were distorted in their own way, and that, I decided during that morning's drive into the city, was the challenge before us: to un-think so we could re-see.

Truth be known, this is how I get before any new project. I freeze up, fearful that I won't be able to pull it off. And each time I forget, like the joke about the fast-food worker who had to be re-trained every Monday, that I was the same way last time. *What am I doing here?* I wonder, to which Beth has a succinct answer: engaging in The Big Whine, her term for my existential wallowing. "Get over it," she advises. "Get out and get to work!" I will say that since I've been researching Matisse, I've found that a certain amount of unattractive hand-wringing goes with the artistic territory. Lydia Delectorskaya, Matisse's longtime assistant, reported that he was petrified every time he approached the canvas. "I'm going to smoke a cigarette to calm down," he would tell her, this after staring at the white canvas for ten minutes or more. Even his little pen sketches tied him in knots. "Don't get so upset," Lydia would tell him.

"I'm not upset," he would say. "I'm scared."

Shut up and do the things that scare you, I told myself as I watched Paris grow large around us. "Make no small plans," said the Chicago architect Daniel Burnham in a quote I keep framed on my desk. "They have no magic to stir men's souls."

When the 21-year-old Matisse arrived in Paris from Picardy in the autumn of 1891, he found the art world as cold as the city. "I was like someone who arrives in a country where they speak a different language," Matisse later recalled. "I couldn't melt into the crowd. I couldn't fall into step with the rest." He bounced around for a while, living in various places and trying to find his way. The first studio he called his own was at 19, quai Saint-Michel, on the left bank of the Seine across from Notre Dame, an address that would be part of his life and art for years. In his poorer early days, the quai Saint-Michel was a decidedly unprestigious address: Notre Dame was a gathering place for the consumptive down-and-out; bodies were regularly found floating in the river in front of Matisse's apartment. Fortunately, the city morgue was right near the church.

Part of my anxiety about Paris was that this time we weren't simply coming for a visit. The extent of what we sought from the city was more than a mere concierge could serve up. Uppermost on my list of things to do while we were there were taking painting classes and seeing Matisse's various Paris studios. But in the bigger picture, Paris was a toehold, a starting point. It would be the place where we would prepare ourselves for the long, ambitious journey ahead.

RUBEN MILOGIS, French Home Rentals' man in Paris, is a thirty-eight-year-old Argentine artist who has lived there some ten years. His dark hair and angular face remind me vaguely of Ricardo Montalban. I can hardly understand a word he says.

Ruben met us at 14, rue du Perche, in the Marais, and helped us haul our luggage up the three-flight walk-up. Then he showed us around the apartment where we would live for the next few weeks. It was nothing fancy but very comfortable, with a spacious sitting area that could be made into two rooms by simply pulling a sliding door, plus a separate bedroom, a split bathroom and toilet, and a small kitchen with counter and barstools. It looked out on a cozy courtyard.

Over the daybed in the sitting room was one of Ruben's artworks, a huge blue collage combining paint, newspapers, and a coil of white wire meandering like centipedes around the canvas. It reminded me of an aerial view of a coastline. When I told Ruben that we were going to follow Matisse around France, he pointed to the blue of his picture and said it was "inspired by Matisse."

He had to leave—"I heeve un appoint-*maw*," he said, a phrase I would soon come to identify with him—but said he had an artist friend we should meet, an American woman named Patricia. He would talk with her and call us soon.

That afternoon Beth and I walked up to the rue de Bretagne to buy supplies. Bretagne is a street of wonderful markets, the kinds of shops in which freshly killed birds hang, still in their feathers, and where thick red steaks, chops, and all manner and size of sausages make a mouthwatering display behind gleaming glass. The street looked especially festive and Christmasy that day, with big white star-shaped lights strung from post to post and lots of people wearing mufflers and fur hats and carrying beautifully wrapped packages. Lines of shoppers waited to get into the charcuterie, the patisserie, the rotisserie with its racks of fat *poulets* rotating on outdoor spits above a pool of potatoes. On the sidewalk, men were selling Christmas trees, whose trunks they sawed and slipped into holes in log stands. Whole gardens of brilliant flowers seemed to sprout from the very pavement in front of the florist shops.

Needing basic groceries, we went first to the Franprix *supermarché,* where I was especially pleased to discover an impressive selection of red wines for the even more impressive price of under four euros a bottle—sometimes even under three. After that, we went to the smaller shops and stocked up with as much as we could carry. That night we sipped wine and sliced cheese while preparing fat Brussels sprouts to go with our rotisserie chicken and *pommes de terre.* We drank toast after toast to our new life, and then settled back on the sofa to watch a French-made Western about a white man captured by Indians who eventually becomes a brave and gets the chief's sister.

The next morning Ruben phoned. "We heeve un appoint-*maw,*" he said, and went on to explain that Patricia had an invitation to an opening for a new exhibit of some kind, I never quite got that, at the Louvre. It was for that night. Would we like to come? (I covered the phone and whispered to Beth, just to watch her face: "Would you like to go to a private soiree at the Louvre?")

"Absolutely," I said to Ruben, and asked what the dress would be.

"Classic French," he said.

"Does that mean a tie?"

"No. Just sometheeng dark."

Our appointment was for 5 P.M. at the Hotel Intercontinental across the street from the museum. Beth and I unpacked and got organized, with special attention to our ensembles for that evening. Beth laid out a black dress, pearls, and the mink coat her mother had given her—assuming the rain let up; I was leaning toward a blue suit and a black turtleneck. Only five days in France and we already had an invitation to the Louvre. We were taking Paris by storm!

THAT AFTERNOON WE began the maddening task of dealing with electronics. Despite our two brand-new $35 adapter kits, none of our electronic gear worked. My beard trimmer hummed down to a hoarse growl, then died. Our nifty new CD player/Sound Soother/clock (which we'd bought to simulate the comforting white noise of my allergist-prescribed air purifier) wouldn't make a sound, so instead of drifting off to any one of twenty soothing virtual realities, including Ebb Tide, Rainforest, or Summer Night, we had lain awake listening to real-life Paris police sirens.

Our first purchase was a French cell phone, which was as easy to deal with as our computers were not. We'd been advised to wait until we got to France to set up international e-mail accounts, since otherwise we would have to pay roaming charges all the time. Rolling our laptops through the rain to an Internet café around the corner, we spent three brain-numbing hours that day—and six and four hours on succeeding days—trying to get our AT&T Global accounts to function. Mine never did, so I stuck with Hotmail.

Back at 14, rue du Perche, I did a couple of sketches of the apartment and brooded about where I might sign up for painting lessons. Before we arrived in Paris, I had fully digested the harrowing account of Henri Matisse's first year at the Académie as he tried to be accepted into the École des Beaux-Arts. New students were not only jeered, they were sometimes forced to stand and sing, and the weakest were even stripped and spat on. The École des Beaux-Arts was, in Matisse's day, where the most talented, most promising art students matriculated, and maybe it was still. I couldn't get in there even if I'd wanted to, which I didn't. I was way too old to be stripped in public.

Wherever my art classes turned out to be, I wasn't looking forward to them. From firsthand experience, I knew there was such a thing as too much information: After taking a night watercolor course at the Arkansas Arts Center, I had found it impossible to do watercolors. Before that class, I'd had great success—even selling a few pictures—doing bold, loose pencil sketches with a watercolor wash. After the class, I no longer considered my technique "watercolor." It felt like cheating—even if I preferred the look of my work to the more classic pictures of the teacher.

Earlier in the year, when our art historian friend Bernadette Murphy had come from France to visit in Little Rock, I had talked with her about Matisse and shown her some of my paintings. "You need to go easy on the color," she said, politely, and I cringed to imagine what she was really thinking. Still, I liked my color—mostly—even if I didn't have the credentials to defend it. When I look back at paintings or drawings I made as a young man, they were as close as I could get them, in both form and palette, to looking like the scene or object I was painting. Today, my work is looser and more colorful, less concerned with replicating reality than hinting at it—progress not just in painting, I think, but also in life: The world isn't perfect, either. A few years ago I painted a scene of the slope-ceilinged corner of my office/studio. I know it could be better, but I still love the painting I made. First of all, I love the *things* in the picture—a strange Middle Eastern chair, a daybed, an old drop-leaf table that used to be in my aunt's attic, an urn I bought in Chicago, a silly Mad Hatter lamp that belonged to my late brother-in-law. I love the composition, and the purely accidental way I depicted the light on the old linoleum floor. And most especially I love the colors—the stripes of the bedspread, the patina of the chair, the blue of the urn, and the blue-green wall behind it all. This isn't even the color of my office—I just liked it, so I painted it that way.

And yet I know that slathering on the color doesn't make you a Matisse. There's so much going on in good paintings that it would almost be enough for me just to understand the questions, never mind the answers. Still, here in middle age, I did hope to become a better painter—better as in gaining *understanding,* especially of mechanics. A grasp of technique allows a painter to reach more emotional depths. The ideal is an apparent effortlessness, even if you sweat blood to produce a certain effect. I wanted to learn to paint with the fuzzy-edged lines of a dream, the better to capture the bright dappled haziness of a summer's day. I also wanted to try to understand what happens when people look at a painting. On the surface, it would appear to be a simple matter—you walk into a museum and see what catches your eye. But I suspect there's nothing simple about it. In some way, that one small act seems to encompass the essence of being alive.

The painter and teacher James Elkins compares painting to alchemy—"the art that knows how to make a substance no formula can describe. And it knows the particular turmoil of thoughts that find expression in colors. Alchemy is the old science of struggling with materials, and not quite understanding what is happening . . . as every painter does each day in the studio."

AT FOUR O'CLOCK I was dressed and ready to go, but Beth had gotten engrossed in some organizational task and let the time slip away. I stood at the bedroom door wanting to tap my foot but knowing it would be suicidal. Finally, at 4:25 we stumbled down the stairs (we hadn't yet figured out how to turn on the stairwell light) and into the gray winter day. At least the rain had stopped. Our subway station was several blocks away, in the opposite direction of the Louvre. "I don't think we've got time to take the Metro," I said. On the other hand, our street was quiet and neighborly, not the kind of thoroughfare taxi drivers find advantageous to cruise. With our thumbs out, we walked in the street to an intersection a few blocks north, where, after about ten minutes, Beth snagged a cab. It was our first one this trip.

Very shortly we were turning right onto the rue de Rivoli, and I began to relax. Then we watched in increasing horror as the cab slowed to the speed of an escargot, inching along block by block by block among the commuters and the Christmas shoppers. Several times we asked the driver how much farther, and the answer was al-

ways *un peu*—a little. We rolled up to our appointed meeting place
at 5:35. Ruben and Patricia weren't there.

But just across the street, at the Tuileries entrance to the Louvre,
all the beautiful people in Paris stood in line to show their invita-
tions. The whole intersection of Rivoli and rue de Castiglione was
jammed with limousines, Mercedes-Benzes, Range Rovers, Jaguars.
Handsome ladies with silver hair and brown furs clutched the dapper arms of well-heeled gentlemen in tuxedos. It looked like the
event of the season. Beth waited where we were supposed to meet, in
case they were still looking for us, while I walked over to see if Ruben
was waiting inside the fence. I couldn't even remember what Ruben
looked like, but clearly no one was straining himself to pass us invi-
tations. I stood outside the gate for ten minutes or so, then gave up

and went back to tell Beth. On the way I was jostled by a fresh-faced fop wearing his incredibly wide-brimmed Borsalino far down over his right ear. He was too perfect, so *haute* it hurt. *Oh, how I hate to miss this,* I thought, and went to find Beth. Not wanting to waste any classic French darkness, we repaired to the nearby Hôtel Meurice and consumed several pricey cocktails.

Late that night we talked with Ruben, whose cell phone number we had forgotten to bring with us. They were still at the party. I apologized profusely, but we obviously hadn't ruined their evening. "We wait thirty meenutes," he said. "Theen we come een and head straight for the champagne." He pronounced it cham-pan-ya. "We luuve the champagne."

OUR NEXT APPOINTMENT was for Saturday evening at a bar called Le Fumoir, which, Patricia had told us when she called, was an "in place." We would make certain to be on time. I had been on the edge of crankiness all day Friday about having missed the Louvre event. Most of my day had been taken up with the difficult business of biting my tongue.

I was also tired. A week after arriving in France, we were still trying to synchronize our inner clocks with our new schedule. At home in the U.S., we didn't go out to dinner much, though we had people over to our house all the time. Now we were going out most nights, leaving for dinner at 8:30 or 9 and coming home just before midnight. Then I wanted to sleep late in the morning, partly because I was exhausted, and partly because the mornings were so dark and gray. Every day I would open the window and stick my head out for a view of the sky, which was invariably the color of putty.

It took a while for me to appreciate that enduring those gloomy days were part of my job. Through them I was seeing what Matisse was formed from. "Color exists only through relationships," he told an interviewer in his old age. Without absorbing—into my very bones—the weighty Old Master tones of the North, would I fully appreciate the brilliant reds and yellows of Matisse's South? Clearly, one of Paris's jobs was to provide that absorption for me. "The search for color did not come to me from studying paintings,"

Matisse also said, "but from the outside—that is, the revelation of light in nature." Now something Bernadette Murphy had said when she was looking over my paintings took on new meaning. She casually tossed off the intriguing notion that Cézanne, being a man of the sunny South, didn't overemphasize color. Matisse, coming from a part of the country where the skies were as heavy as lead, made color more prominent.

Willing my body into the smothering gray in order to sketch (and therefore to *look* at things) still required extraordinary and continued motivation, which I found in our taxes. Matisse or no Matisse, I had to pull them together for my accountant by the end of the month. Anything was preferable to that. Soon, on the frosty streets of Paris, I discovered that my task now was to become a man of two heads—the visual and the verbal. For many years when I've traveled, I've observed the world as a writer. Even when I was an editor, I primarily saw from the perspective of someone reporting on the whole scene. Seeing as a visual artist calls on a different muscle group. In my early magazine days, I often carried two Nikon cameras around my neck, taking pictures as well as writing. The two jobs are not easy to do well simultaneously. As a photographer, you're constantly scanning the vista in front of you in search not of the big picture, but of the small one—the slice of reality that's the essential—and then you compose it instantly with your mind's eye into a harmonious (or dramatic or revealing or disturbing) vignette. You select it with your sensibility and frame it with your mind.

Even more specifically, as a painter you need to switch on your head's stop-action function and really see what your eyes are taking in. Painting a picture, you peel back the world in layers, noticing the colors in a stone, then how the stone reflects the sky, and how the sky looks in the morning, at noon, at dusk. You begin to see how your loved one's face is surprisingly asymmetrical, and how the light at 4:30 in the afternoon makes the yellow room glow like a veil of Chinese silk. You deconstruct drapery folds, flower petals, ears. You pick up echoes of shapes. Painting forces you to notice light, shadow, line, color, perspective. Matisse and his friends used to develop those muscles by sketching quickly. He quoted Delacroix as saying artists ought to be able to draw a man falling out of a sixth-floor window.

The center of that elusive muscle group seems to be located somewhere between the mind and the heart—with a taut stretch of ligament reaching down to the fingertips.

LE FUMOIR WAS a comfortable room with leather sofas and easy chairs and a desirable back room known as the Library. When we walked in, a line of people waited to be seated. The French seem not to mind lines the way Americans do. They queue up convivially for baguettes at the boulangerie, for cheese at the fromagerie, for sweets at the patisserie, for weighing their produce at the super-marché. It seems to me a small contradiction of the so-called arrogance so many outsiders ascribe to them.

Ruben was near the front of the line, wearing jeans, sneakers, and black overcoat, his backpack slung over his shoulder. He and Beth performed the cheek-kiss ritual and then we apologized more for having missed the big evening. Soon we were joined by Patricia, a short blond bundle of energy with a nervous smile. The hostess immediately showed us to a big window table, where Beth, Patricia, and I ordered kir, but Ruben wanted only coffee. He said he was still feeling the effects of Louvre champagne.

Over the next hour we heard two longtime expatriates' eye-opening tales of the artist's life in Paris. I was already guilty of having formed distorted opinions of both Ruben and Patricia, given their apparent sensitivity to "classic French dress" and "in places." Ruben is a committed artist who knows exactly what he does and doesn't want. "Not too much money," he said, because that creates a need for lawyers, tax people, and other hangers-on. "You don't want to become too beeg. Then people want theengs from you." The freedom to do what he wants is everything. "We eenjoy our days," which he spends teaching autistic kids at his atelier, browsing in bookstores, visiting museums, making his art.

An American from California, Patricia grew up in Zurich, the daughter of a pharmaceuticals executive. She went to school in Europe, majored in French, and studied art. In the early 1980s, she came to Paris and got a doctorate in philosophy at the Sorbonne. Later she returned for a couple of months with a boyfriend, "and I've been here ever since." For a while, she said, she worked with Pierre Salinger at ABC. Her "big mistake" was going into freelance production work. "It's impossible to work with the French," she said, and described the typical French business meeting as "no agenda, no minutes, just three hours of people *discussing*. Then they break for lunch and start drinking wine."

Instead of being rich, as I'd thought she might be, Patricia was having the kinds of financial problems familiar to most freelancers. She had even spent four months in her apartment recently with no heat. Finally she appealed to the government, which gave her four hundred euros to get her heat back on. Both she and Ruben have great government insurance, since he has a green card and she's a member of the European Union. They both describe Paris as a hard city filled with hard people—tough, competitive, vindictive. "And yet," said Patricia, "it's a beautiful place. You can have a great quality of life here with not much money. Not like New York."

A young woman named Sophie, who worked at Le Fumoir, came over and brought Ruben a free tart to go with his coffee. She was the wife of another South American artist in Paris, and it occurred to me that there must still be a supportive network of bohemians here, as in the 1920s. We ordered another round of kirs, and Ruben began talking about a major event coming up on Monday night—some kind of all-out artistic charity do, in which there would be a tent for designers, another for painters, yet another for sculptors, filmmakers, and so on. "It's dinner," Ruben said.

"It's *dinner*?" Patricia was very interested. The attraction of public events, such as this one and the Louvre party, is fine food, plenty of drink, and the possibility of useful contacts, not necessarily in that order.

The problem is always credentials. Ruben has a press card from a newspaperman in Argentina, but Patricia has nothing to show. I mentioned that I carry a Writer's Guild card, a vestige of my one professional screenwriting stint. This was apparently thrilling news, and we decided to try to crash the party on Monday. Ruben also made an appointment to phone me "Tuesday at one pee eem," to talk about helping me get set up with a life drawing class.

We said good night to Ruben, and then Beth and I walked across the Seine with Patricia, parting ways near the École des Beaux-Arts. I thought of Matisse and how he had come to hate the dogma preached there. Time and again he rebelled against academy teaching, saving himself and modern art in the process.

On the Left Bank, we strolled along the quai de Conti looking in the decorated shop windows. Christmas was in less than three weeks. We'd already decided that our gift to each other was simply being here—that and having our daughters, Blair and Bret, come visit for ten days. They were due on the 17th. Our friend Holly was coming with them.

Despite the cold, nasty weather, a lot of people were out. Many walked well-behaved and sometimes well-dressed dogs on harnesses. We missed Snapp, our miniature schnauzer, who had turned eleven on the day we'd moved into the apartment on Perche. I still hoped to bring him over at some point when we were settled. He wouldn't believe the life of a dog in France. Years before, Beth and I had enjoyed a fine dinner at the famous Montparnasse brasserie La Coupole. Classic Parisian waiters delivered a stunning array of shellfish stacked on ice-laden stainless-steel trays three high. In the banquette across from us, a lady in a fur fed minuscule crustaceans to the mop-haired dog sitting beside her.

After a too-expensive dinner at a favorite spot that wasn't as good as we had remembered, we walked by the river toward Notre Dame. The big blocky church was all lit up, rendering it ghostlike in the mist. Matisse had studied Notre Dame from his windows half a block away and had painted this vista over and over, endlessly compelled by that most stoic and Sphinxlike of cathedrals. In his hands it changed with the seasons and probably with his moods—snow-blown in winter, blossom-purple in spring, stark under the summer sun, and blue, like a block of ice to be toted with tongs, in a bleak season painted out of season. Matisse told one visitor that the reason he couldn't give up that small apartment, even after he owned other places, was that view.

We crossed the bustling boulevard Saint-Michel and began looking for number 19 on the quai. The entrance was a big dark green door with ornate ironwork, next to a garish bar. An interviewer who visited Matisse here in 1919 wrote that the place "was old and almost a trifle sinister, and it was only with some effort that I could make out the door to the concierge's wretched dwelling in the gloomy entrance hallway." And that was in summer. I shuddered to think what it must feel like on such a night as this.

We were happy to get back to the Marais, an area we were enjoying exploring. It's an arty section of town. There was an art gallery right next door to our building, with two more across the street and another down the block. There must've been fifteen or twenty additional galleries within a two-square-block area. In one, located on the small street behind the Musée Picasso, some artist had constructed a giant pink wooden doghouse. It was bigger even than my blue backyard toolshed back home.

There in Paris, city of light and center of art, most of what I saw in the galleries left me cold. One Friday evening, braced by the red wine, steak frites, and steak tartare of Ma Bourgogne on the Place des Vosges, Beth and I strolled the entire circumference of the Place in the shadows of its ancient archways. All but a handful of galleries were closed, but their lights were on. One artist specialized in large canvases of fishing ports brushed in bright bold primary colors. Another had adopted as his métier bronzy depictions of Venice with Prussian blue water. Several painted soft-edged sunny scenes of mothers and children at the beach, picking up shells, wading in the surf, heavy on the mauve. Others evoked the star-crossed nights of van Gogh, the twisted female nudes of Picasso, the thousand-points-of-light cityscapes of Seurat.

"See," Beth said, I think trying to compliment me, "there's a lot of bad art out there."

There are many, many ways for a painting to be bad. The question is, what makes a painting good? "Be personal above all," Matisse once wrote to a friend, "and for that you must be honest."

The only picture that stopped me—physically, time and again—was a brick-red painting of flowers and fruit on a gallery poster that was taped to the windows of hotels and restaurants all over Paris. I could never walk past it. At the bottom of the picture the tone was rich and deep, like a comforter you could lie under—and, in fact, I often caught myself seeing it behind my eyes before I went to sleep at night. Toward the top left of the painting the color grew lighter, fading to a yellowish orange. I didn't pay much attention to the objects depicted, nor did I commit to memory the name of the gallery or even the name of the painter.

It was only his color that I needed on those dark December days.

3.

Matters of Perspective

IF SIGHT IS the hungry student, perspective is the pedantic school-master, the bullying hall monitor, the officious security guard. Per-spective is all about rules—especially the rule of placing oneself precisely, narrowly, irrevocably in relation to the rest of the world. "You have to put things in perspective" means it's time to see the world from the other fellow's point of view. Where, Matisse increas-ingly believed, is the art in that?

I won't say I was *consciously* positioning myself as a Rebel of Perspective, but a certain familiar stewing was clearly taking place following Patricia's phone call on Monday. The party was off, she said ("It's invitation-only. We don't try to crash gates when your name has to be on the invitation"), and she passed along a message from Ruben, who was preparing his students for their exhibition later in the week and couldn't call me. But he had seen an atelier he thought I might like in the neighborhood he'd just moved to. The address was 36, rue Saint-Sébastien, in the 11th arrondissement. The actual address galvanized my dread.

As for the party's cancellation, we weren't terribly disappointed. We had set up a Web site about what promised to be an expensive project, and Beth, the Webmaster, was busy trying to post her first Web diary, or "blog," which we had recently learned was cyberspeak for "Weblog." She was also writing travel notes that we hoped might entice hoteliers throughout France to give us free or discounted rooms in exchange for a plug. As she figured out how to illustrate these blog postings with pictures taken with our new digital camera, Beth was climbing a steep learning curve, trying to master several new languages at once.

Meanwhile, I had sustained a near-total electronic meltdown: My laptop had simply stopped working. Then, Sunday night—when I'd been using Beth's expensive new do-everything computer to print out an e-mail—I plugged in my printer, about six seconds later heard a *whoosh!* and was suddenly enveloped in thick white smoke. Beth looked up and thought it was coming out of my ears, but in fact it had emanated from somewhere in my printer's viscera. That's when the gravity of distinguishing between adapters and converters was indelibly etched in my brain.

Luckily, we found a nearby computer store, W-3, in which one of the salesmen, Olivier Silber, spoke English. "The printer is dead. Kaput," Olivier said. He opened the lid and showed us the black char marks and cauterized plastic. I felt a tinge of nostalgia: That old Canon had seen me through four books. Beth took a farewell photo as Olivier committed the remains to the trash can. As for my laptop, they would have to look at it. The diagnostic cost was two hours at eighty-two euros per.

But by far the costliest damage from this episode was Beth's intimate, ongoing relationship with the Bazar de l'Hôtel de Ville, a department store known to Parisians as BHV. In the basement of that building right in the heart of Paris, on the fancy rue de Rivoli across from the ornate old City Hall, was a subterranean world comprised of all the Ace Hardwares, Home Depots, Stack 'n' Racks, National Home Centers, and Sherwin-Williams Paint Stores in all the heartland towns of the U.S.A. Not only that, but here were hundreds of *French people* shopping for dowel rods and window frames and tile grout and wall sockets. The concept of the Handy Frenchman wasn't one I was ready to accept. I wanted to flee to the poetic Paris of berets, cafés, and ateliers.

With a compulsion for organization, Beth loved the place. Clearly, we needed converters and a couple of surge protectors. As long as we were there, we might as well get the office supplies we hadn't been able to bring with us—stapler and staples, scissors, yellow sticky pads, more pens, paper clips, neon bookmark strips, tape, thumbtacks, Liquid Paper, batteries, a flashlight (the hall light still baffled us), large manuscript clips, file folders, organizers. And then we needed something to put all that in—how about these clear plastic cases with compartments? That was fine for the small stuff, but what about all the manila folders Beth was filling with information for her Travel Notes & Recommendations? Two big blue plastic boxes soon presented themselves. So did a heavy metal container for my precious research files.

I also needed art supplies. I had brought from home a portable French easel with my oil paints in the drawer, plus sketchbooks, a good watercolor pad, and a small watercolor kit that I could carry around with me. I had shipped, in a huge box full of books and other heavy things, my brushes, palette knives, and pastels. Now, I had to buy pencils, a sharpener, an eraser, some turpentine, and linseed oil. I also needed prepared canvas boards, which would be easier to pack than stretched canvas. Beth insisted that I get a black plastic toolbox to transport my art supplies in.

Our first trip to BHV cost us two hundred dollars. But there was always something else we needed, something BHV could quickly supply. In the apartment at Perche, Beth turned the daybed into her office, with the adjacent coffee table her credenza. She turned up her rock and roll on the CD player (which was now working, thanks to a converter from BHV) and spread her work out just so—every file within arm's reach, every office tool at her fingertips. She was in business, and she worked on her notes and her blog from early morning until we went to dinner at night, and often again when we returned. She was deliriously happy in this temporary home—busy, productive, and in Paris to boot. And her daughters would join her soon.

I shuttled between the bedroom—where I tried to read without hearing Beth's music—and the living room. I was forever losing things. Which bag had I put my notebook in? Where were those refill cartridges for my pen? What the hell had I done with my small sketch pad?

"You need a purse," Beth said. She has a fetish for bags.

"I don't need a purse," I said. "I have a briefcase."

"Most French men carry purses."

"I'm not French, dammit."

"I saw some nice men's purses at BHV."

THE DAY AFTER Patricia's call, I carried my art supplies up to 36, rue Saint-Sébastien. On the way, I recalled reading about Matisse's initial interview with the Académie Julian's William Bougereau, whom Spurling calls "the pope of the French art world." A student had to be accepted into one of the academies in order to try out for the École des Beaux-Arts, whose imprimatur would in turn set students who had excelled in the École's stair-step art competitions on the path—the only path—to a viable art career. Matisse showed Bougereau two still lifes from Saint-Quentin. "Aha, so we don't understand perspective," the master said. "Never mind, you'll learn." Once Matisse was enrolled in his classes, however, Bougereau badgered and belittled him—along with most of the other students—telling Matisse, whose sin had been to place his drawing too high on the page, that not only could he not draw, he would never learn. Matisse changed to the Académie's other teacher, Gabriel Ferrier, who at first publicly praised him—and then, reacting to one of Matisse's drawings of a nude model, said, "It's so bad, so bad I hardly dare tell you how bad it is." Four months after beginning lessons, he submitted, for entrance to the École des Beaux-Arts, a drawing of a male model called *Standing Nude.* It was rejected.

I had a hard time finding the address Ruben had given, and when I finally did, it looked more like a veterinarian's clinic than a Paris atelier. It was a small ground-floor room, a storefront you could peer into from the street. Inside there was no nude model posing, and the students—male and female, all ages, all wearing white smocks, like doctors—didn't drill holes in the world with hollow-eyed intensity. In fact, when I knocked lightly on the glass door and went in, only a couple of them even glanced my way. Then I opened my mouth, and the room turned atwitter.

A pretty, dark-haired woman came to investigate while everyone else watched. Having prepared a cheat sheet, I began reading aloud: "Je m'appelle James Morgan, et je suis ici à la recommendation de Ruben Milogis." I showed the woman his name in my book, but it apparently meant nothing to her. She merely shrugged, then flipped her head back to consult the others. They shrugged too. I tried again. "Je voudrais . . . avoir . . . instruction d'art . . ."

The room broke into laughter, but it wasn't derisive; it was the kind marked by great good glee. As the dark-haired woman went to a cabinet to fetch some information, a square, stocky man, who *looked* like a doctor, asked, in English, what kind of instruction I was interested in. Life drawing, I told him.

"Nudes?"

"Oui."

"Not here," he said. "Not in Paris this time of year. Usually in September."

The dark-haired woman returned with a printed schedule outlining the classes, the times, the costs. She pointed at her watch, and I looked at mine. It was 3:45 in the afternoon, nearly time for this session to be over. Too late for today. "Je . . . *be back*," I said. "Au revoir!"

"Au revoir!" said the atelier in collective bemusement. The dark-haired woman mouthed the words while regarding me opaquely, like our cat.

That night we cooked dinner at home again, and afterward Beth entered her second blog and I did a watercolor of the window at 14, rue du Perche. By then, despite my meteorological lessons on Matisse, my perspective of our dark little courtyard had shifted from cozy to cramped. The weather had been bone-chillingly cold and drizzly almost the whole time we had been there, and while our apartment itself was comfortable, I felt that we lived in a hole. It was still black at 8:30 in the morning, and 11 A.M. wasn't much brighter. As one all too susceptible to encroaching gloom, I wanted to capture this feeling with a watercolor of the apartment's entry hall window, looking out to the taupey walls of the oppressive courtyard.

It didn't work. I hadn't pulled it off. The concurrent delicacy and boldness required of watercolor had once again eluded me. My colors were too bright to be gloomy, too bland to be ironic. Between my heart and my hand there was a language barrier. What I had produced was just a picture of a window, drapes, a hall table, and a funky little Middle Eastern saddle stool, with other windows in the background. Just an empty picture, no meaning at all.

ON THURSDAY WE took the Metro to the rue du Bac and then walked to Place Saint-Sulpice, a little square in front of the ancient church in which Delacroix had spent his last years painting frescoes. On this night, vendors had set up booths from which they were selling jams, honey, wines, rilletes, pâtés, and other wonderful French goods. The festival was an annual affair benefiting the Union Nationale des Associations de Parents et Amis de Personnes Handicapées Mentales.

In a tent in a corner nearest the cathedral hung the artwork of autistic children, several of whom were Ruben's students. We found him inside talking to a group of parents while fending off the adoring attentions of the kids, who clearly wanted to monopolize him. Two white-jacketed bartenders poured champagne from behind a table laden with canapés.

The art was impressive—big and bold and colorful, exuberant declarations of the vibrant world the artists saw around them. And then there were faces, intriguing references to their own inner world. One of the most striking was by a young black man named Malik. He had painted an African mask in ochre tones, with feathery blue fronds fanning out from the top. The eyes behind the mask were haunting.

When Ruben introduced us to Malik, one of his students, he wouldn't look at us directly. He looked up, down, any way but our way. Beth asked if he would pose for a photograph standing by his painting, and he did. His adoptive parents, both white, beamed as Malik coyly revealed a hint of the smile he felt inside. Later his father, a high school teacher, e-mailed Beth to thank her for putting Malik's picture on our Web site.

Patricia soon arrived and we headed for the cham-pan-ya. The *maire* of the 6th arrondissement came and spoke a few words, and there were toasts all around. It was a big night, the kind that made you think of good things and good people. I wished my father could've been there. He knew the hearts of the handicapped and would've been nearly as proud as Malik.

But long after that evening's end, the image still stirring in my head was that of a pretty fortyish woman, the very definition of chic, who had come to tour the exhibit. She was blind, carried an unobtrusive cane, and wore no dark glasses. Patricia, who knew her, said she shows up at many gallery and museum events. We talked with her briefly, about the U.S. and our being in France. She smiled and chatted while looking away, not uncomfortably, into some vague middle distance.

I decided, totally without knowing, that she must not have been blind from birth. The ophthalmologist I'd interviewed had said that such people can remember colors, sunsets, the curve of a tree limb, the sparkle of stars in the night. Anything they've seen, they will always see. Maybe she clings to the memory of a favorite painting, which gallery openings make forever new. Maybe she harbors the moment she first encountered a shade of turquoise that took her breath away. Maybe, even, she lives her life inside the gilded frame of a picture that orders the world into beauty and calm. I knew people with eyes who probably didn't see half as well.

We walked home again that night, ambling through the narrow streets to the river, crossing to the Île de la Cité at Pont Neuf. In my head, the glittering apartments overlooking the island's prow became staterooms on a glamorous ocean liner. I wondered if the blind woman had ever sailed on a ship like the one I imagined. In a way, I felt that she and we were shipmates. People who create live mostly inside their own heads. Those things that engage others most— money, social status, watching TV, fixing meals, getting haircuts— are for the most part unimportant, even unreal, to us. Ours is a parallel, subterranean universe. It's a luxurious way to live, and in my waning days as a magazine editor I prayed that someday I would achieve such a state of grace. I was yearning for a form of blindness, but a blindness that freed me to see only what was important *to me*.

WHEN I ARRIVED at the atelier early the following Saturday, only one student was there. The ancient easels were still lined up on the right, and among the paintings staring down from the wall were a couple I had noticed in progress the week before.

The dark-haired woman seemed not to remember me at first, or maybe she was just surprised that I came back. I suspect she worried about how this exercise was going to work, since she spoke almost no English and my French was, to put it kindly, limited. The other student, a woman, introduced herself in English as Aline. She provided my formal introduction to the teacher—"This is Nadine. Mademoiselle Gauthier. She's the instructor"—after which she asked if I painted. I said I did, a little, and pulled out an envelope containing photographs of my work. Knowing it would come to this, I had stacked the deck: I peeled off the first photo, an accidentally excellent watercolor of a bowl of fruit; next I showed my bold oil self-portrait with palette and paintbrush at home in Little Rock; after that came the vibrant vignette *Corner of My Studio*, followed in succession by *Waiters at Deux Magots, Studio Daybed, Terrace in Havana*, and on and on, ending with a couple of recent pen-and-ink drawings of women, à la Matisse's *Thèmes et Variations*.

Right away, the women began speaking in very fast French. To my delight, the word *Matisse* came up a couple of times. "La palette de *Matisse*," Mademoiselle Gauthier said. Aline asked if I liked Matisse, and I said I did—very much. Whereupon I said that I was about to embark on a journey through France following in Matisse's footsteps—both geographically and spiritually.

She didn't seem to understand. "Chasing Matisse?" Aline said. "Why you are chasing Matisse?" Fortunately, the other students began filing in, so I was saved from having to try a deeper explanation.

I chose an easel and dragged it to the front of the room by the window, my left side and part of my back to the street; if anybody wanted to see how I was doing, they were going to have to be obvious about it. The students began putting on their white atelier smocks.

Feeling not quite part of the club, I stuck with my "Celebrity Bartender" apron from my days as Articles Editor at *Playboy*. It had been given to me one New Year's Eve when a Chicago hotel had run a promotion and was especially pressed for celebrities.

The students were working on all manner of subjects. Over by the sink, a woman was painting a very accomplished picture of a lane with trees and houses. Next to her, a teenage girl was trying to capture the cragginess of mountains. A woman in the center of the room was facing a canvas on which appeared a black scarecrow-like image that I decided was trying to become a tree. A young man who later introduced himself as Jean-Yves was sketching cups and saucers on a blank canvas. Aline was working on the largest canvas of all, a reclining nude against an Art Nouveau backdrop. And right behind me, an English-speaking woman in glasses was doing a still life of a violin and drums, the trick being that you wouldn't know which was in front. She had obviously spent many hours in that maddening perspectival purgatory where the two images collide.

I had decided to work on the picture of our apartment window that I had painted earlier in watercolors. Now I wanted to try it in oils, which, while they're undeniably the masters' medium, are also somewhat forgiving. I had brought along the sketch I used for the watercolor. Placing a fresh canvas board on the easel and propping the sketch next to it, I began lightly drawing the scene onto the canvas. Another problem with the watercolor was that it seemed static; now I drew in the draperies slightly blowing, as though some unseen hand had just jerked the cord and they were swaying in response. In the lower right, I exaggerated the curved legs of the table, giving that section of the canvas a bit of movement. I sketched in the saddle stool quickly, and was working on the open window when I felt Mademoiselle Gauthier at my back.

I turned and nodded. She nodded, then walked away.

Opening my tube of Titanium White, I squeezed a big watery splat onto my palette. Then I pressed out a small mound of Alizarine Crimson and, next to it, some Thalo Green. Years earlier, I had learned that most painters don't use pure black oil paint from a tube, which tends to be too strong. Instead, they mix Alizarine Crimson and Thalo Green to yield a black that works well with other colors. With the blade of my palette knife, I carved out a buttery slice of crimson and began blending it into the green. After I had made my black, I mixed it with some of the white to produce a dull gray. It was still too heavy on the red, so I added more black. I was after cool, dim, muddy colors. To tamp down the concoction, I mixed in a dash of Ultramarine Blue for good measure.

Mademoiselle Gauthier would stop by occasionally to check on me. Whenever I caught her eye, she seemed to be regarding me with extreme caution, as though she expected at any minute to discover that I had been hiding sexual innuendoes in my drapery folds. Finding nothing of the sort, she would nod in a kind of noncommittal okay, then move on. My first indication of trouble was when more and more students began drifting over to see what I was doing. Eventually, the English-speaking woman in glasses came with Mademoiselle Gauthier and a small contingent of other students, including Jean-Yves and the woman who was painting the picture of the lane with houses and trees.

"You want to paint like Matisse?" the English-speaking woman said.

"This makes you think I want to paint like Matisse?" I asked in a joking way, but I don't think she understood me. She nodded, and I pretended to preen. But Mademoiselle Gauthier, locked in her inability to communicate with me, was clearly not happy. She began talking earnestly to the woman in glasses, who translated for me: "She says, 'This is not Matisse colors. Not Matisse palette. *This is not like Matisse!*' "

"Not like Matisse!" I said, and I pretended to x out Mademoiselle Gauthier with my paintbrush. Everyone, including Mademoiselle herself, laughed. Then I explained to the woman in glasses that I wanted to capture what I felt was Paris in December—gray, dull, no sun. I felt a little pompous saying it, but that's art for you. She shrugged.

Mademoiselle Gauthier began pointing to various parts of my painting—the exaggerated table, the ghostly moving drapes, the little saddle stool that now seemed plopped down not so much on the entry-hall floor as against it. The woman in back, she of the tree-lined lane, pointed out for everyone that the line of a painting frame over my table wasn't parallel with the line of the window next to it. The others nodded like dashboard dogs. I wanted to say, *Have you people seen the Matisse-Picasso exhibit at the Grand Palais?* Instead, I calmly explained to the woman in glasses something about wanting this painting to have *movement;* she duly conveyed that to Mademoiselle. They conversed, then she turned back to me. "She just wants to know what your intentions are, so she can help you."

"Ah," I said. "Merci beaucoup."

Mademoiselle Gauthier pointed to a blue vase I had put on the table in my painting. Through our translator, she asked me where the light source was. The window, I said, and she pounced on that. The angle of my shadow was all screwed up, she essentially said. Not only that, but the shadow below the table didn't match up with the angle of the shadow of the vase. Point taken. There was enough going on in this painting already; a couple of accurate shadows wouldn't hurt anything.

They left me alone for a while after that. The lesson was almost over anyway, and pretty soon I began cleaning up. Through the translator, I kidded Mademoiselle Gauthier about whether she wanted me to move my easel away from the window so it wouldn't reflect on her teaching. She and the woman in glasses both laughed, and Mademoiselle Gauthier took my easel and turned it even more toward the window. I was touched.

"Au revoir!" I said, leaving. The atelier responded in kind.

"A bientôt!" I added. And indeed I would see them again soon, a fact that suddenly made me surprisingly happy.

THE GIRLS ARRIVED on Tuesday the 17th and suddenly the apartment mutated into a strange hybrid of sorority house and con-valescent home.

Bret was exhausted after her first-semester exams. Blair was ex-hausted from work and school. Our friend Holly was exhausted from selling her house and moving into ours, temporarily, until she figured out what she wanted to do.

Right now, all any of them wanted to do was sleep. Bret and Blair commandeered Beth's daybed/office and the trundle bed that slipped out from beneath it. Holly took over my living-room center of operations, folding down the loveseat into a double bed, a condition it remained in for six days. Around these nests they stacked their open suitcases, turning the beds into bunkers. In the mornings I would tiptoe out to the kitchen to make coffee, averting my eyes to keep from seeing something I shouldn't. A couple of times I walked through to find Holly in her bra, which unnerved me but seemed to bother her not at all. "I was a model," she said. "I'm used to taking my clothes off with people around."

They regularly slept until 2 in the afternoon, sometimes later. Beth and I had planned to put our work on hold and devote the next week to them, but they didn't seem to want to do anything—not unless you could start doing it around 4. Beth set up her laptop on the kitchen counter, and I stayed in the bedroom and hid. *Christmas in Paris*, I thought. *Magical.*

The undercurrent here was that Blair and Bret were feeling homeless. They didn't want us to sell the house they loved, even though they were admittedly in various stages of leaving home. Even though they knew we needed—for our own sanity and self-fulfillment—to go other places and see other things, and that it made no sense, financially or otherwise, to hold on to that house any longer. "You guys just want us around to wash your dirty laundry," I joked, and they laughed through their tears. "This is what we get for being such good parents," I said. More laughter, more weepiness, which at any second could turn to anger.

At least Blair and Bret could tell us how they felt; Snapp and Cleo, our other guilt center, could only stare at us. Our pets had lived their entire lives in that Little Rock house. Snapp had had his routine, waking me early to let him out, taking himself for a walk in the neighborhood, then yipping *one time* on the side steps for me to let him back in. He lay at my feet while I wrote, followed me downstairs to get coffee, then followed me back up again. He took naps with me. Cleo spent most of her days outside hunting, but at night would climb onto our chests and purr. I was still haunted by the look in Snapp's eyes when we left for the airport. What kind of people were we?

On Thursday, after the girls had had a couple of days' rest, we managed to get ourselves together and walk over to the Centre Pompidou. I had been there once, nearly two decades before, but it had been closed for renovations my last few visits to Paris. I was essentially seeing it for the first time, then, and it was a shock. The Pompidou looks like God's boiler room, or maybe a German Expressionist steamship that somehow managed to dock in the middle of eighteenth-century Paris.

I was surprised at how the Pompidou turns the city itself to art. We paid our admission and entered the glass tunnel that rises with the escalators on the outside of the building. With each floor, you see more of the Paris skyline—until, at the top, the sixth, the city spreads out around you like a toy town. To the north, the bright white Basilique Sacré-Cœur occupies the highest point; to the southwest, the Eiffel Tower rises like a golden charm; straight south, Notre Dame clutches the earth like an anchor.

Like making art, viewing art is pretty much a private activity. Even when I'm just with Beth, her pace seldom matches mine. Now there were five of us. We launched a ragtag invasion of the Max Beckmann exhibition, mingling among the floating hordes lost in polylingual headphone lectures, confronting in our individual ways Beckmann's tortured images of sex and triage and death. I was particularly taken by his self-portraits, which nearly always depicted a blondish flat-faced man smoking a cigarette and looking away from the viewer. In my favorite, he wore an orange shirt, maroon sweater, gray slacks, and a brilliant blue sport coat. A vast dark canvas loomed behind him, and his cigarette arm was propped on a chair the color of tropical seas.

Beth once asked me why painters did so many self-portraits. *Why do I write books?* I started to say, but it seemed a little too true. Besides the obvious advantages of free and available models, artists are by nature and necessity self-centered, if not outright narcissistic. They're also loners who spend an inordinate amount of time staring into the eyes in the mirror and wondering what in the hell is that person's truth *today*. If the ultimate act of creativity is a painter's own life (you first have to create the conditions for creativity) then self-portraits are a legitimate part of his oeuvre—van Gogh's frightened eyes and bandaged ear; Vuillard's blush in the portrait embracing his sister; Matisse's shocking erect paintbrush at the Beau Rivage in his first season apart from Madame Matisse. As windows into the artists' souls, self-portraits are irresistible.

On another floor we rounded a corner and two large Matisses filled a wall in front of us. One was an interior of a woman with flowers; the other, obviously painted at 19, quai Saint-Michel, showed a bowl of goldfish sitting on a small table by a window. The light in the room was tinged with tones of turquoise and Prussian blue. Outside, the blue Seine flowed beneath the Pont Saint-Michel. Sun fell on the classical old building on the corner beyond.

I started to sit down on the bench in front of the Matisses, but then Beth called me to come look at a painting in another gallery. Together and apart we all ambled through the Picassos, the Roualts, the Kandinskys, the Derains, the Braques. Only later, once we were back in the apartment, did I find out that I had completely missed the Matisse Room.

MY PAINTING WAS still on the easel by the atelier's front window, and I was happy to see it. You never know. Part of the torment of trying to make art is having to confront it after an interval away, like a night's sleep. You want to look, but you're also afraid. So you try to catch it off guard by popping in unannounced, or you carry it into different rooms to see how it looks in different settings, or you go see it before you even brush your teeth in the morning. Quite often you resort to the old mirror trick, in which you hold the picture up to a mirror in order to see it more clearly. If you don't have a mirror handy, you can simply turn the painting upside down. This doesn't change the hackwork you've committed to canvas, but it does change the way you read it. It shocks you out of your accustomed left-to-right scanning and allows you to see without expectation. This is probably the secret of originality—maybe even of genius. Those people hold the world itself upside down. Some of them couldn't turn it right if they wanted to.

Mademoiselle Gauthier was standing at the back of the atelier talking with a pleasant-looking blond woman when I arrived for class. As I laid out my brushes and paints, I could tell that they were talking about me. In a few minutes the blond woman came over and offered me a cookie. "Mincemeat," she said, in English. I declined, having just consumed a ham-and-Roquefort panini on my walk to the studio, but I asked if mincemeat was big here at Christmas the way it was in the States.

"Yes," she said. I'd known it was a stupid question even as I was speaking the words.

A dour, dark-haired woman came in, and then another man. No one else showed. Mademoiselle Gauthier began the session by demonstrating perspective on a chalkboard. She marked out a horizontal line to indicate the line of sight, and then she drew a glass to show how, at eye level, the opening of the glass looked flat. Below that, she drew two more glasses. The lower the glass was from eye level, the more rounded the opening appeared. I paid polite attention, making a show of taking notes. Even with the language barrier, I could tell that this mini-lecture was primarily for my benefit.

After she finished, I went back to my painting. I was pleased with it. I still liked the warm red-gray color and the ghostly blowing drapes and the strangely placed saddle stool. I liked the exaggerated legs of the table. The folds of the drapes could still use a little fluffing, I decided, so I mixed up some paint and began working.

Before long, I felt the presence of Mademoiselle Gauthier behind me. I kept piddling with the curtains, touching up the windowsill, strengthening the line of shadow from the vase. Was I painting or acting? Finally I turned and looked at her. She was scowling. She pointed at the table legs and the saddle stool and called the blond woman over for a conference.

Soon the blond woman translated for me. "She wants to know if you *know* that these things are . . . off-kilter."

"Yes, I do," I said. She translated for Mademoiselle Gauthier, who shrugged in the French way and went off to help others.

"Okay," said the blond woman. "She just wanted to know."

"You speak very good English," I said.

"I'm British," she said.

"Oh. Then your people have been speaking good English longer than my people have."

Thank goodness she chuckled. She was married to a Frenchman, was a "mum," and painted a very good pear.

After that, I was amazed at how comfortable the afternoon was. The radio was tuned to classical music, then shifted to American jazz. Meanwhile, I stood there marveling at the fact that a grown man could be spending a rainy weekday afternoon in Paris contemplating the folds of a drapery. Never mind that, thousands of miles away, my house wasn't selling and I was no doubt running out of money. You can lose yourself in the paint, which is part of the wonder of it. I kept trying to do what I had been taught long ago—to hit the highlight on the outermost fold, then grade it down to dark in the crease. It's harder than it looks, and I ought to be better at it.

At the end of the session, Mademoiselle Gauthier came to study my work. As she took it all in, she scuffed at a spot of paint on the floor with the toe of her impossibly pointed boot. A lot of French women were wearing that style this season, I had noticed.

"Your painting is better now," she said, and she actually smiled.

4.

A Sub-Department of Paradise

THE LONELY ARTISTS' garret has always held great appeal to me, which probably ought to be cause for concern. "It is important never to forget how crazy painting is," writes James Elkins in *What Painting Is,* and he goes on to talk about "the self-imprisonment of the studio" and "the allure of insanity." "Working in a studio means leaving the clean world of normal life and moving into a shadowy domain where everything bears the marks of the singular obsession.

. . . The studio is a necessary insanity. Perhaps writers have insanities of paper, or of erasers, but they cannot compare with the multicolored dementia caused by fluids and stone."

Yes, writers do have their own insanities, which they must embrace as painters embrace theirs. But once that hurdle is cleared, this world of private psychosis—this place where the quotidian cares of the day-to-day world end and the intoxicating alchemy of creation begins—can become deliriously fulfilling. Matisse, whose work spaces were elegant and well appointed, but still inhabited by demons, once called the studio "a sub-department of Paradise."

In our cramped apartment on Perche, I was missing my studio back home. Even when I wasn't creating, it was a good place to hide from whatever distress was lurking in the rest of the house. In Paris, that distress was something akin to displacement. Holly had left with three days to go until Christmas, and if her departure had given us back family and space, it had also underscored the hollowness that accompanied this year's Christmas. I had first felt it the previous Saturday when the girls were shopping at Le Bon Marché and I was standing outside the store listening to a Salvation Army duo sing Christmas carols, the older of the two men also accompanying on violin. They played "Silent Night," "O, Come Let Us Adore Him," and an especially heartfelt "Gloria in Excelsius Deo." I watched people sing along as they passed. The music made them smile. Later I went across the street to a café and sat outside sketching. Right next to me was a decorated Christmas tree whose fresh scent reminded me of home.

On the day before Christmas Eve, Beth decided we needed to have a party. Holiday celebrations had been part of her tradition for as long as the girls had lived. Beth decorated the house for nearly all occasions, and on every Christmas Eve for a dozen years at home in Little Rock we invited friends over—especially those who didn't have nearby family—and served champagne, caviar pie, baked oysters, and Beth's standing rib roast with Yorkshire pudding. Some days before that, we usually invited another group for eggnog, using a recipe by Tennessee's John Edgerton that was heavy on his home-state sipping whisky.

"Yes," I said to Beth. "A party sounds great."

"We'll invite Ruben and Patricia for Christmas dinner," she said. In no time, it was an appointment. The girls left soon after for rue de Bretagne to begin hunting and gathering.

I had planned to force myself to work on our income taxes, but even in my little bedroom hole I could see that the sun was finally shining—the first time in three weeks. I opened the window and stuck out my head. The air was almost balmy. I quickly slipped on my light parka and, dispensing with my usual bulky briefcase loaded with notebook, large and small sketchbooks, pencils, sharpener, camera, and watercolors, I stuffed only my small sketchbook and pen into my coat pocket. Hands free, traveling light, I headed to the Pompidou to see the Matisses on my own terms.

At the top of the escalator, I stopped for a few minutes on the sixth-floor landing to make sketches of the skyline. The sun was shining on Sacré Cœur, white as bone, but the sky behind was a deep winter blue. Once inside, I made a quick run-through of the entire permanent collection, then planted myself in front of the Matisses for a couple of hours. I had seen, in person, a lot of Matisse's paintings over the years, and yet I still couldn't quite understand why they affected me so. When I was young and my parents suggested going to an art museum, I resisted with all my adolescent might. Why now— especially now—did painting in general and Matisses in particular seem so essential to me?

I had been slogging through several dense books about art, which wasn't nearly as much fun as looking at it. But I was slowly beginning to isolate a few interesting ideas, one being the basic human need for *equilibrium*. "We cannot bear chaos—the disturbance of equilibrium," writes Gyorgy Kepes in *Language of Vision*. Many times at home, when my writing wasn't going well, I would tell Beth I had to go to the Arts Center "to look at pictures." Equilibrium isn't the same as symmetry. In *Art and Visual Perception*, Rudolf Arnheim explains how a horse traveling from right to left in a painting appears to be working harder than if he were moving from left to right. He also says that if you have two equal objects in a picture, the one on the right appears larger. All this has to do with the way our brains cause us to take in images, and with our intrinsic need to recast our world into something that feels balanced. Color, line, shape, mass, even the size and configuration of the canvas and the frame around it—all have crucial roles in whether we see a painting as formed and ordered. "The eye especially demands completeness," wrote Goethe.

And maybe the eye sometimes tries to compensate for the soul.

I sketched Matisse's *Interior with a Goldfish Bowl,* appreciating for the first time the brilliant strip of brick red on the windowsill. I doubted it was that color in real life, but it echoed the warm tones of the fish. This was one of the paintings done at 19, quai Saint-Michel in his second—actually his third—incarnation there. He had first moved into the attic with a painter friend. Then, in 1895, a struggling Matisse and Camille Joblaud, the girlfriend who would become the mother of his first child, Marguerite, moved into an apartment on the fifth floor, which would be his home until 1908. But in 1913, by then a financially secure family man with three children, he would return with his wife, Amélie, to that building, taking an apartment on the fourth floor directly below the one he had formerly occupied. He found the views from those windows compelling, and he painted them over and over again.

From *Studio Under the Eaves* forward, windows and doors—portals—would be a major theme in Matisse's art. Their presence haunts the stories he tells in paint. Because of them, his pictures become scenes of an interior world, with the exterior world glimpsed through the window or door. Sometimes—as in *Studio Under the Eaves*—the portals seem to imply yearning and hope, but other times, in lush paintings like *Interior with Aubergines,* they simply reveal the stark contrast between the outer world and a fabulously rich inner life.

One winter morning years ago I left my Chicago apartment in the predawn darkness to take a taxi to O'Hare. As the driver climbed the ramp to the expressway, I glanced at an adjacent row house in which a single light was burning. A young woman, framed by the window, stood nude before a mirror. It proved to be an unforgettable image, and some of Matisse's paintings of the window at 19, quai Saint-Michel stir the same feelings. *The Studio, quai Saint-*

Michel, shows a dark-haired nude—Lorette—reclining on a daybed spread with a red flowered coverlet. Before her is an empty chair positioned before a canvas. Outside we can see the workaday world continuing on its plodding path, while inside this window—one window among thousands—this snippet of intimacy is taking place. The inner life is a sensual life—without rules, without masks, without clothes.

After leaving the Pompidou, I caught the Metro from Rambuteau to Châtelet and crossed the river to quai Saint-Michel. Outside the big green door of number 19, I stood sketching a not-very-successful view of Notre Dame. The perspective was catawampus, as my mother would say, and I tried to put in too much detail. Look at the best painters' pictures of Notre Dame—they capture the massive square sum of the place, not its architectural fine points. Amateurs always fall into the trap of too much detail.

Lots of people were out enjoying the afternoon, which entailed dodging an amazing number of tour buses and the streams of sightseers pouring out of them. On the river, the bateaux were cruising along with customers on the top deck for a change. As I was sketching, a young man with glasses stopped and pressed the door buzzer right next to me. I asked if he spoke English. "Un peu," he said. I tried to explain that I was a writer working on a book about Matisse, who once lived and worked in that very building. The young man smiled blankly and asked me a couple of questions, which I didn't understand. We both shrugged. Finally he opened the door and said what I took to mean, "Come on in."

I followed him into a long corridor and waited while he keyed in the combination that would open the glass door to the small lobby. Once inside, he walked straight toward a door at the rear, but indicated that I should follow the wooden stairs curving up to the right. A dark little Christmas tree stood at the base of the staircase.

On the second floor, the stairs stopped at a wide landing whose black and white diamond-shaped tiles were larger and bolder than those in the lobby. This second-floor mezzanine spanned the width of the building, with apartments opening onto it from the street side. I wandered down the hall to the left and saw that the stairs continued up at that end. Probably they did on the opposite end as well. Of course I had no idea which side Matisse's apartments had been on, but, judging from his views of Notre Dame and the classical building on the Pont Saint-Michel, I guessed he would've been to my left.

I was excited about the possibility of seeing the rooms Matisse used as a studio, no matter how they looked today. I tried to recall how many artist's studios I'd been in: Cézanne's in Aix, Delacroix's in Paris, Monet's at Giverny, my friend Thom Hall's in Little Rock. The latter was an especially rare privilege, since Thom is still alive. Back in the early 1970s another Thom—this one Thomas Hart Benton—both allowed me in and kicked me out of his studio. Having just talked my way into my first magazine job, as editor in chief of *Kansas City Magazine,* I was extremely ill equipped when it came to journalistic savvy. Granted an audience with the notoriously crotchety artist, I figured we'd just have a nice chat. I went in wearing a three-piece suit and carrying no notes, no questions, and precious little background knowledge about Benton or his art. He kept painting while I stood around grinning like the young fool I surely was. Finally he said, "Look, Sonny. Go back and do your homework, then come see me." I was too humiliated to follow up with him. But never again did I show up for an interview without prepared questions.

The old building did feel spooky. It was dark and warrenlike, with no sounds of life. "No. 19 quai St-Michel was a massive stone building, put up in the early years of the century . . ." writes Spurling, "let off and sublet into apartments so numerous it was more like a vertical village than a single dwelling." The staircase, much narrower on the sides, curved up a very few steps to another landing, with an apartment straight ahead and another branching off to the right. This still seemed to be the second floor, but maybe it was the third; in France, the first floor is what we in the States call the second. On the next story, three more apartments opened onto another landing, and two of them—one on the street side and one at the back—had massive double wooden doors. The next level was the same. On the top floor, the doors weren't massive, and janitorial supplies littered the landing.

I tiptoed back down one flight. Through the double doors on the Seine side, I heard a woman talking, perhaps on a telephone. I screwed up my courage and knocked. In a few moments she was on the other side of the door. She wanted to know who I was. "Je m'appelle James Morgan," I began, but couldn't remember how to say I was a writer. "Je suis . . . *escrivier*," I finally stammered. "Un livre de Matisse . . . c'est maison de Matisse?"

"Oui," she said. It was the right apartment—one of them.

Then she kept repeating the same phrase over and over, something that included the word *merci*. Maybe, I decided, she was saying she would thank me to get the hell away from her door before she called the gendarmes. Instinct told me that I better not stay around any longer.

Cursing the camera at home in my briefcase, I dashed off a couple of quick sketches—the landing leading up to her door, the tiles on the mezzanine—and then made my escape to the quai outside. *Almost!* On the other side of those doors was either Matisse's first real studio, the fifth-floor room in which he painted the porcelain neck of his paramour, Camille Joblaud; or it was the one he moved to later with Madame Matisse, the studio in which Lorette lay nude on the red bedspread an arm's length from where goldfish sometimes caught the glint of a Paris sky. I was betting on the former.

I made a detailed drawing of the door at 19, quai Saint-Michel. Then, plotting my return, I strolled slowly homeward, taking my sweet time, cherishing every moment of that unexpectedly perfect day.

THE GIRLS SPENT most of Christmas Eve shopping, but I finally had no choice but to barricade myself in the bedroom and pull together numbers for the tax man. I was still working on it that afternoon when Beth announced that we were all going to get our "tree"—everyone was to choose some branch or plant or flower that we would put in the center of the table and decorate. Shortly before we were to leave, I checked my e-mail and opened a message from Lloyd, who wrote that our bank account was nearly dry.

I suddenly felt almost physically ill. According to that vague back-drawer-of-the-mind accounting that I'm always engaged in, I thought we had plenty. Of course I had forgotten a couple of big checks I had written before we left. Plus, I was having trouble getting access to cash in France. Since the advent of the euro, banks won't touch traveler's checks; when I needed cash fast, I had to fall back on my trusty Regions Bank ATM card, which worked with the same deceptive ease on the rue de Bretagne in Paris as it had on Markham Street in Little Rock. I was keeping receipts, but they had been arriving faster than I was entering their totals in my expense book.

Beth noticed the change in my mood, but she chalked it up to normal income tax angst. I walked with them, surly but surely, to the rue des Archives to buy greenery at a snooty shop called Art et Nature. Then we stopped at a wine store to stock up on champagne and *vin rouge* for Christmas Eve and Christmas Day. Going in, I held the door for a middle-aged man who was leaving with his arms loaded. "That's so sweet of you, darling," he said, looking me square in the eye. I was in no mood to be flirted with.

That evening, we had dinner reservations at a wonderful old brasserie, Vagenende, on the boulevard Saint-Germain. During dinner I tried, not successfully enough, to hide my feelings about money as we ordered a better-than-middling champagne and two dozen Brittany oysters, which were slurped down faster than Lance Armstrong's metabolism. A couple of times I caught Beth's eye and it almost brought me to tears. She was trying so hard—she *always* tried so hard. She wanted nothing but the best for her girls, and for us. She had the biggest, most generous heart of anyone I had ever known. I needed to aspire to that.

We had planned to walk, after dinner, to Notre Dame for midnight Mass, but a terrorist bomb threat at the cathedral that afternoon had changed our minds. It would be just our luck getting blown to bits and everyone at home feeling sure we were okay. No one would imagine that we were in church.

Back at 14, rue du Perche, we opened a bottle of Veuve Clicquot and I made Christmas tree decorations with watercolor crayons—stars and icicles, trees and Santas, and a bizarre vegetable series featuring bright orange carrots. Beth was pleased, which was good, because I was consciously sucking up for my notable absence of charm at dinner. While I painted my offbeat ornaments, I thought of Matisse's struggle in 1892 following his first failure to qualify for the École des Beaux-Arts. He went back to Picardy to meet with his father in the coastal city of Lille. Henri was depressed and Monsieur Matisse was distressed, and there were long uncomfortable silences between them. One day they went together to a museum of art, where Henri saw his first Goyas. Until then, "I believed I would never be able to paint because I didn't paint like the others," Matisse said later. Seeing the Goyas changed everything. The Goyas brimmed with real life, unlike the cold, perfect paintings his teachers wanted him to turn out. "That was when I understood that painting could be a language; I thought that I could become a painter." He returned to Paris with renewed hope, and soon found an academy teacher— Gustave Moreau—who shared his sensibilities. Moreau believed that art came from within, from the spirit, and not from the tricks of the hand that the academies taught. Under Moreau, Matisse was encouraged to explore, to experiment, to go his own way and see where it led.

After so much champagne, it was easy for me to put myself in Matisse's shoes. What I needed, I thought, was a Gustave Moreau, someone who would nurture what came naturally to me. At the atelier for my last session before holiday break, I had started to put my Perche picture back on the easel when Mademoiselle Gauthier shouted "Stop!" What she meant was, *It's finished. Don't touch it!* I could see a few things I could fiddle with, but she was probably right.

Unfortunately, I had forgotten to pack another canvas. I had, however, brought along a book of black-and-white photographs that I'd found in the apartment. Taken by Iris Wolf, a Los Angeles photographer and friend of the apartment owner, the pictures were of Paris street scenes—a couple walking in the Luxembourg Gardens, an arty view of the Eiffel Tower taken from inside a Metro entrance, a man and his dogs sitting at an outdoor café. I had responded to the photos immediately. They were the kinds of vignettes I would've sketched more if the weather hadn't been so dreary.

I took out the book and my pad and seated myself at the end of a long table. The atelier was very crowded. Aline was there again, working on her Art Nouveau nude, and also the woman who had made such a big deal about the frame in my painting not being parallel with the window. It had snowed on her lane-and-tree scene since I'd last looked. Two women next to me were doing basic art exercises—painting vases, bowls, and glasses from photographs. A woman in the center was dabbing tiny brushstrokes on an ebony-toned nude with close-cropped hair. The stocky man I had talked with on the first day was back working on a portrait, from a photograph supplied by Mademoiselle Gauthier, of choreographer Merce Cunningham. I wondered if he even knew who it was. In the rear, a woman I'd never seen before was painting sailboats. And across the room from her, a woman in a neck brace was carrying on about three conversations while painting an Arab and his camel against some distant mountains. At the beginning of the session, she had come up to me and said, "In the U.S., they call me Hortense. In France, they call me Or-TONCE!"

The photo I chose to sketch was the one of the man and his dogs at the sidewalk café. Soon Mademoiselle Gauthier came over to see what I was doing. She stared blankly. When I asked if she had a canvas I could use, she went and got a loose piece of raw *toile*. We clipped the fabric to a board on my easel and then she brought over a bucket of white stuff with a big brush. Gesso, I guessed, but I didn't know for sure. I had read about it but never seemed to have a need for it personally, since I don't stretch my own canvases. But I began slapping it on, filling in the little holes between the weaves of the linen. The gesso was like glue mixed with white paint.

No one had told me I had to actually dry the gesso, so when Mademoiselle Gauthier saw me standing around waiting for the concoction to prepare itself, she led me forcefully to an ancient hair dryer splattered with layers of paint. Both sides, she said, demonstrating. I blew on it as long as I thought necessary, then clipped the canvas to the board and started sketching.

It wasn't dry enough. Some of my pencil lines came out clear while others hardly registered. I also got the old man too low on the canvas, which meant that his poor dog, whom I had decided to paint yellow, was lying curled up on the bottom edge. By then it was 2:45, halfway through the session. Mademoiselle Gauthier looked worried, and mentioned something to the stocky man behind me.

"She says you need to use acrylics. Oils won't have time to dry."

"I've never used acrylics," I said. Now I too was worried. This was mostly a new audience, and I didn't want to be the class goat.

"They're basically watercolors," he said, and showed me how to dilute the pigments with water. No one had ever explained acrylics quite that way before. They had only talked about drying time, not the paint itself. What I soon found was that I could apply the paint thick and creamy, as with oils, or I could dilute the consistency until it was almost like a wash. Passing the brush with its quick-drying paint over the rough raw canvas produced a looser, less finished effect than I had been used to achieving. Acrylics were a revelation.

Before long, I was proud of the painting, though Mademoiselle Gauthier scowled at the angle of one of my tables.

CHRISTMAS DAY DAWNED with more than its usual dash of anticlimax. Blair and Bret had long since slept later than Beth and me on the big day, and, not having plans till evening, we let them snooze. I declared a moratorium on income tax, and even on worry. Beth and I dressed and walked up to the rue de Bretagne to pick up the things she had ordered for Christmas dinner—plump quail and capons, pungent cheeses, savory *petites tartes* and slim *haricots verts*.

That evening she threw a fabulous dinner party. Ruben and Patricia arrived bearing chocolates, and we popped the champagne, all the while conducting tag-team phone conversations with family back home. Blair talked to her boyfriend, and Bret seemed very pleased to have heard from some new boy we didn't know. We played Latin music in Ruben's honor, and Bret and I, who together had been studying his big painting on the wall, gave him our analysis of it: It wasn't an aerial view of a lakefront; it was a man throwing off the bonds that had bound him. Ruben sipped his wine and smiled in amusement; he probably couldn't understand a word we said, either. I enlisted Patricia's help in my new plan to crack the Matisse studio

at 19, quai Saint-Michel: She wrote out a note for me, in French, explaining who I was and that I wanted to visit that apartment for *just a few minutes*. When the time was right, I would post this note above the buzzer and wait for yet another kind stranger, like so many we had encountered on this journey, to call.

Our guests left early, about 9:30, and we celebrated a little family Christmas. Beth had bought the girls hats and perfumes and other things over the past few days, and that night she had them reopen the packages while all of us looked on. She even had a small present for me—a black moleskin notebook with thick creamy pages suitable for both writing and drawing. It came with a J. Petermanesque legend invoking the names of all the luminaries—van Gogh, Matisse, Hemingway—whose "sketches and notes, ideas and emotions . . . have been jotted down and harboured in this trustworthy pocket-size travel companion before being turned into famous pictures or the pages of beloved books."

In a couple of days the girls left for home. Once they were gone, Beth and I fell back into bed. That afternoon I called Lloyd. Lloyd Cobb is a godsend. He and I must think as differently as two people possibly can, and yet—and I hope this won't destroy his accounting business—he seems to have a streak of the romantic in him. By that, I mean he understands dreams and how money can be employed to fulfill them. Lloyd may choose to put his own funds in cement plants instead of wild book schemes, but he understands that I have no choice. "You're *supposed* to do this," he told me over dinner one night before we left. "You're *supposed* to go to France and chase Matisse."

Now he said, "Don't worry." He aways figures out a way to make things work. After he and I hung up, I felt both relieved and depressed. I hate not being financially self-sufficient, which is different from being financially independent. Until I elevated myself to Author, it was never an issue. After that, some of my most creative writing was the checks I penned twice a month.

ON THE SUNDAY after Christmas, we awoke to a wonderful new world. It's amazing how sleep rests the spirit. For the first time in a couple of weeks, we were able to see and think clearly. We had loved being with the girls, but now it was just us four again—Beth and I, Matisse and Paris. Incredibly, we had been there nearly a month. Where had it gone, what had we done? Sometimes after we had stayed in the apartment all day, we would go out in the evening and I would be surprised to hear people speaking a foreign language. Getting our systems established and our inner clocks working properly had taken longer than anticipated. Now our time in Paris was coming to a close. In January, we would begin traveling around the country. Though I was dying to see the sun of the South, there was still unfinished business in Paris.

That Sunday, we went out and walked for seven hours. High on Beth's list of things to do was to find a hotel that we could call our "home in Paris" once we were on the road. We needed a place to receive mail, store a couple of suitcases, and put up from time to time if we were back in the city. The goal was to get that in exchange for promotion on our Web site. Our top choice was the Hôtel Saint-Germain, number 88 on the rue du Bac, a small, homey inn where we, the girls, and Beth's mother had stayed for a week in 1998. Adding to the family ambience was a funny little white French bull-dog, named Jules, who spent most of his day dozing in the lobby.

We strolled down the rue Vieille du Temple and over the Pont Louis-Philippe to the Île Saint-Louis, where we watched a young man, egged on by his beer-drinking buddies, strip down to only his glasses for a frigid swim in the Seine. From there we crossed the little walk bridge to the Île de la Cité and turned behind Notre Dame toward the Left Bank. Beyond the plane trees, the little streets split off this way and that, curving coyly toward secret surprises. No wonder artists love Paris. Walking those streets is like chasing a thought, or a dab of paint, toward whatever mystery lies at the end. On my first visit, in 1974, I spent one entire day searching out doorknobs and door knockers to photograph. There's no better city for exploring on foot, and on this trip I had figured out why: From the sixth floor of the Centre Pompidou, you can look over the buildings toward any horizon you want. Paris is scaled for humans.

We ended the day as tourists, sitting outside among our fellow sightseers having a drink at Les Deux Magots. Across the street, in front of the church, a spirited jazz ensemble played for euros. Sunday evening wasn't quiet on the Left Bank the way it was over around Perche. The whole world seemed to be passing by, and much of it struck us as funny. We sipped our drinks and giggled at the outfits, the hairstyles, the husband-and-wife spats, the sullen teens and har-ried parents who'd clearly had about an hour too much togetherness.

On the way home, we cut through the little Place Furstenberg, where Delacroix lived at the end, and ambled up rue Mazarine to-ward the river. Darkness was on us now, and it had started to sprin-kle. Still, we were in no rush. I had popped open my umbrella and was strolling along, visually grazing on nothing and everything, when Beth stopped cold and said, "Look." She was pointing to a win-dow, a gallery window. Inside it, spotlighted on a heavy-duty studio easel, was the red painting whose posters had caught my eye all over Paris.

It was larger than I had imagined, which made the color even bolder. I couldn't stop staring at it. There on that gray winter street, it seemed to be giving off light. The artist was someone named Pierre-Humbert. The window was that of the Galerie Daniel Besseiche. The address was 33, rue Guénegaud.

I was supposed to find this painting, the way Lloyd said I was supposed to chase Matisse.

WE BEGAN THE year with a concert of Vivaldi, Mozart, and "Ave Maria" sung by a powerhouse soprano at a church near boulevard Saint-Michel. And we did find ourselves a hotel. A few days before we left the city for our driving journey, we had a meeting with Monsieur Michel Malric at the Hôtel Saint-Germain. He was the classic charming Frenchman, impeccably attired in ochre wool hopsack slacks and a rich plaid wool vest with a silk saffron back. Beth had sent him her best sales-pitch e-mail, and I had followed up with a phone call. Now it was clear that he still didn't know quite what we wanted.

We repaired to his office to dial up www.ChasingMatisse.com on his laptop. Beth took the liberty of putting it on his favorites list, and indeed he, as an art lover and collector, did seem to like the project and the idea of being connected with it. "But what can I do for you?" he said, and we enumerated: receiving mail, storing bags, complimentary rooms, if available, when we're in Paris.

"How big are your bags?" This was his main concern. "We have not much space."

"Oh, not so big," we said together, as though reciting an overly rehearsed lie. I drew a picture in the air: bigger than a bread box, smaller than a Louis Vuitton steamer trunk.

He thought on it. His mother popped in for a minute and said hello. We remembered her from 1998. That led us to asking about Jules, the white French bulldog, whom we now noticed had a black female bulldog pal, named Ogun. "It was Colette who made the French bulldog trendy in the salon," Monsieur Malric said, and explained that he had bought Jules years before for his mother, who lived in a beautiful apartment near the hotel. "She kept complaining that he was doing bad things in her house."

" 'No,' I say, 'he is a good dog.' But she keeps complaining. Finally, she give me back the dog. At *my* house, he does nothing bad!" Jules and Ogun now live with Monsieur Malric, and he brings them to the hotel with him every day.

Speaking of baggage.

"How many bags?" Monsieur Malric was saying. He was teetering on the edge.

"Two," we promised. "C'est tout."

He smiled. "Okay, you have a home in Paris," he said, and opened his arms in gracious welcome. "On the rue du Bac. Not bad."

Not bad indeed.

In early January, I took my note over to 19, quai Saint-Michel, and posted it above the buzzer. My thinking was, *Now that the holidays are over, people can focus.* The note was printed neatly on white cardboard and encased in tight plastic from a kitchen bag. I used Beth's tape from BHV to secure it to the wall.

From there, I went back to the Galerie Daniel Besseiche. The painting looked as stunning in daylight as it had at night. The colors were brilliant—red, blue, and yellow flowers in a silver-gray pitcher, at whose base lay a bright yellow something, perhaps a lemon, next to a red sliced pomegranate with black seeds. To the left of the pitcher was a yellow-orange plate of whole pomegranates, and above that, clearly in the background, was a cup that looked like pewter, with crisscross marks on it. In tone, the cup echoed the pitcher. All these items were positioned against a field of deep brick red graduating to yellow-orange at the top.

I wanted to know why this painting appealed to me so, very much in the way that Matisse's works do. The summer before we left Little Rock, my old teacher, David Bailin, had invited me to sit in on a weekly "artists lunch," a loose bull session that I first attended at a downtown pizza place on a scorching day in July. Bailin, Warren Criswell, Sammy Peters, and a couple of other guys talked about everything from George W. and terrorism to whether it was better to destroy your bad works so your spouse won't ruin your reputation by selling the stuff after you're dead. There was a lot of laughing.

At one of the lunches Sammy Peters put this question to the table: Have you ever cried at the sight of a painting? ("Only my own," I replied.) Some of them had, most of them hadn't. I had shed no tears over Pierre-Humbert's *Anemones et Grenades,* but it had certainly lodged itself in my consciousness. I wasn't a hundred percent clear on this business of equilibrium, but it seemed to me that *that's* what's in the eye of the beholder. There are people whose soul responds to Picasso's gleeful bent toward dissonance and people whose soul responds to Matisse's eternal struggle toward serenity. "In a balanced composition," writes Arnheim, "all such factors as shape, direction, and location are mutually determined in such a way that no change seems possible." On some level, then, Pierre-Humbert understood *me,* just as Matisse did. I thought we ought to have a talk about it.

The gallery door was locked, but when I pressed the buzzer it was answered in short order by an attractive woman with blondish-brown tousled hair. I guessed her age as late thirties, early forties. She worked at her desk while I toured the Pierre-Humbert exhibit. In a glance around the main gallery, I saw a lot of nice paintings but nothing that overpowered me the way the painting in the window did. There were a couple of appealing pictures of doorways and, on the opposite wall, a red table that caught my eye. A dark blue portrait of a nude in the artist's studio was intriguing. He painted a lot of nudes.

Downstairs, a couple of canvases of flowers generated a mild buzz, but it was only when I entered the final room that I experienced a feeling similar to that produced by the painting in the window. This canvas was large, horizontal, and damned near pink. The focal point was a fuzzy bowl of cherries. Behind them, the artist had obviously painted some flowers in a vase, then changed his mind. He had blocked them out, but not completely. Oddly enough, it was this pentimento of long-gone flowers that made this picture captivating.

When I went back upstairs, the tousled-haired woman looked up from her work. "Parlez-vous anglais?" I said.

"Yes."

I introduced myself and explained how I had been strangely attracted to the painting in the window. It would really be great, I said, if I could interview Pierre-Humbert.

She smiled, shook her hair slightly, and told me how appreciative she was of my interest. Unfortunately, however, Monsieur Pierre-Humbert had died ten years before. As she said this, she glanced toward the inside of the front window. On a panel behind the easel hung a large black-and-white photograph of a handsome man with a bushy gray mustache. Obviously the artist.

"But if you'd be interested," she said, "his widow is coming to the gallery in twenty minutes. I'm sure she'd be glad to meet you."

IN THE END, the studio I visited wasn't Matisse's. A few days later I discovered that my note had been rudely ripped from the wall at 19, quai Saint-Michel. It had taken some paint with it. But within the week Beth and I were riding the Metro to Anne Pierre-Humbert's apartment near the Place d'Italie. We had already met with her twice at the gallery, with tousled-haired Alice Pennington–Mellor interpreting, and we liked her immensely. Anne was short and pretty, a former actress and reader of radio plays. When she met Charles Pierre-Humbert in the early 1960s, he recognized her voice from the radio. Pierre, as he was called, was a struggling artist torn between his life and a living. A school in Orléans had offered him a teaching position. "What should I do?" he had asked.

"Refuse it," Anne said, and so he had.

I'd asked Anne if their life together had been hard. "Yes," she said, "but just when we thought everything was over, a miracle arrived. They always came just in time." That undying belief in miracles allowed Pierre to spend all his days making art. His works were shown in galleries in France, Switzerland, Germany, and once in the United States. He and Anne even managed to acquire a small house in the south of France in addition to the apartment in Paris. When she asked if we would like to see his studio, we accepted it as a gift.

Alice, from the Galerie Besseiche, met us at the Place d'Italie. She was bundled up, with a thick fur hat pulled tight over her head. Jan-

uary had brought record cold to Paris, but at least the sky had
cleared. I was amazed at the colors in it—golden in the morning and
pink in the late afternoon. No matter what the time, the light always
seemed like that at the end of a day.

After stopping at a chocolatier to buy Anne a present, we walked
about three blocks to her place. Beth and Alice were curious about
each other and hit it off immediately. Beth quickly ascertained that
Alice was English, early forties, and commuted via TGV between
Paris and Auray, in Brittany, staying in the city from Tuesday to Saturday and returning home for Sunday and Monday. She lived with a
nice man named Guy, a veterinarian with whom she was about to
buy her first house.

What Alice ascertained from Beth about us and our lives, I had
no idea. I also had no way of knowing whether this was a unique situation or just Alice, but she volunteered to call around and see if she
could find a hair salon that carried Beth's particular red. She would
help us get some printing done. She said she knew of a good hotel in
Belle-Île, our next destination, and would e-mail the owner to see if
she would give us a discount. She even had friends back home in England who owned a house near where she lived in Brittany. They
weren't using it during the winter, and in February we would need a
place to light for a few weeks so I could write. Maybe something
could be worked out. We were stunned by Alice's generosity. After
all, I had just walked in off the street.

Or maybe I had followed the light in her window.

The building in which Anne and Pierre had lived together, from
1970 until his death in 1992, was modern and boxy, probably dating
from the late '50s or early '60s. Alice buzzed and Anne appeared in
person to let us in. Soon she ushered us into a small apartment
whose furnishings were simple and compact, like on a boat. Anne's
desk was on the left as you entered, and a sofa backed up to the picture window. A cabinet beyond that held books and curios, including a butterfly whose wings were almost too blue to look at. Matisse
had owned one like it that he had bought in a shop on the rue de Rivoli, paying fifty francs when he had nearly no money to his name.
"Blue, but such a blue!" he later said. "It pierced my heart!" He had

always gone out on a limb for beauty. "This was precisely the kind of daredevilry [his wife] could never resist in her husband," writes Hilary Spurling. "The story of the blue butterfly became a family legend, standing for all the risks the pair had taken together when young."

Anne served coffee on a round table next to her sleeping area, which was set off by a curtain of beads. The handleless cups had been made by Anne herself. They were as thin and delicate as French cookies, and mine was a beautiful mottled azure that reminded me of the sea. She didn't work with clay much anymore, she said—at least nothing as fragile as these.

Two of Pierre's paintings, a blue nude and a red still life, hung on the wall behind us. Anne said that for a time he had made his art in a government-sponsored communal studio that Pierre referred to as "The Reservation." Later he had done his work here at home. His studio was just upstairs, Anne said. Were we ready to see it?

One of the books I cherish most, given to me by Beth and the girls for Father's Day 1991, is *The Artist in His Studio,* by Alexander Liberman. A writer, sculptor, and magazine executive, Liberman visited the work spaces of many famous French painters in the years following World War II. There's no pattern to these havens. Bonnard's was cramped and dirty. Leger's was bright, like his paintings. Kandinsky's was as ordered as a *pharmacie.* Picasso's was a show waiting for applause.

Pierre-Humbert's studio was up a flight of steep narrow stairs with no rail. The room, about the same size as the one below it, was wonderfully cluttered with boxes, bottles, brushes, books. The furniture included a daybed, a couple of cabinets, and some bookcases stocked with art reference books. In one, Matisse occupied a large portion of the top center shelf. A heavy paint-splattered easel anchored the small open space. The windows looked toward the northwest, as best I could tell. A shaft of pink late-afternoon sun sliced across a nearby building. "He was always looking for light," Anne said. "Even in the dark colors, he was looking for light."

The far end of the studio was taken up by alphabetized bins containing Pierre-Humbert's many canvases. I was surprised to see such order in relation to the rest of the room, and Anne explained that this was a system she had set up. She and a helper were cataloging all of Pierre's works—in other words, his life. She showed us folder after folder of drawings, from large tight charcoals to loose pen-and-inks. It was a big, difficult job. As she flipped through the works on paper, so many were nudes. I glanced at the daybed. They must've been posed right there.

Most painters I've known protect this precious personal turf, either because they don't want it compromised by external judgments, or they want to maintain the aura of enchantment that surrounds it and their work. Maybe both. At the artists' lunches in Little Rock, I had tried to get them to talk to me seriously about things like that. Mostly, they deflected my questions with jokes. After one of the lunches, Criswell sent me an e-mail: "Your questions are good, and brought us back to thinking about art philosophy and theory, which we haven't done in a while. Since the government was hijacked by oil tycoons with IQs in the double digits, and then 9/11, we've been preoccupied with politics, but our normal conversations include history, literature, music, archeology, astronomy, quantum physics, paleontology, sex, and all kinds of things not directly connected to art. It's like art is almost too painful to talk about. Jokes are easier. All my answers were honest ones and I'll be glad to elaborate on them, but if you interviewed each of us separately, I'll bet you would get a different set of answers from everybody. It's because we don't really know what we're doing. Art is informed by intellect but driven by intuition. The whole bundle of needs, desires, ideas, and emotions that go into a creative act is a nonlinear mess, but the only way we have of explaining it is linear, so the explanations you're after will always be distortions of what really happened."

Later I kidded Warren about his evading my questions. I told him I had decided that artists make their studios off-limits because they want to hold on to the mystery. "But it's a mystery to us, too," he said. "The problem is, you have to approach art from the side of going with the mystery."

5.

Standing on the Edge

THEY CALL THE wild west coast of Belle-Île-en-Mer *la côte sauvage,* and standing on the windswept cliffs watching the roiling waves crash against jagged rocks, I understood. It is a very beautiful, and very dangerous, place to be. Beth and I arrived in Belle-Île on January 24, 2003, my fifty-ninth birthday. There's not much to recommend a fifty-ninth birthday except the alternative of not having one. Observing it on a piece of schist overlooking the abyss felt somehow right.

Precipices must have also weighed on Matisse's mind when he first spied those craggy headlands. In the summer of 1895, at age twenty-five, he was already a father and just five years away from the cut-off age for study at the École des Beaux-Arts. If real life wasn't exactly looming, it was at least shimmering on the horizon. Fearful that his father would end his allowance, Matisse had put himself on half rations to hold out twice as long. His friends were astounded by his dogged determination to succeed, and he was making progress. He had just that year passed the Beaux-Arts entrance exam and so was a full-time student of Gustave Moreau, who had set him on a course of copying the masters at the Louvre. Matisse particularly responded to the works of Jean-Baptiste Chardin—again, they were "an open door" through which he glimpsed an extraordinary power and mystery. From Moreau he had learned that "color has to be *thought,* passed through the imagination. If you have no imagination, you will never produce beautiful color."

Never having ventured farther from home than Paris, Matisse was no doubt jarred by the journey to Belle-Île. Just *getting* there was an adventure. With Camille Joblaud, baby Marguerite—who was less than a year old—and several fellow artists and their girlfriends, Matisse had ridden the train from Paris across the heart of Normandy into strange, insular Brittany. At Quimper, they transferred to a relatively new line that took them southeast along the Atlantic Coast to the tip of a scrubby peninsula jutting into the ocean. This was the port of Quiberon. From there they boarded a paddle steamer for the nearly twenty-kilometer voyage to Le Palais, the island's capital and most populous town. A hundred and eight years ago, Belle-Île was wild and isolated. The people who lived and worked there, speaking their own Celtic-influenced guttural language, Breton, shared their small thatch-roofed houses with their cows, pigs, and chickens. They made the denizens of Bohain look as delicate as Picardy silk.

Matisse found himself paralyzed creatively, hardly able to paint. Ensconced in a top-floor room overlooking the back harbor, he managed one view of Le Palais from his window. And he and Émile Wery, his friend and neighbor in Paris, went into a local bar and each painted what he saw. Matisse's canvas was subdued, even somber, a perfect example of the traditional palette he was still using. In Wery's picture, light poured in, bathing the back-bar bottles in tones of red, green, and orange.

That first summer, Matisse fled Belle-Île after only ten days, retreating with Camille and Marguerite to the safer mainland. But it wasn't the wildness of the land or the people that finally spooked him so. It was the sight of Wery, an advanced and more adventurous artist, painting with primary colors squeezed straight from the tube. Today, with our lives permeated by color, we have a hard time understanding why this would have been so shocking. But in the 1880s and 1890s, most of the industrialized world was very drab—black suits, black dresses, black automobiles. Color implied frivolity and materialism. Color was freedom, and therefore dangerous.

Matisse was baffled, disturbed, and excited by Wery's recklessness. Witnessing it must have felt like standing on the edge of the savage coast, looking down at the churning surf. The really frightening thing was, he knew he was going to leap. More than half a century later, he vividly recalled the moment. "I noticed that [Wery] could get more luminosity from his primary colors than I could with my Old-Master palette," he told the editor Tériade in 1951. "This was the first stage in my evolution, and I came back to Paris free of the Louvre's influence and heading toward color."

BETH AND I were cold on the deck of the ferry to Belle-Île, but we stayed topside anyway. We turned up our collars and wrapped scarves tight around our necks. The sun was out, and for the first part of the forty-five-minute trip we sat looking back at Quiberon so it would warm our faces. The sky was a brilliant blue. Gulls soared overhead, and occasionally one of them would drop like a bullet into the water, coming up with a fish.

I've never enjoyed birthdays, but this one was starting out okay. In fact, all the days since Paris had been easy and carefree. We had taken our time driving through Normandy and Brittany. The first night we had stayed in Rouen, where we'd had dinner in a restaurant said to have been open since 1345. Jeanne d'Arc was burned at the stake right outside its front door, and I later told my brother the history buff that we had eaten at a barbecue place. He said he was glad that being in France had lent me such added sophistication.

We spent a couple of nights in Honfleur and three in Etretat, where Matisse had spent the summers of 1920 and 1922. By then he was a wealthy man. He could have, and had, gone practically anywhere—to Corsica, Morocco, Italy, Germany, Russia. But he chose Etretat because of its drama, and because Monet and other artists he admired had painted there before him.

One of those sites Nature has smiled upon, Etretat nestles in a natural gap among miles and miles of high cliffs, the *falaises*, which stand tall against the English Channel. At Etretat, the cliffs also perform geological tricks. On either side of the village they fan out majestically, revealing matched arches through the chalk. On the west, the Falaise d'Aval boasts a 200-foot needle rock. Atop the east cliff, the Falaise d'Amont, stands a picturesque seaman's chapel, the Notre-Dame-de-la-Garde. We studied this view, endlessly, from our hotel room. The striped cliffs seemed alive—one moment orange like the back of a tiger, the next moment gray like a zebra's hide. The afternoon sun ducked in and out of pink clouds, projecting its magic on the chalk screen that was the cliff face. *How do people live in places like this?* I wondered. *You can't work, you can't sleep, you can't eat. All you can do is watch.*

The drive from Etretat to the Atlantic Coast was familiar terrain, evocative of a very good time in our lives. In the summer of 1998, Beth, Blair, Bret, and I (accompanied by my son Matt for a too-short portion of the trip) had spent six weeks in France—two in Provence, two in Normandy, with a week between and a week in Paris at the end. So we had traveled those highways all together. We already knew to what wonders the turnoffs to Caen and Bayeux led. We reminisced about driving up a long road to a farm where we bought Calvados from the man who had bottled it. We could still taste the plump salty oysters we'd gotten in Cancale and brought back, in seaweed, to our rented house near Saint-Hilaire-du-Harcouët.

Now, in late January, the countryside was green and rolling, and the clouds staged an incredible show in the western winter sky. They were huge, fluffy, constantly changing shape and color. I wrote in my notebook: "The clouds here are worth spending a lifetime trying to capture on canvas. I ache to be able to do it."

Just past Avranches, we decided to make a detour through some of our old stomping grounds. We were headed for Quiberon, but we could just as well stop in Dinan for the night. The day was still early, and Dinan wasn't far away. We drove out to take another close look at Mont-Saint-Michel, which is visible from miles away, perched on that rock at the end of the earth. When we got there the tide was out, and sheep were grazing in the marshy grass. There was much less traffic now than in summertime, but tour buses were still lined up like dominoes. Beth got out and took pictures, but we didn't go to the walled city. Instead, we drove along the Emerald Coast toward Cancale.

The tide was out there, too, of course. Fishing boats sat on the mucky bottom, and one fisherman had somehow driven his car out into the bay—I guess to work on his oyster traps. There was no fish market, and very few restaurants were open. In the summer, Cancale is a wonderful place to be. The people selling oysters will give you a dozen just to sample.

We entered the gates of Dinan about four o'clock and checked into a hotel across from the statue of a brave but homely knight. With its well-preserved ramparts and castle, Dinan is one of the most picturesque villages in France. One afternoon years ago, Beth and I had wandered into one of its antique shops and found a set of twelve silver beakers. We both loved them, and Beth really wanted us to buy them. I've forgotten the price, but in any case it seemed too much. We walked away, and I had regretted it ever since.

Now, not wanting our afternoon of nostalgia to be over, I suggested we see if we could find the shop again. We did, and of course the set of beakers was long gone. But in a glass cabinet were several handsome individual silver cups. "Why don't we each pick one?" I said. "It'll be a bit of elegance we can carry on the journey with us."

"You know we shouldn't," Beth said, but I persisted. We opened the case and began touching the cups. They were heavy and cool and felt good in our hands. All of them were engraved—most with initials, but some with names. Beth found a small beaker marked "Robert," the first name of her late beloved brother who had advised us to use "Matisse colors, Vuillard patterns." She kept looking, but always returned to that one.

My own selection was harder, since none of the names or initials seemed to carry any special meaning. I just concentrated on the cups themselves and, in time, narrowed the possibilities down to two. Both were handsome and larger than Beth's cup. She didn't mind. The one I liked best had a field of latticework around the bottom two thirds, then a solid line, and finally a small band of leaves and flowers at the top. I couldn't even make out the initials.

The proprietor lowered his light and held his jewelry glass to his eye. "Hmmm," he said. "Aish." He wrote it out—H.

"Et eem." He wrote that, too—M.

"Oh well," I said to Beth. "At least it's got an M."

We couldn't tell the order of the letters. "H.M.," Beth said, "M.H." She was thinking. Then: *"Henri Matisse!"*

The bill came to 275 euros. Without a flinch I went to an ATM and got the money. The crazy thing was, I felt great about the purchase. *My blue butterfly.* That night, as we sipped aged Calvados from our silver cups, I had said to Beth, "Guess what I just found in Hilary Spurling's book!" Then, opening *The Unknown Matisse,* I pretended to read: "Henri Matisse visited the village of Dinan only once, and it changed the course of modern art. It was there that he lost his favorite silver beaker. He spent the rest of his life painting elegant and beautiful scenes out of his sense of loss for this wonderful cup."

AS I STOOD at the prow of the ferry, Belle-Île appeared first as a possible apparition, a hint of a shape on the horizon. Slowly the contours began to come clear. From the boat it looked long and flat, with gnarled fingers of rock knuckling down to the sea. In January, the foliage was mostly brown. At the far north end, seemingly cut off from the rest of the island, rose a high plateau, with something white in the middle. I took out my binoculars for a better look. It was shaped like a country church back home, but in fact it was a lighthouse—a house with a square light tower attached. The very top of the tower was orange.

I liked islands and had been looking forward to going to Belle-Île ever since I'd read about Matisse's summers there. Beth and I had even thought about trying to rent a house on the island so I could begin writing. "In winter," Alice said, "you'd be out of your minds in two weeks." We weren't so sure. Writing is a kind of island existence anyway. We were certainly enjoying the island life we were living at the moment, this driving around alone together in a car in a country whose language we didn't understand. You can cut out a lot of crap by not knowing what people are saying. "I'm happy not to be involved with others for a while," Beth had said one day recently as we passed through a shuttered village in Brittany. In that way, the island of Belle-Île had great appeal.

As the ferry eased into the main harbor at Le Palais, we went below with the other car passengers. Soon the big steel door was lowered and we drove off in a line of what appeared, by their backpacks and bike racks, to be weekend visitors. In contrast, we looked like arriving homesteaders. Beth had her map handy, plus Alice's directions to the hotel where she and Guy liked to stay. We found it easily, but our room wasn't ready. Unloading enough luggage to approach inconspicuousness, we headed back to town for lunch. Even in winter, Le Palais was invaded by tourists, who strolled the quaint streets snapping photos of the quai and the massive citadel that looms over it.

We wanted to do the same, but first things first. At the restaurant in the Hôtel Le Bretagne, a sunny table with a harbor view was waiting. We paired a cold bottle of local Muscadet with a dozen oysters each, the treat we had missed this time in Cancale. Then Beth ordered us a piping hot pot of her new favorite French winter dish, *soupe de poisson*—fish soup. She had first encountered it in Audierne, a pretty little port town dotted with white Breton houses overlooking a blue harbor; it was one of the villages Matisse painted when he fled Belle-Île that first summer. We had happened, late for lunch, into an almost empty roadhouse by the water. Le Grand Large, it was called. Besides sandwiches, all that was available was soupe de poisson, which Beth ordered. It came with cheese, home-made croutons drenched in garlic, and a thick buttery rouille the color of terra-cotta. On that day, a mission was launched. The fish soup at Le Bretagne was good, but not *as* good. On the other hand, the crème caramel was spectacular. Yes, I said to Beth as we clinked glasses, this birthday was shaping up just fine.

We could hardly wait to drive around the island. At eleven miles long and between three and six miles wide, it is compact; nothing is very far from anything else. But that first afternoon, sleepy from the wine, we decided to stay in town until we could get into our room and take a nap. In the meantime, we went up to the old citadel de-picted in so many of Matisse's paintings of Le Palais. It was our in-troduction to the work of the famous engineer Vauban, the foremost builder of forts and battlements in France. In the coming months, we would see his name nearly everywhere there was a seventeenth-century castle or fort. This one was built in 1549 and redesigned by Vauban in the 1680s. It was attacked several times in the eighteenth century and even captured by the English in 1761. The Germans oc-cupied it during World War II. In 1960, a very wealthy couple bought the then-crumbling fort and have been fixing it up ever since.

Beth and I pretty much had the place to ourselves. We wandered around by the barracks and the parade field and the powder maga-zine, and even stuck our heads into the prison. It didn't have a bad view, which I suppose was one of the punishments. From the ram-parts you could take in the whole port. I spent a few minutes sketch-ing from one of the corner guard towers. But the best part was the historical museum, with its nod to some of the luminaries who have loved Belle-Île. Notable among them was the actress Sarah Bern-hardt, who so craved escape from her public world that she bought herself an old fort on the other side of the island and made it her summer home.

THAT NIGHT WE drove to the nearby village of Sauzon to a restaurant Alice had recommended. Véronique, the hotel owner, had made our reservations. "They have a surprise for you," she'd said. When we opened the door to La Maison, a wood fire was going at the far end of the room. People were sipping aperitifs in front of it, light from the flames dancing on their glasses. *We're home,* I thought. Philippe, the proprietor, looked like the actor Jean Reno. Showing us to our table, he said, "I want you to meet someone," who turned out to be Johey Verfaille, the young wife of La Maison's chef, Stéphane Gawlowícz. Johey was from Baltimore.

She talked with us a few minutes at our table. A chef in her own right, she had met and married Stéphane in the States. In time, he got homesick for France. They'd spent a year working at La Rochelle, on the coast north of Bordeaux, but hadn't liked the feel of the city. In October, they'd moved to Belle-Île. "How do you like living here?" we asked.

"Let's have a drink after dinner," she answered, and took our orders—Thai crab bisque, Corsican charcuterie, fresh stuffed crab, a nice Bordeaux. I was having a birthday fit for Louis XIV.

The restaurant, reasonably busy for a Friday night in winter, was nearly cleared out at 11. By then, a few locals had showed up to drink with Philippe and sing a few boozy French songs. We bought Johey a glass of wine while we waited for Stéphane to finish up in the kitchen. In fact, she said, she liked Belle-Île very much. "It's very friendly, very close. Everybody knows everybody."

We could feel it. La Maison felt like our own living room in Little Rock, complete with singing.

"The only problem is, sometimes Stéphane and his friends get to talking so fast that I can't follow, so I feel left out." When that happens, Johey makes jokes at the expense of the French. "The term for local products is *produits terroir,*" she said, "which I find very funny and Stéphane doesn't. '*Terroir,*' I'll say to him. 'Ooooo, scaaarryy.' "

Stéphane came in and Philippe fixed him a drink. He seemed like a nice guy, though he didn't say much. It was hard to talk over the singers, who were at the next table. They had gathered quite a head of steam. Johey did tell us a little of Philippe's story. He had been in the ad business in Paris but got sick of it, so he and his wife came to Belle-Île and opened La Maison. He had a strange sense of humor, which showed up in the restaurant. Water glasses were designed to tilt. Meal tabs were slipped into mouse traps, which sat on the tables. In the spring, Johey said, Philippe was going to open another place across the island, and she was going to be the chef there.

Johey seemed to want to talk more, and we did too, but it was impossible. We exchanged e-mail addresses and phone numbers and promised we would see them again before the weekend was over.

"How about that?" I said to Beth on the way to the hotel.

"She seemed lonely," Beth said.

OVERNIGHT THE MIST rolled in. Without the sun, Belle-Île came closer to my preconceived notion—an image engineered by Matisse. *Open Door, Brittany,* painted in gray-greens and mottled creams, shows a squat, square double door open to a bleak wasteland seemingly on the edge of the sea. The house appears to be built for hobbits. What sun there is remains smothered by heavy clouds. One of the most famous of Matisse's Belle-Île canvases, this picture infused in me a combination of curiosity and foreboding.

The painting was made in 1896, the summer he returned with Camille, Marguerite, and another group of artist friends. The year had started well for Matisse, who had sold eight pictures and been accepted as an associate member of the Société Nationale, an alternative salon formed in protest against the restrictive policies of the establishment Salon. In Belle-Île the Matisses stayed a short time in Le Palais, again in an attic room above a patisserie, and then moved—with the Werys—across the island to the small village of Kervilahouen. There they lived on the top floor of a stone house owned by a boat pilot and his family. It was in that house that *Open Door, Brittany,* was painted.

The attraction of Kervilahouen was the nearby presence of the charismatic Australian painter John Peter Russell, a former friend of Vincent van Gogh. Independently wealthy, Russell had come to Belle-Île in 1886—the first outsider to settle there—and had built a mansion above the creek at Goulphar. This house was the social center for all visiting artists. For Matisse, it was perhaps the spiritual center as well—Russell's life was about painting, and his painting was about color.

I turned on the car lights and we drove toward the top of the island, a direction that felt like north but is actually northwest. At Sauzon again, we got out and photographed the picturesque little harbor. At the entrance to the port the remnants of more modern fortifications looked like the German bunkers we had seen in Normandy.

Even in the gray of winter, Belle-Île had an undeniable, almost mystic, beauty. We saw very few cars. At La Pointe des Poulains, I parked in a circle where the road ran out. On a flat hill beyond an inlet that becomes flooded during spring tide stood the lighthouse I had spotted from the ferry. It was splendidly isolated, and apparently empty. We walked down some steps and across the sandy natural moat and climbed up the bank to the plateau. "Wouldn't this be a great place to write?" I said to Beth. I had found myself applying that criterion to every place we went, even—so perversely romantic was my self-image—to broken-down side-of-the-road brush-covered stone hovels filled with bat guano. She suggested instead that we buy a fortress she'd just spotted on a nearby hill. It was abandoned and a little run-down, but very elegant in a medieval sort of way. In such a house King Arthur's round table wouldn't be out of place as your writing desk. We would later find out that this was Sarah Bernhardt's Belle-Île retreat.

Turning back the way we'd come, we drove a couple of miles and then cut right toward the western side of the island—the *côte sauvage*. The road stopped at a parking lot at the site of the Grotte de l'Apothicairerie, a giant cave at the foot of a nearby cliff. The lot was entirely empty except for a purple motor scooter. Beyond that stood what had to be the world's ugliest hotel, which by modern French architectural standards was saying a mouthful. So wild and remote was this location in Matisse's day that painters often stayed overnight in the inn run by a friend of Russell's. There, in that summer of 1896, Matisse painted the famous *Breton Serving Girl*. We got out and walked around, and Beth peered over the edge to see the grotto. All I wanted to do was get back in the car and drive away.

About halfway down the island another road branches off to Kervilahouen, a hamlet of white cottages clumped in the shadow of the Grand Phare, or great lighthouse, which dominates that flat landscape approaching the sea. I had read that Kervilahouen means "sound and fury," and I imagined living in one of those little houses during the kind of ferocious storms they're supposed to have out there. In my mind, I heard the howl of the wind and the roar of the ocean, and I peered out a window and saw the pounding rain caught for an instant in the beam from the tower.

We had a photograph of the pilot's house that Matisse stayed in, and Beth recognized it immediately. It was by the main road on the right. Someone was doing a lot of work on it, and there were wheelbarrows and sawhorses in the yard. We parked and walked up and looked in the window. In the living room I placed Matisse in the approximate spot he would've been in to paint *Open Door, Brittany*—though based on that painting, I would never have imagined such an imposing house.

John Peter Russell's mansion stood half a mile away. Today that's the site of two swanky hotels, one with a spa. They sit high on a ridge overlooking a narrow bay. No one was around, so we walked out to the terrace and watched a boy and girl down below who seemed to be trying to catch crabs. Then we drove around the point to the next cove, Port-Coton, to see the famous rocks known as Les Aiguilles (needles). Monet painted them, Matisse painted them, Russell painted them, I sketched them. And I noted to myself that the lonely look of the land there at the edge gives gravitas to the word *barren*.

In summer, though, Belle-Île is said to be astonishingly beautiful, with wildflowers blanketing the meadows and cobalt waves spinning cotton froth on majestic rocks. Writing to a friend, Matisse described the Belle-Île sky as "made of mother-of-pearl." Under the influence of John Peter Russell that summer of 1896, he opened a door between his old life and the one he would live forever after. A letter he wrote that season from Belle-Île encapsulated what he had absorbed from Russell: "We painters shouldn't be galley slaves. So don't worry about your neighbor. Pay no attention to anything except what interests you (anything else would be impossible in any

case). And enjoy working. Work with white, with blue, with red, paint with your feet if the whim takes you, and if anyone doesn't like it, send him packing."

Two 1896 Matisse paintings of the port of Le Palais tell the story of Russell's influence and Matisse's progress. The first canvas, painted at the beginning of the summer, is dark and muddy—the "Old-Master" palette of the previous year. The second, from summer's end, is bright and airy—the palette of the Impressionists.

WE ATE SUNDAY lunch at La Maison, waving to Johey and Stéphane, who were both working in the kitchen. The restaurant was crowded, and the people at two tables had brought their exceptionally well-behaved dogs. It made me feel bad about Snapp. The night before, we had phoned Beth's mother, Bobbye, to see how things were going. I thought Bobbye would wish me a gushing happy birthday, but she didn't even mention it. All she could talk about was Snapp's thyroid pills and his flea treatments and how the vet she'd taken him to had said that schnauzers were "high-maintenance dogs." Bobbye wasn't comforted by my stories of all the times I had forgotten to give Snapp his pills. She wasn't complaining, she was worried. She wanted to do everything just right. In the meantime, Snapp hadn't had a haircut in three months and Cleo was terrorized by a neighbor cat and afraid to go outside. I felt guilty about all three of them.

We'd also received an e-mail from our Realtor reporting continued "price resistance" and recommending that we come down another ten grand. That would put us $60,000 below where we had started the previous summer. Her six-month contract would soon be up, and we were considering a change. But clearly—at least clearly to me—we had priced the house too high. Beth believed fervently that the right buyers would come along eventually, and that they would be lucky to get our wonderful home at any price. After all, a book had been written about it. People called it "The Book House." It had twice been photographed for magazines, the second of which feature had come out just as we put the house on the market. It was perfect—wasn't it?

These are Sunday subjects, I thought. Sundays had always depressed me. If weekends were islands in time, Sunday marked the approach of the ferry to carry us back.

After lunch we took our wine to the other room and finished it in front of the fire. Johey and Stéphane came and sat with us for a little while. Instead of saying good-bye, we made a plan for them to spend the night with us on the mainland in a few weeks when they went to pick up Johey's cousin at the train. "We don't know what kind of space we'll have," Beth said, speaking of the borrowed house we were about to move into, "but we'll make do."

WHEN MATISSE LEFT Belle-Île at the end of the summer of 1896, he returned home with something perhaps even more important to his future than John Peter Russell's infectious commitment to color; for the first time, he had actually seen a life built around the freedom of creating. Russell had it all—peace and quiet, splendid isolation, and the comforting support of family and friends. The cacophony of Paris was wearing on Matisse, and it wouldn't be long before he would begin his search for a different way to live.

Even though I hated leaving Belle-Île, I also looked forward to working in the welcome seclusion of our borrowed house in Brittany. We were to meet Alice in Auray in front of a drive-through boulangerie on the Quiberon highway. Projecting forward from the time the ferry landed, she estimated we would be there Monday afternoon about 2. "I'll be in a silver Volvo station wagon," she said.

The problem was, we were starving. I had already gotten lost in one small town trying to find a place to buy sandwiches, and now we were running late. As we drove into the outskirts of Auray at nearly two o'clock, we saw a McDonald's. "Oh my God," Beth said, and I swerved into the parking lot. We pulled up behind Alice about 2:20. "Hide that McDonald's cup," I said, as Alice ran toward the Peugeot to give us hugs. It was great to see her. The sixteen days since Paris had seemed like forever.

We followed her through a couple of roundabouts, by a spanking-new housing development, then onto a road that took us into open country. Cows were grazing near a pond. We passed a stately old mas, then a row of new houses, then more farmland. Finally we came to a place in the road where four houses were built close together—two newer houses and a huge old one on the left, and on the right a single neat white cottage. Alice stopped in front of the huge old house and we parked behind her. She stuck her head out the window. "Wait here while I open the gate!"

Two minutes later we were in a vast yard staring dumbfounded at the wonderful farmhouse that was to be ours for the next month. "Come on in," Alice said. A blue gate opened onto a sprawling stone patio that surrounded the house on two sides. The stone outbuildings had periwinkle doors. She let us into the house. In the foyer was a hall tree hung with hats. To the left was the living room, furnished with two white sofas and two leopard-print chairs. Propped against the bookshelf was a gut-string guitar like the one I'd had in high school.

Across from the living room was the kitchen/dining room, a large open area with a working fireplace, bookshelves with books (in English!) and a CD player, an old sideboard set up as a bar, and a long white wooden dining table with eight blue chairs. Upstairs were four bedrooms and a big bath. The master bedroom had a fireplace. When we flung open the shutters, one entire wall framed a view of rolling Breton farm country.

After Alice left, Beth and I unpacked the car and went grocery shopping. "I go to LeClerc," Alice had said, so we did too. Located ten minutes away next door to our surreptitious McDonald's, LeClerc was a giant supermarket with its own cleaners, bank, florist, shoe repair shop, and probably others I've forgotten. In that respect, it was similar to the Wal-Mart Supercenters that have taken over the U.S., but in every other way it was utterly, inimitably French: Three hundred different cheeses, two long aisles devoted to wines, champagnes, and liquors, and, just inside the entrance, a big circular bar where people were drinking and smoking and telling stories in a dialect that depended not so much on the tip of the tongue but on a nether region of the neck. "Clear your throat," I told Beth, "and the Bretons think you're a great conversationalist."

We quickly settled into a comfortable routine. Aside from my writing, I had one household chore in Auray that I had to perform without fail. The boiler for the heat was in one of the outbuildings, and once a day I had to empty the bucket that the condensation drained into. "Going to do my chore," I would say to Beth, slipping on my coat, and while I was outside I might wander around the yard for a few minutes. The property was vaguely pie-shaped, with a high stone wall angling in on the back side and a fence with heavy foliage running down the side parallel to the road. The house owner, a sailor, had built his children a funny wooden play boat near a swing set by the wall. Far down at the point of the pie was a run-down stone building almost covered in vines. Where the door had once been was now just a black void. One day I ventured down there to inspect it, and when I got close something inside started making a terrible racket, thrashing around and beating the floor. I ran. Whatever lived in there could have it. I hurried back to my writing.

The way the rear of the house butted up to another high wall, we couldn't see either of the houses next to us. Except for the little cottage across the road, which I could look down on from the bathroom window, we had the illusion that we were alone in the country. But lying in bed in the predawn we would hear shotguns pop very near us, and dogs bark. Later in the morning we heard farmers herding cattle in fields close by. For a couple of hours at the end of the day, the road by the house became a shortcut for whooshing commuters eager to get home to one of the hamlets outside Auray.

In the winter, the days were short but beautiful. One morning Beth woke me up to look at a pink glowing sky. From the window by my writing table, I could watch the continuously changing clouds and light, their colors shifting from slate gray to ultramarine to golden pink. One amazing day brought, in quick succession, rain, sleet, snow, hail, and then brilliant sunshine. At night the stars were as clear and bright as I had ever seen them.

While Beth worked, I took on evening cooking duties. I turned on Chet Baker or Billie Holiday, opened a bottle of wine and poured us each a glass, and then, while she wrote to the white noise of *Zorro* reruns in Italian, I busied myself in the great kitchen for the next couple of hours chopping beets, turnips, carrots, tomatoes, and even pumpkins, which Beth had figured out would cook down to something resembling our beloved Southern sweet potatoes. I sautéed duck breasts, roasted chickens, broiled heavily herbed loins of pork. I insisted that dinner be at the dining room table by candlelight.

On the first Saturday morning we were in the house, Beth plugged in our new printer and blew the electricity. Nothing I did seemed to work, so I was forced to phone the owners in England and ask their advice. "You've flipped the breaker? You've tried the fuses? Well, I can't really help you, now can I, Jim?" said the owner, Mike, speaking in that funny British way that always ends with a consensus-seeking question. "The French electrical system is a bloody abomination, isn't it, Jim?" Denise, Mike's wife, called André, her French handyman in Auray, and left a message on his answering machine for him to get in touch with us.

Unable to write, I set up my easel in the dining room by the windows and did three paintings that day. The first was a loose picture based on a sketch I'd made of the antique table and chairs in our room in Honfleur. The second was a nearly all reddish-orange still life of pomegranates that I called—because of the color of the painting that I had been so taken with in Paris—*Homage to Pierre-Humbert*. Finally, I got out the Max Beckmann book we had bought at Pompidou and painted my version of the picture he did of himself in that bright blue sport jacket, except I put in my face. "Look, Beth," I said, "it's *Self-Portrait in Max Beckmann's Coat*." I was feeling positively brilliant.

The next evening, Alice and Guy came to dinner. With first champagne and then good red wine, we toasted Alice for all her kindnesses. Over the many lives in a lifetime, friends will become strangers and strangers will become friends. Guy's English was better than our French, but I worried that he felt left out most of the night. At the end of dinner he said, "I don't understand all the words. But I understand the language of the heart."

Such were the joys we were experiencing in this beautiful borrowed home. Very early on, I made a note in my book: "The rhythm that takes over everything. Enjoying cooking again after so long. Making great ambitious dinners, eating late, listening to music, working, reading, painting. It's heaven."

THEN WE GOT an offer on our house. It came on February 4, a week before our Realtor's contract was up. The offer was so far below our asking price that we didn't take it seriously. Our Realtor cautioned against that. "Come up with a counter," she said, and suggested a number that was breathtakingly below where we had started.

I gave Beth the news. She was furious. She wanted to murder someone, and as the messenger I was in the running. We agonized for hours, then faced facts. "Okay," Beth said, "but not a penny less."

The people brought their offer up to within four thousand dollars. Our Realtor volunteered to donate $1,500 from her commission. This was our first offer in nearly six months. We wanted—*needed*—to sell. Were we going to blow the deal for $2,500?

As long as I live, I will never forget the scene that played out that night in that borrowed house in Brittany. It was after midnight. All the lights were off. Beth lay in bed crying while I sat at the top of the stairs trying to figure some way to make either of us feel better. I couldn't. We were the characters in Matisse's haunting canvas *Le Conversation*, the man in his pajamas, the woman in her bathrobe, a gulf of blue between them. In that picture the window looks like an escape hatch.

I phoned Lloyd, whose advice was to sell. Then I called our Realtor again. My voice cracking, I told her we had to have another $1,500. She called back in a few minutes with a yes. That was it, no more wiggle room. We agreed to sell our house for $75,900 under where we had officially started.

The next day, Beth e-mailed Blair and Bret and apologized for selling their home out from under them. And in her diary, she wrote:

> We always knew the sale of our house would be emotional and hard, even though it was what we'd chosen to do in starting our new lives. But this is thornier than I thought. I think that even though it's what we intended, as long as the house was still ours, we had a home whether we lived in it or not. I haven't been unhappy with our nomadic existence. To the contrary, I've enjoyed every step of the way, but somehow it does feel different now. At least at this moment, I am sad. I feel on the edge.

For much of the next month, this was the undercurrent. Beth worked like a fury, and for one five-day stretch didn't set foot outside the house. I told her she needed to ease up, but she wouldn't hear of it. Planted morning to night on the sofa with her laptop, she listened incessantly to a plaintive CD by David Gray that she had found in our hosts' cabinet. *"What you gonna do when the money runs out?"* he sang, seemingly every time I came downstairs for coffee. Something in his nasally whine evoked dusty images of all the down-and-out southerners I'd ever read about making their desperate way to Detroit, or Chicago, or L.A.

I stayed upstairs as much as possible, closing my door and trying to lose myself in work. Occasionally, in the bathroom, I would stand at the window and watch the old man who lived in the cottage across the road. A couple of times a day he and his little dog would make a tour of the lawn, studying the bushes, examining tree branches, inspecting the steps and foundation and the condition of the gate. *Is that what I want?* I thought, *or is this?* I was one of the lucky ones—I'd always known that I wanted to write. The downside was that I could never be happy doing anything else. Matisse once said that "the genuine creator" wasn't just a person with talent, but one who had managed to arrange his existence in such a way that art could flourish. For four decades I had struggled with that proposition, trying to achieve the right combination of time and space and money to live the life I had to live. In that sense, I'd been chasing Matisse since before I knew about him.

Even my painting seemed to suffer a greater-than-usual malaise. Having tried to absorb Matisse's words about visualizing a painting, thinking it out, building it like architecture, I attempted a *nature morte* of an old white pitcher, yellow tulips, and a blue chair in the dining room, having first boiled down the composition—through a series of tight sketches in my notebook—to a finely balanced whole. The result was an embarrassingly bad Matisse knockoff, which felt like it wasn't mine, and I wished it weren't. I would have to forget the planning and instead just face the canvas and see what happened. What happened when I tried to capture shadowy trees in the late-afternoon Breton light was that Beth said it looked like I had used Halloween colors. "Your painting isn't as natural as it was at home," she said. "You're trying too hard."

FINALLY WE CAME to our senses: Brooding alone together in this house wasn't going to help matters; we had to get off our island. We made a pact to go somewhere one day a week. One Saturday, we drove over to the big market in Rennes. In a huge *place* surrounded by quaint half-timbered houses, hundreds of vendors set out beautiful fruits and produce, while one whole pavilion is devoted to meats and cheeses and another to fish. Between the pavilions, a boy played guitar better than Django. We stocked up on vegetables, cheese, and sausage, and bought a capon from a jolly lady who held the bird up by its neck so we could see its little curled claws dangling and its milky white eye staring at us upside down from its floppy head.

"Whack! Whack!" Beth said, making chopping motions at her neck and ankles.

"Coupé?" the jolly lady asked, her own eyes dancing at her fun with the squeamish Americans.

"Oui! Oui!" we said, and she laughed heartily and sharpened her cleaver.

After a long lunch at a classic brasserie across from the Hôtel de Ville, we headed home in late afternoon. The early February sunset was spectacular. "It looks like the sun is setting fire to the clouds," Beth said. In Kepes's *Language of Vision*, I had just read a quote from someone called M. Luckiesh: "A cumulus cloud in the sky may be hundred thousands brighter than the deepest shadow. However, the artist must represent a landscape by means of a palette whose white is only about thirty times brighter than the black." No wonder Matisse dated his chronic insomnia to his summers on Belle-Île; once you make the leap to color, you're already halfway to madness.

Early in February we learned that the French Tourist Network was going to feature our adventure on its Web site. That was our introduction to Louise O'Brien, who would become one of our staunchest supporters—in spite of the fact that the FTN article called us "brave . . . some would say foolhardy."

On Valentine's Day we had dinner at the Port de Goustan in Auray. The next week we went to the market in nearby Vannes and still had enough daylight to drive toward the coast to see the megaliths at Carnac. On a gray Saturday morning we drove east to Brocéliande, the enchanted forest of the Arthurian legends. We enjoyed lovely dinners with Alice and Guy at their new house, and one Sunday went with them to the home of their friends Jean-Pierre and Véronique, where we celebrated J-P's birthday over a four-hour meal that began with seven dozen Brittany oysters and ended with tipsy group hugging. A few days later, Johey from Belle-Île came for a night with her hilarious Dutch cousin Yolanda. Stéphane had had to work, but Johey brought wine and *coq au vin* and I built a fire in the dining room fireplace. Beth and Johey stayed up till nearly dawn talking about islands and marriage and the challenges of life in a foreign country. The next day, after they left, Beth said we have it easier than Johey and Stéphane, since we're both left out together.

As the weeks ticked by, I found myself feeling better about the house sale. Maybe Beth did, too. We wouldn't end up with much money, but we would pay off our debts. I was proud of that. Fresh start, new life, another chance. In Brittany, the days were getting longer. Red buds and forsythia were blooming along the fence. Jonquils had appeared beside the driveway. Standing by the bathroom window, I could watch the little man in the cottage across the road kneeling down to pry dandelions one by one from his lawn.

The house closing was scheduled for February 26. We didn't know what time on the 26th, but all that evening in Brittany we were tense and edgy. The next morning, I dreaded opening my e-mail. Having bought and sold several houses, I knew that closing day often brought surprises. Sure enough, when I scrolled down my e-mail list, this was the message from our Realtor: "Little Rock is shut down by snow and ice. Everything is delayed indefinitely."

WHEN HENRI MATISSE returned to Paris with paintings he had done on Belle-Île in 1896 and 1897, many people said, essentially, that he was committing career suicide. "Anyone," writes Spurling, "could see that the strange, bright, highly simplified paintings Matisse produced on the island in 1897 were frankly unsaleable." But Matisse had made his stand: He would follow the path of color wherever it took him, even if it led to personal darkness. For her part, Camille Joblaud thought he had lost his mind. Weary of struggling to make ends meet with this rebel who did everything possible to avoid playing the game, she made a stand of her own—she left him.

In a few days we got an e-mail from our friend Patti in Little Rock: "Well, they're in," she said, meaning the buyers of our house. Our old life was officially over. Looking around for solace, I found it in Beth's resilient hope. "Underneath my distress, I realize the tiniest spark of excitement," she had written in a recent diary. "The real adventure begins."

Part II

BORROWED LIGHT

6.

The Being of Things

MATISSE PAINTED A luminous picture of oranges in Morocco, but I always think of it as a true product of Corsica, the first place he ever saw oranges growing on a tree—and a light that could make them glow.

In Corsica, the sun commands your full attention. From dawn to dusk it delivers a forceful sermon on its own stunning centrality, and after a few moments in its presence you wouldn't dare dispute it.

When I first felt its power I thought of something I had read in Arnheim's *Art and Visual Perception*. "Physicists tell us we live on borrowed light," he writes. "The light that brightens the sky is sent through a dark universe to a dark earth from the sun over a distance of ninety-three million miles. Very little in the physicist's description accords with our perception." Then he goes on to recount the historical debates, biblical and philosophical and otherwise, about the nature of light and darkness, ending on the side of art over science. "Knowledge," he writes, "has made us stop talking like children, ancient chroniclers, or Polynesian islanders. . . . We have trained ourselves to rely on knowledge rather than our sense of sight to such an extent that it takes accounts by the naïve and the artists to make us realize what we see."

I pulled my cap down over my eyes and edged my chin toward the sun that had changed Matisse's life. Once he had seen it, nothing beneath it looked the same. That must be the curse of the true painter, for whom the right light is home. Until he found his, this man from the dark plains of Picardy was compelled to chase after it, tracking it from one shore of the Mediterranean to another, searching for the perfect wave, the perfect ray, the perfect beam, which he would then attempt to trap in the nanospace between color and canvas, or between color and color. Straining to imagine the experience, I remembered how, as a young boy in Mississippi, I collected balls of mercury from a gas meter at a house on the street where we lived. With that quicksilver light in the palm of one hand, I pinched gently and watched it explode into silver BB's, like a miniature Milky Way.

IN FEBRUARY OF 1898, newlyweds Henri and Amélie Matisse steamed into Ajaccio for an extended working vacation. They had met only four months earlier at a wedding for a mutual friend, and each had been immediately taken with the other. "It was Matisse's boldness that attracted her," writes Spurling, "the glint of devilry that overcame him all his life at moments when the lure of risk and danger compelled him to stake everything, both personally and professionally, on an uncertain future." For his part, Matisse was nervous and uneasy beneath his jaunty facade. He was more than ready to embrace an ally who would unconditionally champion him and his work.

Corsica was the beginning of their grand adventure together, come what may. At the Académie Julian in Paris, he had been promoted to the level of associate. "What a fine civil service career opened before me!" he said, sardonically, a quarter century later. "In effect, painting, even academic, was a poor provider at that time. I was going to be forced to take up some other profession. I decided to give myself a year off, without impediments, in which I would paint as I wanted to. I no longer worked for anyone but myself. I was saved."

Amélie, a southerner from Toulouse, had chosen as their launching ground this ruggedly beautiful island awash in clear, penetrating light. For the rest of his days, Matisse credited the four months they spent in Ajaccio as pivotal to his development as an artist. "Here is a country where light plays the leading role, color comes second," he said in 1947. "It's with color that you put down this light of course, but above all you must feel this light, have it within yourself."

Beth and I arrived by ferry on a Saturday evening in spring. This ferry wasn't like the one to Belle-Île; it was more of a floating mall, with food court and bar and at least a couple of shops. Despite having comfortable assigned seats, people milled around aimlessly. We sat by the window on the port side; the movie *Spider-Man* was playing on the monitors hanging at intervals from the ceiling. Most of the passengers were dressed as though they were going to a NASCAR race. There was one strangely notable exception, a couple in black who appeared to have stepped through a time warp. They could've been on the same boat that brought the Matisses to Corsica: She wore a long dress, and he wore a black suit with velvet trim on the collar. His sideburns were long for current fashion, and he carried a cane and gloves and topped his ensemble with a boater. Waiting to embark, we had seen them at the marina strolling in that getup, the lady idly twirling a parasol.

At about 7 P.M. we passed several jagged rock islands on the port side, one with a watchtower on it and another with a lighthouse. Thirty minutes later we docked in Ajaccio and drove off into bright

sunlight past lines of cars waiting to take the ferry back to the mainland. Corsica was a very popular tourist destination, judging by the
trouble we'd had getting a hotel. The difficulty had been baffling—
often, we hadn't even received a response to our e-mails or faxes.
On this wild and insular island they apparently didn't care if we
came or not.

Our three-star hotel was downtown a block from the port. The
street was narrow and appeared to be restricted to pedestrians, so
our first glimpse of the hotel was from half a block away. "Good
God," said Beth. "You think that's it?" The building was dingy and
unpainted. But in comparison to the one across from it, it was a
palace. Beth waited with the car while I went to check in. Outside the
hotel door I looked up at the building opposite. Windows were wide
open, single light bulbs hanging from the ceiling. In one apartment,
a black garbage bag had been rigged up on the light for some purpose. Hollow-eyed people with lots of kids hung close to the windows, hoping to catch a breeze. A man in a wife-beater undershirt
stood smoking at one, his foot propped on the sill.

In the hotel lobby—which was small but clean—a sweet, attractive young couple manned the desk. They had our reservation and
seemed genuinely glad to see me. It was okay to park in front to un-
load, the man said, so I went to get the car. "How is it?" Beth said.

"There were a lot of people in the lobby," I said.

We carried in a couple of bags and stopped for the key. The pretty
woman said, "You're going to be with us five nights?" and pushed the
key to room 64 across the counter.

"Yes," I said, with a glance at Beth, who looked none too pleased.

"You have a room with a terrace," the woman said proudly, as we
lugged our bags up the flight of stairs to the tiny elevator. It stopped
half a flight below our room. I inserted the key and opened the door.
The room was almost impressive—large, with two pairs of French
doors, a fancy antique daybed and a big armoire. Then: "Oh God,
what is *that*?" Beth said. It was an extra wide chair, apparently, although it could've been a hibernating animal. It was upholstered in
long, fuzzy, matted fake brown fur. My first thought was, *Naked people have done unspeakable things there.*

"Let's look at the terrace," I said, and opened the French doors. Again, it was a perfectly nice terrace—big and wide, with potted flowers. But forty feet across the street, at eye level, the smoking man took a long drag of his cigarette and stared at us. I pulled over one of the mildewed plastic chairs and sat in it, but my head was still above the railing. "I've got to go inside," I said.

"This isn't going to work," Beth said. She—we both—knew me: The room was one thing, but I would never set foot on that terrace with those eyes trained on me. I was chasing Matisse, not Walker Evans. That's why we had stretched to stay in nice places. Was I now supposed to set up my easel and capture the serenity of a naked lightbulb?

We weren't sure which scenario would make us the Uglier Americans—bolting at the sight of poverty, or staying and living it up in front of the poor. In any case, we decided not to bring in any more luggage but to park the car in a nearby pay garage while we figured out what to do. On the way, Beth saw a sign with an arrow saying *Route des Sanguinaires.* "Turn right!" she said, and I cut across a lane to do it. "This is where all the nice hotels are."

Within half an hour we had stopped at four different hotels that she had sent letters to, and every one of them had sea views and availability beginning the next day. We finally settled on Cala di Sole, which was priced at 122 euros a night—only nine more than our downtown hotel. The Cala di Sole had a seaside saltwater pool, its own beach, and our room would have a private balcony looking directly out to the islands we had passed on the way in to Ajaccio—the Îles Sanguinaires, named for the spectacular blood-red color they turned at sunset. Matisse had been particularly taken by the beauty of the Îles Sanguinaires.

We found a restaurant down the coast and had dinner by the sea. Beth was ebullient that night; I was a little subdued. I felt that we had made the right decision, but I dreaded telling that nice young couple that we were fleeing in the name of art.

ON SUNDAY WE made a fast and early exit. "I'm writing a book on Matisse," I told the man at the desk, "and for that I need a view."

He seemed to understand, but the pretty woman wouldn't even look at me.

Our new room wouldn't be ready for hours, so on Place Foch, a nice shady square near the port, we claimed a comfortable table by a big plane tree and ordered *deux crèmes*. The weekly market was in full swing half a block away. From another direction someone was playing gentle tunes on an accordion. Beth opened her guidebook and read to me about Corsica's history of bloody vendettas and the "honorable bandits" who acted against the Republic. Formerly controlled by the Italians and now the French, the islanders just couldn't seem to stand being under anyone's thumb, and those who committed crimes against the state were often protected—for years—from arrest and prosecution. The outlaws hid out in the *maquis*, the notoriously scrubby undergrowth that gave the island its distinctive scent.

Lowland maquis was composed of briar, arbutus, mastic and yellow broom, wild garlic, potent thyme, rosemary, and marjoram, and a variety of wildflowers, including orchids. In the mountains it became taller and thicker, mixed with trees and high shrubs. "I would recognize my island with my eyes closed," said the Emperor Napoleon, Ajaccio's most famous native son, "by nothing more than the smell of the maquis carried on waves."

"Remember that Corsican charcuterie you had on Belle-Île the night we met Johey and Stéphane?" Beth said. I did—it was strong and spicy. "It says here that the native pigs, including wild boar, graze on the maquis and that's what gives the meat its flavor. I think we should go to the market and get some." I paid for our coffees while Beth went to the corner and tipped the accordion player. A few months in France had turned us into admirers of the discreet accordion.

At the market we bought several sausages, a few slices of *prisuttu* (dry, salty ham), a couple of cheeses, and three bottles of Corsican wine. The man who ran the wine booth said the reds from the village of Patrimonio were the best on the island. On the way to the car we saw a boulangerie and picked up a fresh baguette. That would take care of lunch. Once we reached our hotel, with its pool and its balcony overlooking the sea, I didn't want to tear myself away until dinner—if then.

In full daylight that part of Corsica didn't look much different from the mainland coast. The distant mountains were greenish brown with dots of yellow—broom, we guessed. The sea varied from blue to blue-green to turquoise. One difference was the beaches— they were wide strands of pink sand, not the usual Mediterranean pebbles.

Our room was ready early, so we checked in and changed into our swimsuits. From our balcony the sea was probably thirty yards in front of us. The sun beat down ferociously. Out to our right, successively lighter hills sloped to the surf one behind the other, until the Îles Sanguinaires broke off from the rest like loose links in a keychain. Closer in was a modern hotel whose descending tiers echoed the hills behind it. To our left was our hotel terrace with its blinding disks of white tables. Beyond that was the clear blue pool.

Before long the sun became unbearable, and we took our books and went down for a swim. We were out there a long time. The water was cool but not cold, and Beth swam laps while I fell asleep on the chaise. When I woke up she was gone. The sun had moved lower, toward the hills, but it was still too bright for anything beyond the most fleeting glance.

At about 7 P.M. we opened a bottle of the wine we had bought at the market and I sat on the balcony waiting for the fabled Îles Sanguinaires sunset. Really seeing had proved difficult in the searing Corsican light, so I decided to cheat by documenting in my notebook every nuance of what my eyes beamed back from the scene before me. At 7:33 I saw the first sign of pink above the mountains. Higher in the sky there was only a heated white, centered on the sun.

7:38: More pink over the mountains. Not a full pink, just a hint. The mountains nearest the sun are darkest. To the left, the far Île Sanguinaire, the one with the lighthouse on it, seems almost faded to gray. In front of me, the waves pound the rocks.

7:41: Lots more pink now, especially to the left and below the sun. A seabird seems to fly into the sun, then disappears. I have to rest my eyes. Bright reflection in the water below the multitiered hotel.

7:48: The sun has moved a bit to the right. Instead of at the hump of the mountain, now it's in the trough between two hills.

7:54: Sun has faded in intensity. You can look at it, just about.

7:57: The sun has moved farther right and is no longer in the trough. It's now climbing the other cliff. In the cove the reflection is choppier, and pinkish in a reverse crescent.

7:59: Sun touches rising slope.

8 P.M.: Sun partially hidden.

8:01: Sun 3/4 hidden.

8:01:30: Sun gone. Pink/orange clouds where it disappeared. Far left, blue/gray/purple warming to the right—hottest (orange/pink) where the sun set. "The palest hint of aubergine," Beth corrects. I think of aubergine as nearly black. Must pay more attention to food if I want to be a writer.

8:08: The sky above the blue mountains a warm persimmon.

8:10: There is apparently to be no blood red tonight. The sea begins to reflect warmth as one surface. The sky drifts away. It's as though the universe has turned us upside down.

ON MONDAY I went to find where the Matisses had stayed in Ajaccio. According to written descriptions, their rooming house was at the southern intersection of the boulevard Sylvestre Marcaggi and the rue Miss Campbell. In 1898 that was far out, but today scores of apartment buildings and hotels rise between the site and the *centre ville*.

The villa they stayed in was no longer standing, but I parked the car on boulevard Marcaggi across from a small church and walked around the area hoping to get some sense of the Corsica that Matisse saw. Spurling writes that he didn't stray far from the neighborhood, and no wonder—the apartment they rented connected by winding staircase to a flat roof, upon which he set up his easel and painted nearby buildings. When the Matisses did go out, they often followed a path leading down the hill to the sea, and from there they could stroll along the coast road between lush gardens and the sparkling surf.

On the gray windowsill of a faded terra-cotta house on what was once that path to the sea, two orange lilies seemed to burst in a fusion of light and color. If nothing else was the same, I had to believe that in 1898 Corsican lilies exploded with just such intensity. So must have the butterfly orchids, the white flowering heather, the pink rock rose. And for Matisse it was all astoundingly new. He was seeing as a child, and his senses were assaulted by the color, the fragrance, and especially the light of the South. The paintings I've seen that he made in Corsica were all colorful landscapes infused with light, two of them scenes of an old mill that is no longer standing. In the months immediately following their time in Corsica, he painted several still lifes of oranges.

I photographed the pot of lilies on the windowsill, and then I made a small sketch, noting the colors—the light yellow orange on the outside, the gray fading to black inside away from the sun. I had been thinking a lot about something Matisse had said, quoting Delacroix, about seeing as an artist: He said you needed to look at a subject so long and so hard that it no longer appeared the way that subject had ever been seen before. I knew—felt—what he meant. You could do that with words, pronouncing, for example, the word *home* over and over so many times that it ceased to have common meaning. I could often make myself remember how I had seen a place—a room, a house, a street—for the first time, which was always different from how I later came to see it. We start to see what we expect to see. That's what the artist has to combat and what the rest of the world is doomed to embrace—seeing as others see, the better to market to them.

After I finished sketching, I stood across the street in the shade looking hard at the lilies on the windowsill, but apparently not hard enough. They still looked like lilies when I left.

When I got back to the hotel we decided to go find some lunch,

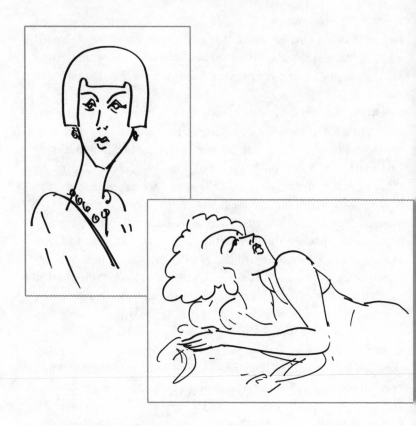

but instead of driving back to Ajaccio we headed farther out the Route des Sanguinaires. I had thought the highway would continue on around the island, but in a few kilometers it petered out in the parking lot of a restaurant at the Îles. The lot was full of classic cars—old MGs, Triumphs, Austin-Healeys, a Morgan. There was even a 1971 Mercedes 250C like the one I had bought in Little Rock in 2000 and unloaded—thankfully—while I still had a dollar left to leave for France.

In the restaurant the garrulous antique-car club, husbands and wives, commandeered a long table containing a surprising number of wine bottles. One woman had her head on the table. After mediocre salads we left and walked up the trail toward the old watchtower. This was the last hump in the chain before the links broke loose. Up close the maquis was fascinating—succulent growths of everything from wild asparagus to garlic to lilies. The rocks were granite with delicate sienna lichens growing on them. The views were stunning: Coming around a turn, we would be hit squarely in the senses by a hillside of yellow flowers against the blue-green sea. Thousands of blue buds of some kind had blown from the maquis into the water, making a periwinkle surf. As we came down the final path, the car club was getting ready to roll. Their cheeks and the Corsican sun glowed impressively.

In the afternoon, I got out my sketchpad and made some drawings from the balcony. One was a crisp clean view of the modern hotel stair-stepping down from the hills to the sea. Another was of a small red fishing boat that bobbed in the turquoise water like a Derain painting. The colors were so beautiful that I almost felt guilty just drawing. It was an internal debate that had been going on for eons. "Poussin and Rubens had this general fight," my old art teacher, David Bailin, had told me the previous summer. "It's color versus line. Rubens was the colorist, Poussin the linear guy. The line tends to be the real classical approach. In fact, Poussin established some of the issues of the French academy, in which artists would train according to an incredible hierarchy: historical and religious paintings at the top, portraits next, then landscapes, and finally still lifes.

"Of course," Bailin said, "this gave younger artists something to rebel against. For example, the Impressionists—consciously or not—took the lowest end of the scale of the classical academy and made their paintings of landscapes and still lifes. It was an art of negation."

In his book, Arnheim discusses a Rorschach inkblot test designed to determine if you're a color person or a line person, depending on whether what you see favors one at the expense of the other. "Rorschach found that a cheerful mood makes for color responses," writes Arnheim, "whereas depressed people more often react to shape."

I liked that—then read on. "Color dominance indicated an openness to external stimuli. Such people are said to be sensitive, easily influenced, unstable, disorganized, given to emotional outbursts. A preference for shape reactions in patients goes with an introverted disposition, strong control over impulses, a pedantic, unemotional attitude." No wonder William Blake insisted that all good artists are mad.

Actually, I had been concentrating on my line work. The summer before we left, I decided I needed to learn to draw women. I don't want to take a Rorschach test for this, but most of the females I had drawn in my life had looked like bad drag queens: chins too strong, jaw lines too prominent, shoulders too broad. Matisse was a master at capturing the delicacy of the female form, so I photocopied some of his drawings from *Thèmes et Variations* and set to work the way I had at age twelve when I had committed myself to learning to draw Elvis Presley.

For some reason, I knew instinctively that I needed a large sketchpad. The larger you work, the looser you can be. Looseness leads to fluidity, which seems to be the key to drawing women. I laid the Matisse pages out on my art table and studied them. Amazing: He could render a perfectly beautiful woman in about fourteen strokes of his pen. "One must always search for the desire of the line," he used to tell his students, "where it wishes to enter and where to die away." Most of the time, it apparently wished to enter on the hair, which was depicted as a simple curvy line. It liked to die away in the fingertips. The face was constructed of eight lines: the roundness of the forehead; the jut of the nose; the cheek, chin, and jaw; two quick eyebrows; a line for the eye; a blip of a nostril; and a bow-shaped line for the lips. For Matisse, the desire of the line was always toward a truthful simplicity.

Working fast with a bold black pen, I filled my sketchbook with a surprising number of—if not beauties, at least womanly women. Even my also-rans looked better than female forms I had drawn in the past. My plan was to move down the body until I had learned to draw the whole woman. "Remember that a foot is a bridge. . . ." Matisse said. "This straight leg goes through the torso and meets the shoulder as it were at a right angle. . . . The other leg . . . curves out and down like a flying buttress. . . ." Unfortunately, we started packing before I got beyond the hair and the head.

My ultimate goal was to draw and paint Beth. All along, I had told her that she was going to be my model on this journey. "You better make me look good," she said. In our apartment in Paris, she spent whole days in her ice-blue silk pajamas, a silk flowered robe tied tight at her waist, looking as if she'd walked out of a Matisse painting. I thought of asking her to pose many times, but always lost my nerve. "I was afraid I should never do figures," Matisse told the writer Louis Aragon. "Then I put figures in my still lifes."

Not me—not yet. Painting someone is a very intimate act. Deep in my head I sometimes found myself in an artists' locker room complete with towel popping, soap dropping, and *bon mots* bouncing off the wall: "It ain't the size of the brush, it's how you handle it!" At times like that, you keep your towel tight around you and make sure not to meet anyone's gaze.

THE LOCALS CALL Corte, a mountain village in the center of the island, "the soul of Corsica." On Tuesday we got up early and set out to explore it. Thank God for French roundabouts: Several times on our way out of Ajaccio, Beth searched the map for the right route while I circled, once as much as four times, waiting for instructions. We tried not to fight. The spoke we finally took was a straight two-lane that led us through the junky transition from outlying commerce to lowland farms. On bus stops, power stations, houses, and trees, the word *Indepenzia* was slapped on angrily with red paint. Some rebel had been on a rampage.

In short order the road began climbing, winding ever steeper into granite mountains, passing beneath thick canopies of chestnut trees, barely skirting drunken plunges into treacherous gorges. The maquis lived up to Napoleon's claim, its scent riding sweet and savory on the cool mountain air. We were glad to be driving in the mountains, whose charming villages came on us suddenly from over a rise or from around a turn. One was a lazy-looking town shaded by big trees. People sat at a café and peered out over the peaks, snow shining on the farthest ones. "What would you think about spending a winter here?" Beth said. The very words activated the View-Master in my mind. Click: The Mountain Retreat—*roaring fire, flannel shirts, good books, red Corsican wine.*

Now that we were officially homeless, where—how—were we going to live? There were so many View-Master favorites. Click: The Paris Apartment—*parquet, exotic tiles, French doors, elegant moldings.* Click: The Provençal Mas—*stone farmhouse, massive beams, terrace, lavender, vineyards.* Click: The Beach House—*white walls, blue shutters, cool tile, old rattan.* And what about Italy, Ireland, the Greek Isles? Cost aside, for the first time in our lives we could live wherever we wanted. The problem was, we wanted to live everywhere and nowhere.

An old aqueduct appeared around the last curve out of the village, and we began climbing again. Closer to Corte we negotiated a descending hairpin into another charming village. There we stopped for a photo beneath a wonderful terra-cotta terrace overlooking a statue of a cloaked woman supporting a limp child—a monument to the *enfants* lost in World War I. From the statue, we could see the highway winding down into and through the town, and beyond that the interlocking mountains framing the sky. We came around one turn to find a herd of goats crossing the road. The young girl who was their goatherd shouted for them to hurry, but they seemed pleased with their own pace. A gap-toothed man in a plaid shirt appeared from nowhere and watched us make our way through the goats. Then he smiled and waved as we passed by.

Corte was a pretty college town nestled in a valley. It reminded me of Fayetteville, Arkansas. There were a lot of young people, and except for that, it seemed like a place where time might stand still. The air certainly did. We found a restaurant with a shaded second-floor terrace that caught what little wind there was. Over lunch of pâté of pigeon, salad, and veal ragout, we watched the kids coming and going on the street below. I wondered how they felt living in so isolated a place—a village in the mountains on an island in the sea. The soul of Corsica struck me as short of oxygen. "Maybe we'll live in a lot of places," Beth said as we left Corte. "Not for good, but for a few months here and there. It's the way artists have always drawn fuel."

"What about all our stuff?" In spite of myself I sometimes missed the blue of my old Chinese rug. We had enough wonderful things to furnish all those View-Master dreams, and Beth loved them—I knew she did. What I hadn't known was how much all of it had tired her out after so many years. For the moment, what she really loved was not having the responsibility of a house.

"I don't know," she said.

We wound down the mountain past sheer cliffs and mossy woods and rushing streams. Rounding a curve, we spotted two wild pigs rooting on the side of the highway. "Stop the car!" Beth said, and I did. She got out and tiptoed toward them, intent on taking their picture. Whatever they were rooting must've been really good, because they hated to stop. They looked up at the approaching menace, then stuck their heads back in the ditch, snout down but ears perked. As she got closer, one rooted and the other watched, and then they switched. A couple of times they reluctantly moved their rooting place, ambling off while looking back over their shoulders. Beth kept coming and they started trotting. In the end they were galumphing awkwardly at full gallop up the road like men in high heels. Beth gave chase, snapping her camera on the run, but they were gone.

A few kilometers farther we saw a roadside pen full of pigs and stopped for a calmer look. Nobody seemed to be home but the animals, so we got out of the car and walked to the fence. The Corsican pigs weren't fat like the ones I was used to seeing in the American South. These were trim and muscular—fit. They gave pigs a good name. One black-and-white show-off of a sow trotted over to the gate and stared directly into Beth's camera. Later I studied her picture. She looked sweet and trusting, and her questioning eyes reminded me of Snapp's.

That night we went into Ajaccio to the Restaurant de France, renowned for its Corsican pork, but we seemed to be in the mood for lamb. Not that our encounters with charcuterie on the hoof had killed our appetites. We started with *paysanne* vegetable soup, then moved on to cannelloni stuffed with *brocciu* cheese (from goat or ewe's milk), pâté of *figatelli* (liver sausage marinated in wine, garlic, and peppercorns), and finally the lamb, all washed down with a *pichet* of good local wine. Chestnuts—*marrons*—are a delicacy in Corsica, so for dessert we felt it was only proper to split a *coupe* of chestnut ice cream drenched in chestnut liqueur and topped with whipped cream. We lingered over our coffee for a long time. Then we forced ourselves into the night feeling like pigs from home.

OUR LAST FULL day in Corsica we devoted to art, beginning with a visit to the Musée Fesch in Ajaccio. Cardinal Fesch was Napoleon's uncle, and he amassed a fine collection of Italian paintings through the plundering of his nephew. We stopped for a precultural coffee at our favorite café on Place Foch. The day was already hot, and the shade felt good. We ordered a second coffee. The accordionist was in his accustomed spot beneath the tree on the corner, his old-world melodies blowing down the block with the breeze.

In that way we almost missed the Fesch. When Matisse visited in 1898, it was a shoddy operation open only a couple of days a week during lunch. Today, the Fesch is a fine museum and lunch is an inviolable French institution. We got to the ticket counter at 11:45 and a young lady with glasses said we couldn't go in because they were closing in fifteen minutes. We didn't want to come back at 2:30. "We can do it," we said, and she gave us a cut-rate fee. Recognizing a travesty even as we ran through the beautiful rooms of the cardinal's palace, we did our best to locate the Botticellis, the Raphaels, the Veroneses. We were especially struck by the lighting of the paintings: The salons were dark and the pictures seemed to glow.

That afternoon I set up my easel on our balcony. The space was a little tight, and I dropped one tube of acrylic paint and subsequently stepped on it, but it was only green. Landscapes have never appealed to me; they require so much green and brown, colors I find boring. But looking out at the Îles Sanguinaires, I painted a quick, loose landscape of the near and distant mountains. If I had picked up anything from all my intensive looking and reading, it was that less was more. Hemingway had said a similar thing about writing—that what was important wasn't what you put in, but what you leave out. I wasn't sure quite how the idea translated to painting, but that was how I was leaning. I had begun to like seeing the white of the canvas coming through in places, and in the painting of the mountains I left a rough unpainted outline along the peaks. I laid in some Yellow Ochre for the hills and then, with the tip of a square brush, dabbed in a little green on top of it. In some places I slapped down a hint of Primary Yellow to indicate the broom. Splotches of Burnt Sienna mixed with Yellow Ochre became the rocks along the shore. For the water I painted a base of Ultramarine and then went back over it with areas of Primary Blue.

My other painting that day took its cue from the strange tree by the swimming pool. Called a "parasol pine," it stood just in front of the wall separating the swimming area from the terrace. The trunk had separated into three gracefully curving tendrils that rose and disappeared beneath a dark green canopy that was almost cartoonish in its perfection. It was a child's version of a tree, with a brown trunk and a green circle as the bough—except this bough wasn't circular, it was umbrella-shaped.

Starting with the stylized tree, I enhanced the fantasy with brighter colors—the distant hills became ochre, purple, and blue, the stones in the wall almost orange. The umbrella by the pool took on dizzying stripes of red and turquoise, and the roiling surf became a frothy blue-green. The grass was yellow in the sun and green in the shadows, and in blue *chaises longues* lolled four pink topless bathers that if I had taken myself more seriously I might have called nymphs. I did give the picture a Matissean name—*Le Bonheur de Corse,* the happiness of Corsica.

Beth had been at the pool during my painting session, and when she came inside I showed her what I had done. She said she "liked" the landscape and thought the tree picture was "interesting." I was a little disappointed by her tepid response, and in time closed my paints and went to the pool myself. I carried Arnheim's book with me so I wouldn't feel like a slacker.

The sun was scorching. After my swim, I forced myself to open the book to the only thing light about it—the chapter on light. Arnheim explained the light-related properties of objects, such as "illumination," "luminance," and "glow." He wrote about "attached" and "cast" shadows and explored the symbolism of darkness. I found my mind wandering to the light shimmering three feet down in the swimming pool, or to the different color whites in the chaises, the lamp on the stone wall, and the flowers cascading down from the terrace. I perked up when he left physics and wrote about painting it. Trying to paint light was a case of creation challenging Creation.

Matisse said that a painting "must possess a veritable power for generating light." I couldn't say that the pictures I had made that day *generated* light, but at least they didn't smother light with thick paint. That was something I was learning by studying Matisse's work along the Mediterranean: To depict luminance, he sometimes thinned his pigment, covering his canvas with translucent oils.

According to Arnheim, the way painters have painted light has confirmed or denied human ideas of basic existence. Before the nineteenth century, painters attempted, through the use of glazes and other tricks, to delineate between separated illumination—external light shining on an object—and object color and brightness, "intent on distinguishing properties of the objects themselves from transitory effects momentarily imposed upon them." But nineteenth-century painters "represented the sum of local brightness, local color, and the brightness and color of the illumination through a single shade of pigment. This technique not only confirmed the purely visual sensation as the final reality; it also asserted philosophically that the being of things is not untouchably permanent. Accidentals are seen as participating in the essence of things just as much as their invariant properties."

After a while I closed the book and ordered a *pastis,* though the drink didn't have the desired relaxing effect. Watching water turn the amber liquid to milky white, I felt that somewhere in this murky subject of luminance was not just a lasting lesson about Matisse's truest instincts as an artist, but also, if Arnheim was right, maybe an illuminating hint about our new impermanent status. Lying on a chaise in the middle of the Mediterranean, I looked far beyond my feet to a road peeling a distant hill like an apple. The whole scene rippled in the heat. Light, the ultimate life force, is also the ultimate mystery. It's as central as the Corsican sun.

7.

Beautiful Jungle

SOUTH OF PERPIGNAN the new grapevines looked like black as-
terisks. To the west were the mountains, heavy in clouds, and to the
east the sea was a slash of bluish gray. Sturdy olive trees with silver-
green leaves were dug in, like good little soldiers, on either side of the
highway.

I recognized Collioure by the coppery-pink bell tower of the
église in the harbor. This was a scene I had looked at scores of times,

in paintings by Matisse, André Derain and the other artists who put this former fishing village on the map with the outrageously colorful canvases that horrified the French art establishment and earned the painters the name *les Fauves* (the Wild Beasts). But no matter how many pictures I'd seen or how many books I'd read, none of it prepared me for the real Collioure. A cozy harbor where the Pyrenees meet the Mediterranean, it had all the artistic requisites: the gray-green mountains, the cobalt sea, the church, the fort, the chateau, the castle, the windmill, the fishing boats, the gnarled plane trees, the game of *boules*, the portside cafés, the tile-topped village houses in hues of pink and ochre and turquoise and terra-cotta and even periwinkle, all with brilliantly coordinating shutters that were often closed handsomely against the midday sun. There was even the doddering old Monsieur with beret and cane and the impossibly petite Madame rolling home her fresh legumes and *fromage* from the open-air market.

We had reservations at the Hôtel Madeloc, which is up a hill near the train station where Matisse first stepped off with his easel and brushes in May 1905. At age thirty-five he arrived in Collioure looking dapper and self-confident—professorial, even—but in fact he was gripped by a fever, whose origins can be traced to the preceding year in Saint-Tropez, when he had spent the summer working with the painter Paul Signac.

Erstwhile protégé of the late Neo-Impressionist Georges Seurat, Signac was a tireless proselytizer for color. Matisse had read his book *From Eugène Delacroix to Neo-Impressionism,* in which Signac spouted such Delacroixisms as "Grey is the enemy of all painting!" and "Banish all earth colours!" He also laid out the movement's philosophy of building paintings through a *scientific formula* of placing small strokes of contrasting colors next to one another, a technique that could produce a particularly luminous effect. The technique was called Pointillism or, as preferred by Signac and his followers, Divisionism.

I had known next to nothing about Signac until a few years ago when a Little Rock collector named James Dyke donated his Signac works on paper—the largest such collection in the world—to the

Arkansas Arts Center. At the show's opening, I was stunned by the energy of the Signac watercolors, which were mostly harbor and sailing scenes. "I should write James Dyke a letter and thank him for this gift," I had told Beth, but of course I never got around to it. Then, just before we left for France, we happened to be at a dinner party with the Dykes. I thanked him for the Signacs, and that led to a discussion about our project, including Matisse colors and Vuillard patterns. "You should see this book I've got on Vuillard's interiors," I said.

"I just bought one," he said.

"You bought that book?" I was excited that James Dyke and I had so much in common.

"No," said Dyke, "I just bought a Vuillard."

Like his fellow colorist John Peter Russell on Belle-Île, Signac was a die-hard sailor who had made his Saint-Tropez home into a kind of salon. Artists from all over France gravitated to what was then a small fishing village bathed in incredible southern light. Situated on a hook of land actually facing north, Saint-Tropez enjoyed magnificent sunrises *and* sunsets. Signac's oil paintings of the village and harbor look like so many gold coins floating in luminous seas of orange or pink, depending on the clock.

The sunrises and sunsets are still a big draw, but today their glitter is rivaled by the gold hanging from visitors' necks. On our first night in Saint-Tropez, Beth and I sipped whisky outside the Café de Paris and watched a yachtload of drunken Brits have their photos snapped by a hired photographer, who then collected his fee and scuttled down the gangplank like a rat. At the next berth, the brooding midnight blue *No Escape* rocked quietly, its only sign of life dim salon lights behind nubby curtains. "Wonder if it's a movie star," Beth had said. Just up the Côte d'Azur the Cannes Film Festival was about to get started, and every time a newer, larger yacht motored into the harbor, we expected to see Harvey Weinstein at the bow looking like the king of the world.

I frankly hadn't expected to like this slick village, with its Kenzo and Hermès shops and its jet-set clientele. The concierge of our elegant but unpretentious hotel, Le Yaca, had confided that people could be "snobby" during high season. We were not shocked. In our room was a lavishly produced magazine called *La Revue (du Golfe de Saint-Tropez)*, which contained see-and-be-seen photos of the international set engaged in a lot of cute cutting up.

One day we paid eight euros apiece to take a boat around the bay looking at the fabulous homes. Our master of ceremonies was an engaging young man who had his patter down in multiple languages. French and English were enough for our voyage, Beth and I being the odd couple. As our boat navigated through the harbor into open sea, a giant cruise ship was unloading customers into rubber rafts so they could go shop in town.

We skirted the near coast, our guide pointing out the *maison* of the founder of L'Oréal cosmetics and the house where Paul Signac's granddaughter lived. At the top of the bay he showed us the set of a TV series called *Saint-Tropez,* a glitzy nighttime soap opera that Beth and I had seen in some hotel during our travels. On the other side of the bay was the surprisingly small house of Brigitte Bardot, whose film *And God Created Woman* put Saint-Tropez in the limelight in the 1950s. Called the "Sex Kitten" in those days, she had become an animal-rights activist and now lived in that house with her husband and an obscene number of cats. Atop a cliff beyond Bardot's place was the home of the head of Opel cars, and, conveniently close by, the villa of the American inventor of the car wash. At one point, our tour guide proudly called our attention to a not-so-big villa that had been occupied in the past, he told us, by Sylvester Stallone. "That house," he said, "rents for *one hundred thousand American dollars a month!*" We all acted appropriately flabbergasted.

Later that afternoon, just as we were about to write off the village as nothing but a pretty face, we wandered into the Musée de l'Annonciade, a converted chapel by the port. Dedicated—with the encouragement of Paul Signac—to the work of the painters who came to the village in the late nineteenth and early twentieth centuries, it contained quite simply the best collection of modern French painting that we'd seen anywhere in France. Nearly everybody was there—Signac, Seurat, Bonnard, Vuillard, Matisse, Derain, Vlaminck, Braque, Dufy, van Dongen, Camoin, Manguin, Marquet, Puy, Rouault, Cross, Vallotton. You could take in the beauty of Signac's glowing *Saint-Tropez, the Quay* and then glance out the adjacent window at the real thing. Matisse was represented by a wild picture, called *Seated Nude,* in which the woman's lips were blue, her cheek brick-red, one breast orange and the other blue-green. That recklessly wrought painting told the story of Matisse's experiment with the prissy premeditation of Divisionism.

He did produce a few notable Divisionist pictures that summer, including the makings for what would become the famous *Luxe, calme et volupté,* his oil mosaic of nude *pique-niquing* on the shore of Saint-Tropez. Signac bought that masterpiece and hung it in his dining room, but, mostly, the two painters didn't see eye to eye. Signac criticized Matisse's "large" brushstrokes, and Amélie had to take Henri on long walks to calm him down. In the end, Matisse discovered in Saint-Tropez that he wasn't cut out to be part of any school or movement. "One can't live in a household that is too well kept, a house kept by country aunts," he told the editor Tériade years later. "One has to go off into the jungle to find simpler ways which won't stifle the spirit."

Which brings us back to Collioure, to the train station, and to a red-bearded stranger shielding his northern eyes from the blazing southern sun.

I LIKE TO think of Matisse that first season in Collioure starring in his own version of *Apocalypse Now,* a crackling chronicle of his descent into the heart of darkness in search of truth about color and light. "Ah, how wretched I was down there," he later told a student who asked about the struggles he'd been waging during that time in his life. It's probably a wonder that he and Amélie survived that summer intact.

Between his months in Corsica and the time he arrived in Collioure, Matisse's life and career had been wrenched like a wet rag, and at times he had thought himself completely dry. Following his flash of success in 1896, Matisse had suffered agonizing setbacks even as he and Amélie were adding to their family. Besides Marguerite, there was Jean, born in 1899, and Pierre, who came along in 1900. Matisse was committed to shouldering those responsibilities "with courage," but they did make his stand as an artist all the more difficult.

Near the end of 1899, Amélie had opened a hat shop in Paris to try to bring in money, while Henri landed a job painting decorative panels for the 1900 Paris Exposition at the Grand Palais. The year 1899 was also when he had gone out on a limb to buy Paul Cézanne's painting *Three Bathers,* in which he clearly saw another open door— one the art establishment longed to close. The Cézanne that so captured Matisse's imagination shows a trio of chunky bathers in and about a small body of water framed by perilously leaning trees. A rising presence in Paris at the turn of the twentieth century, Cézanne had nevertheless chiseled out his hard-won mark by risking an outsider's vision. His crude, wallowing nudes—situated more in an untamed jungle than a manicured *bois*—could hardly be more different from the porcelain nymphs and cute cupids that were the trademark of Matisse's old teacher William Bougereau, who just happened to be president of the Société des Artistes Français, a body that for two decades blocked Cézanne's applications to the official Salon. Different was always scandalous at first, and when writer Émile Zola's Impressionist collection was displayed in Paris in 1903, both the collector and one of his favorite painters, Cézanne, were denounced as "diseased minds, traitors to their country, lovers of physical and moral filth." "If Cézanne is right," wrote journalist Henri Rochefort, "then . . . Watteau, Boucher, Fragonard and Prud'hon no longer exist, and nothing remains as the supreme symbol of the art dear to Zola but to set fire to the Louvre."

As this debate was raging, the Matisses were in the waning days of their *Studio Under the Eaves* stint in Picardy, the years during which he was ridiculed as a fool who couldn't even turn out portraits that looked like their subject. This was the low point, and had been immediately preceded by another of Matisse's strange and telling intestinal attacks and Amélie's closing the hat shop due to her own ill health. In those dark days Matisse drew strength from Cézanne's painting—probably both from the bold stance of the artist and the refreshingly awkward stance of his three bathers. "If Cézanne is right, then I am right," Matisse later recalled thinking. "And I knew that Cézanne had made no mistake."

His fortunes began rising in 1904, just before he left for Saint-Tropez. That June, he had his first one-man show, encompassing forty-five paintings and one drawing, and the influential critic Roger Marx wrote that he "delights in capturing anything that pleases his profound and lucid sight." In 1905 he showed eight paintings at the Salon des Indépendants, Signac's group, and on the basis of *Luxe, calme et volupté* was hailed by the Neo-Impressionists (who still regarded art as a team sport) as "the movement's most prestigious convert since Pisarro." The 1905 Indépendants exhibition was also notable for offering the first-ever retrospective of the works of Vincent van Gogh, which Matisse helped Signac stage. Matisse owned two van Gogh drawings that John Peter Russell had given him on Belle-Île. Like Cézanne, van Gogh was one of Matisse's heroes. So even as the Neos were celebrating Matisse's membership in the club, he was headed south, into the wild, searching for the next stage. And if the door wasn't open, he was going to open it. "Van Gogh and Gauguin were ignored," Matisse wrote in an essay forty years later. "A wall had to be knocked down in order to get through."

Collioure was the place I had looked forward to the most. In all the months before I finally saw it, I had spent long winter evenings poring over the paintings from that period in *Henri Matisse: A Retrospective,* from the famous Museum of Modern Art show in 1992. Even to my twentieth-century eye, Matisse's Collioure canvases were shocking. They were essentially loose drawings in paint—thin, spontaneous, unbridled, some just this side of garish. His greens were shades of soft spring mixed with hard mineral. His pinks and violets were almost sinfully ripe. His blues vibrated, his oranges glowed. And the world these colors depicted was both lush and sinewy, a tropical jungle bursting with sensual fury—banana and date palms, orange, lemon, and fig trees, agave fronds slicing soft air like scimitars. "Is this France," Hilary Spurling quotes a traveler from Matisse's day writing about Collioure, "or already Africa?"

By late afternoon, Beth and I checked in at the Madeloc, and a mist had settled over the mountains. From the tiny balcony adjoining our room, I could just make out the bottom half of an old watchtower atop one of the peaks. Once settled, we strolled down rue Romain Rolland toward town. In no time, we came face to face with a reproduction of Matisse's painting *Fenêtre à Collioure* bolted to the wall of a house where rue Rolland meets avenue Aristide Maillol. The colors in the picture were very bright—red chair, red floor, and through the window the layered ranges of the Pyrenees in green, pink, and blue. "This must've been painted right around here," I said, and went back across the street to get a higher view of the mountains. Sure enough, I could make out the same pattern of peaks to the southwest.

Farther down avenue Maillol we met up with a reproduction of Matisse's famous *Interior with Aubergines*. At the bottom of the hill, passing through a small *place* where leafless plane trees looked like gnarled hands reaching toward heaven, we crossed the street and turned toward the harbor. There, on boulevard du Boramar, where the sea had scooped out a picturesque cove between the thirteenth-century chateau and the seventeenth-century church, pictures hung one after another as in an outdoor art gallery: Matisse: *Vue de Collioure, l'église.* Derain: *Le Faubourg de Collioure.* Matisse: *Barques à Collioure.* Derain: *Le Phare de Collioure.* Matisse: *Porte-Fenêtre à Collioure.* They were mostly wild-eyed views of this very harbor dating from that summer of 1905 when the two artists attacked tradition with color as hot as their blood. All, that is, but the last one, the *Porte-Fenêtre*—the open window, the broad black void between stripes of blue-gray, yellow, and green. That was from 1914. I had just seen it at the Pompidou in Paris and hadn't understood it. Unlike most Matisse windows, this one looked toward someplace very bleak.

Only one café was open on the waterfront—the Copacabana. We took a couple of chairs beneath a broad yellow umbrella and ordered bourbon, a weighty antidote to the transitional weather. The pebbly beach was deserted, the church lit by warm floodlights, the sea and sky deep blue and run together like watercolor. In three months, women would be sunbathing topless there at that time of day. For now, though, we had the place pretty much to ourselves.

One morning maybe a year before we left Little Rock, Beth had dreamed that we were in a small fishing village with a fine view of the sea. There was a terrace with flowers and herbs. We were both working well. Over time that had become her loose template for the life we were searching for—in addition to our indescribably fabulous Paris apartment and all our other dwellings.

I often wonder if other people spend as much time as we do thinking about such things. Down deep where I really live, I tell myself that my desires can be defined in five words: *Read, write, paint, think, travel.*

Not that it's ever as simple as that.

WE AWOKE IN the morning to light rain. Slipping on our parkas, we made our way down the hill to the village, where the wet walls of the houses were the colors of ripe melon—watermelon red, cantaloupe gold, honeydew green. It was apparently the same in Matisse's day, when the fishermen had painted their houses with colors left over from painting their boats. For all its African flavor, Collioure was deeply Catalan. After centuries of dispute, Catalonia was split between Spain and France. Spanish Catalonia stretches south to Valencia and west to Andorra; in France, the region runs as far north as Salses. Catalonians are proud of their heritage and—at least a hundred years ago—were standoffish to strangers. Unlike Beth, and with typical New World narrowness, I knew precious little about them upon our arrival in Collioure, and I quickly simplified their culture to a couple of graspable elements—tapas on the menus and rope-soled espadrilles on the men.

We walked in the village most of the afternoon. The streets were a labyrinth, a life-size puzzle whose face was color. Whether down by the romantic church or up by the medieval fort, whether behind giant double doors scaled for kings or through short single ones befitting fairies, an intriguing world hid there. On a back street above an art gallery we saw a large bright picture of a woman with these words written onto the painting:

> Watanabe
> ART
> The gate of
> SOLACE—
> I have arrived—
> I am home—

"You need to talk to her," Beth said. "I'll bet she's American." I peered through the glass on the door and knocked, but nobody was there. Most of the shops in Collioure were still closed for the off-season. We walked around a while longer and then came back. This time the gallery was open. A tall, thin fortyish woman rose from behind a desk when I entered.

"Bonjour," I said. "Parlez-vous anglais?"

"Yes," she said.

Her name was Tessa Harris, she was British, and she had lived in Collioure for about six months. For four years before that she had lived in the Pyrenees on a farm. She was a painter and worked part-time in the gallery, which was in fact owned by an American painter from California, Carol Watanabe. The gallery was mainly devoted to Carol's work, but there were a few of Tessa's pictures hanging, too. I particularly liked one of a plane tree against bright-colored houses. "You saw pink in the tree," I said, pointing to a small section of the painting.

"Yes I did," Tessa said, visibly warming. It was nice, the pink. The average person would see a plane tree as putty gray, olive green, and off-white, like desert camouflage. But there are vibrant colors in most any surface if you attune your eyes to them.

We talked a while, told her what we were doing, and asked about rental prices in Collioure. I heard her say, "They're generally very high. I have a small flat for eighty-five-hundred euros a month."

I had to lean against a post to keep from crumpling. Through what sounded like a rushing river in my head, I listened to Beth asking Tessa if she knew of any apartments for rent. Yes she did, Tessa said, and picked up the phone. A friend of hers had just redone the top two floors of his house. "He's German. His name is Gerd Pfeiffer, but here he calls himself Gerard." She waited, then left a message on Gerard's answering machine, including our cell phone number. After that we chatted a few minutes and then made our exit.

"That was great, wasn't it!" Beth said outside.

"Great? She rents a tiny apartment for nearly ten thousand dollars a month! Are you out of your mind?"

"She said five hundred euros."

"I don't think so."

"Go ask her."

So I did, and Beth was right. Not only that, but as I was talking with Tessa, Gerard called. We could come over immediately. Tessa drew us a map. "It's around the chateau on the quiet side of town."

Ten minutes later we were ringing the bell at 10, rue Edgar Quinet, a three-story mustard-colored village house with faded green shutters. It was a couple of blocks away from the sea, but the mountains rose right behind it. On the way over, we had passed another Matisse reproduction—the famous *La fenêtre ouverte*, the open window, hanging on the very building in which it was painted. To my mind it was the quintessential Fauvist painting, a window opening onto a world in which clouds were purple and seas were pink.

When the door opened, a tall older man in jeans and house slippers was standing there. I had expected someone nearer Tessa's age, but Gerard was nearer mine. "You found it," he said, and added a funny little rising *umm?* like a doctor asking if it hurts here, or here, or here? He was *very* tall, maybe six foot six. He had white hair and gold-rimmed glasses. "You come up to my place and we visit awhile," he said. "Then we go see the apartments, umm?"

Waiting on the sofa in his apartment was an attractive woman whom he introduced as Pamela. She was Canadian. We took seats in two club chairs that were facing away from the sofa, so we had to sit sideways and crane our necks to converse. As a potential landlord,

Gerard seemed very interested in what we were doing and told the story—I took it as a parable—of a couple of American friends of his from North Carolina who retired and moved to France. They bought a house and everything. "Then the wife didn't like it. 'The Frogs are so different,' umm? So they sold their house and moved to Evanston, Illinois. The husband felt a terrible loss when they left. He loved France."

At some inscrutable moment he felt the time was right. "Yeah, so," he said, standing. "Let's go see the apartments, umm?" and led us to an elevator in a vestibule just beyond his dining area. *An elevator!* I pictured myself loading our mounds of luggage onto it and simply pressing a button. Gerard explained that the lift had been installed for the previous owner, who had become quite ill.

We stepped off first at the second floor, which had three bedrooms, two baths, and a view—from the room in which I would write—of the Pyrenees. The apartment was air-conditioned and nicely painted in white with turquoise trim, and it would be large enough to accommodate my work and the large number of visitors we thought we might have during the summer. The drawback was, it was unfurnished.

Then we went to the third floor, the onetime attic. It was essentially a loft. New skylights bathed the space in light. Handsome old beams were exposed on the ceiling. A large balcony opened to the mountains, atop which you could see a castle, a fort, a windmill. Through an arched doorway was a big sunny room with a bed, a bath, and an enormous shower with one of those trendy big curved heads that spray water straight down as if from a gigantic sprinkler can. As below, the apartment was white with turquoise trim. It also had air-conditioning. The furnishings were tasteful, comfortable, and new.

Back in Gerard's apartment, he consulted his price book. He had turned both apartments over to an immobilier—a Realtor—but they hadn't gone on the market yet. Neither apartment quite fit our needs—the top floor was too expensive (and probably too small) and the other was unfurnished; we had six huge storage units full of stuff back home. Were we going to buy a houseful of furniture—and not *just* furniture: knives and forks and cups and saucers and pots and pans and sheets and towels—for one summer? Still, it was a very nice apartment. It had fallen into our laps. Nobody knew about it yet.

We made notes, exchanged cards, and Pamela served us tea and cake that they had bought at the market that morning. During the conversation, Gerard told us he had begun looking for a place to retire to in 1992 "when my wife decided she'd had enough of me." He had been an engineer in Germany, a director of a company. He knew of many men, he said, who couldn't let go of their past lives—the clubs, the directorships, who they had been. "Finally, after a couple of years, they might as well die, umm? They were caught between a life that no longer existed and one they had failed to invent."

ON MONDAY THE sun returned, making the day surprisingly hot. After placing several phone calls about other apartments for which we had seen signs, I packed up my notebook and sketchpads to go work over coffee at the Copacabana. We were elated by the opportunity presented by Gerard's apartments and were happily enjoying the euphoria; on the other hand, we seemed strangely inclined to extend the tease without progressing to consummation. Our loaded automobile had become perversely comfortable, in that it required no further commitment. "Four or five months," Beth said, tellingly. "That's a long time in one place."

It was on Monday that I finally figured out the Matisse painting on the waterfront. At midday I happened to glance at one of the windows above the reproduction of Matisse's *Porte-Fenêtre,* and it was as though I was seeing his painting come to life: The building was a washed-out ochre, the shutters greenish-blue. They were partially closed to keep out the sun. The space between the shutters was a black void. I had always assumed that Matisse had painted this window the same way he had painted so many others—from the inside out. That's why the darkness at the center had baffled me so. But there it was, black as an evocation of the cool dark *interior* compared to the searing Mediterranean exterior. It was Matisse reducing his vision to the bare essentials. And by then he had begun treating color

and light as the inextricable forces they are—he had begun painting light.

But that first summer in Collioure, he and Derain were crazed by color itself. I was too on that afternoon at the Copacabana. A man walked by wearing a cobalt shirt, and the woman with him sported a Derain-orange parka. They looked fabulous against the sea.

Color is its own language, which makes it hard to discuss in any other. When I was a magazine editor, talking hue, tone, and intensity with art directors was useless; we had to look together at pictures. Even scientists have difficulty describing colors. "When observers are presented with a continuum of the rainbow colors, e.g. with a light spectrum," writes Arnheim, "they do not agree on where the principal colors appear at their purest. This is true even for the fundamental primaries, especially for pure red, which may be located by observers anywhere between 660 and 760 millimicrons."

If it's that hard deciding which shade is red, imagine trying to discuss what red *means*. ("When it comes to color," said the crusty New York School painter Milton Resnick, "nobody knows anything.") And yet different colors do clearly evoke different responses in viewers. When Matisse and Derain displayed their outrageous Collioure canvases at the Salon d'Automne in Paris in October 1905, the crowds all but bayed at the moon. Paintings are more than the sum of their colors, of course, but I wondered if it was possible to analyze the specific effects of the Fauvists' specific colors. "There are ways to scale emotional responses, and there is no reason color couldn't be the stimulus for such experiments," says Mark D. Fairchild, director of the Munsell Color Science Laboratory at the Rochester Institute of Technology in Rochester, New York. "But my sense is that the results are more inconsistent than people would like to believe—i.e., red might make one person feel more angry and another more calm. I would guess that any consistent trends are due to consistent societal influences—essentially peer pressure. If all your friends are outraged by a color and tell you so, you're more likely to have the same emotional response."

This factual Black Hole of Color has never lacked for experts rushing in to fill it. In his thoroughly entertaining but discredited book *Theory of Colours,* first published in English in 1840, Johann Wolfgang von Goethe weighs in across the spectrum: Of the color red, he writes, "The red glass exhibits a bright landscape in so dreadful a hue as to inspire sentiments of awe," and he goes on to point out that "history relates many instances of the jealousy of sovereigns with regard to the quality of red. Surrounding accompaniments of this colour have always a grave and magnificent effect."

But he really begins to touch on the Fauves in his discussion of yellow-red: "In looking steadfastly at a perfectly yellow-red surface, the colour seems actually to penetrate the organ. It produces an extreme excitement." He could have been describing the ear of the model in Matisse's Collioure canvas *Woman in a Hat.* "A yellow-red cloth disturbs and enrages animals. I have known men of education to whom its effect was intolerable if they chanced to see a person dressed in a scarlet cloak on a grey, cloudy day."

For more up-to-date color theory, I consulted an interior decorator friend, Ellen Kennon, about the effects of color on our moods. A very successful decorator who creates beautiful, comfortable spaces, she had just developed her own line of house paints based on the growing field of "color therapy." The following is from her online newsletter, *Living Well*.

"Red is the color of power, strength, action, passion, and desire—the epitome of vitality, energy, and independence."

"Orange is also associated with energy. It brings thought (from yellow) to action (from red), thus promoting balance, unity, and wholeness."

"Gold is the color of divine awareness, spiritual healing, and positive change. It radiates love, compassion, and understanding to all who come into contact with its radiant light."

"Purple, also associated with spirituality . . . should be used with discretion or in small doses as it can be tiring on the eyes. . . . It can produce a high state of exhilaration, but is followed by a letdown or intense state of irritation. . . . Research shows it is also very good for curbing anti-social behavior."

"The color violet is found on the planes of consciousness associated with the great masters of music, art, and literature. It raises personal values, seeks perfection in life, and encourages self-sacrifice and work without selfish aims."

"Pink is a calming shade of red. . . . Its healing qualities make it good for children and convalescents, and is supportive for divorcees."

"Turquoise is bold and compelling yet restful at the same time. It . . . is an ethereal, healing color that is particularly useful in reducing stress without depleting energy."

"Green [is] the most healing color of all, and blue [creates] calmness, tranquility, and serenity."

Regardless of how much stock you put in the meaning of colors, you wouldn't have wanted either Henri Matisse or André Derain to decorate your bedroom in the summer of 1905. They were bomb throwers, squeezing out copious amounts of red and orange like so much plastic explosive. No calm blue for their seas—red and hot white were the colors of choice. In their portraits of each other, pigment appears to blow up in their respective faces. Matisse painted Amélie with one cheek pink, the other cheek yellow, and with a screaming chartreuse line that split her face from her hairline to her lip. "At the time," writes Spurling, "he felt himself cracking up. Sleep became impossible."

At the start of this journey I questioned why people paint. Writing is an act of inspired reason in an existing man-made language. Composing or playing music is an act of gifted logic in an existing man-made language. But painting—taking ground plants or stone and mixing their dust with oil to fill a surface with a picture from your heart—is, said Matisse, "an act of belief." It pits man against nature, the unknowable against the imponderable. The more I read about Matisse and Derain that first summer in Collioure, the more I began to suspect that the particular images they produced weren't even the point. It was the boldness of their palette that reflected their hope in wresting order from chaos. It was the brave slashes of paint that immortalized their elemental struggle to rewrite the rules. Their paintings weren't even *finished*, in the then-accepted understanding of the term. These artists were searchers, and the search was an end in itself.

Why paint? Why live? Like getting up and going out to meet life anew each day, painting was insanity and therapy all wrapped in one.

TUESDAY MORNING WE met Tessa at Copacabana for coffee. While we were there, we spotted Gerard and Pamela at a table a few rows closer to the water. As they were leaving, they stopped and sat with us for a while.

We told Gerard that we liked his apartments very much, but that the one was too expensive and the other was unfurnished, so we really had to think about it. "You make your decision and let me know, umm?" he said. "We can come to an agreement." He was much more interested in talking about books. "Under the Nazis, there were no American books or authors. I was eight when the war was over, and I immediately read Hemingway and Thomas Wolfe. I thought all Americans must be like Hemingway characters."

It was a little surreal, having this conversation on a sunny day in the south of France in the year 2003. As I was listening to Gerard talk, my mind called up images of the three German men living it up at the next table at the restaurant in Rouen, the bunkers we had seen at Omaha Beach, the Vauban citadel that the Nazis had occupied on Belle-Île. I fleetingly wondered how Germans felt traveling in the countries their government had once so hideously invaded, and then I caught myself. Europe had had hundreds of years of wars to get past. Everybody had attacked everybody else at one point or another. Time marches on, relationships change, alliances are redefined. People aren't governments and vice versa. In the States, we had a hard time understanding that. Segregated on our side of the world, we were stuck in our moldy biases or our blissful ignorance. I had recently read that only 14 percent of Americans have passports. "Do they celebrate Christmas over there?" a fortysomething American lawyer had asked me when he heard we were going to France.

"Have you been following your war, umm?" Gerard was saying, and I realized he was talking about the American and British invasion of Iraq. Suddenly the old war and the new war had become entwined as a single thread. In fact I had not been keeping up in great detail, much to the dismay of U.S.-based acquaintances who insisted on letting us know what they thought of our being in France when France wouldn't even back the war. In Auray we had had no newspaper, no CNN. We did occasionally watch the news on BBC, but the news was counterproductive to our purpose. We were there contemplating beauty, creativity, serenity. We watched the news to get the gist of what was happening, but we didn't linger over it. And, naively perhaps, we didn't think it had much of anything to do with us.

Then, in mid-March, we started receiving strange e-mails from the States. One touted "French Vacation Spots We Missed," and on a map of France were such villages as Lilie Livere, Faux Amis, and Petit Balles. Another e-mail included a quote attributed to General George Patton, who said he "would rather have a German division in front of me than a French division behind me." Still another alerted us to this scoop: "Breaking news! Ten earthquakes in France! It's the American dead rolling over in their graves." Finally came this word from my disgusted brother, Phil, a newspaper reporter in Tampa: "One of our state politicians is proposing that all American war dead in France be exhumed and brought home."

Good God.

I did happen to be aware that one of the battles the Allies had hoped would be quick and easy had turned into more of a challenge, and that was apparently what Gerard was referring to. "Bush must be biting the rug," he said.

"Pardon me?"

"Our illustrious Adolf, when things weren't going well, was said to get so angry that he would bite the rug."

After they left, Tessa told us that Pamela was going home that coming weekend. Tessa hated it because she and Pamela had become best friends. "She's a jazz singer," she said. "When she and Gerard met, he had been on his own a long time and she hadn't been in a relationship for a while. They agreed to see how things went, with the stipulation that he would pay her way back to Canada if the relationship didn't work. The relationship didn't work."

Over lunch Tessa told us about farm life with a former boyfriend in the Pyrenees. We talked about art, about "finding your line," and about the art community in Collioure. In summer the village was very crowded, she said, but there were nonstop festivals—people singing, playing jazz, dancing the *sardane,* the traditional Catalan dance. "That was where Matisse got the inspiration for *La Danse,*" she said.

It was nice for us to have someone else to talk with; Tessa seemed to feel that, too, and we got the impression that she was gently nudging us toward Gerard's apartment. She had a lot of furniture in storage in the Pyrenees, she said; if we decided on the unfurnished flat, we could go get her things. It would save her the storage fee and help us at the same time.

More and more, as Beth said, it seemed "meant to be." And yet inertia is always the easier choice, no matter whether you're staying or going. Who knows? Maybe there was something better waiting around the next cove.

"Do you think you ought to call Gerard?" she said.

"Nah, he's not in a hurry. Let's see if we hear from any of these other people."

That afternoon I took my sketch pad and made drawings of the église, trying to capture the way the buttresses jutted out on the side by the sea. I was using a big black felt tip, so I was sketching quickly, with broad strokes. I dashed off a few chairs and umbrellas from Copacabana with the church in the background. Behind the church was a wonderful flat-roofed, Moorish-looking castle, with faded turquoise shutters, that I drew with the church in the foreground. Then beyond the church on the sea side was a little chapel on a hill. One of Matisse's reproductions hung there, and I stood in the same spot and sketched the church with the far harbor and the mountains behind it. I could already tell that one of the challenges of being a real painter in Collioure, as opposed to a tourist-postcard painter, would be to avoid placing this church front and center in every picture. One of Matisse's Collioure landscapes that I most admired was a 1907 view of the harbor seen through a clump of sinuous trees on the side of a nearby hill. If you know Collioure, you might recognize the church bell tower in the distance, but overall grace of line and color—not the church—was the point.

I needed to be working with color in the birthplace of the Fauves, and I wished I could paint with oils, whose smell and consistency I love. But with our pile of stuff, there was no way to carry wet canvases. Acrylics were the best I could do on the run, and watercolors were even better for location painting. After a while I tired of the waterfront, so I climbed the hill to the old windmill. There I took out the small watercolor kit that I had bought a couple of years before but hadn't used much until now. I liked its compactness—I had carried billfolds larger—and the ingenious way the little water holder popped out and snapped into a slot on the side. Then you could slide out a bottom panel to form a second mixing tray. The kit held fourteen colors. On watercolor paper I made a pen-and-ink sketch of a couple of houses by the sea and then applied a watercolor wash to it. The result wasn't great, just a watercolor sketch. But I liked how the ink ran and mixed with the watercolors. The sea looked muted and gray, the way it actually was.

In early evening Beth phoned her mother and they had a long happy conversation punctuated with much laughter. Bobbye even admitted missing Snapp, who was now at Blair's apartment in Little Rock; we were going to bring him over soon. Beth told her about Collioure and about the apartment. "You would love it here, Mother!" she said, and they talked about Bobbye's coming to visit.

Later I went to buy soft drinks at the grocery store, and while I was out I ran into Tessa and Pamela. The encounter felt strange. There was a distance that hadn't been there earlier in the day. I told Beth about it when I got back to the hotel. Beth discovered that Tessa had sent her an e-mail encouraging us to "check out the immobilier" before committing to Gerard.

"What the hell is that about?" I said. "Is she trying to send us a message? Did Pamela tell her something weird? Is Tessa trying to *warn* us?" Suddenly I had an overwhelming feeling that we too had ventured deep into—if not a jungle, then certainly dense woods. The colors had been so inviting; now they had turned murky.

Beth e-mailed Tessa and asked point-blank if she was trying to tell us not to rent Gerard's apartment. She responded quickly. Not at all, she said. She just wanted to make sure we had done our homework before we committed.

But by then we were spooked.

WE CHECKED OUT of the Hôtel Madeloc on Wednesday morning, having made reservations at Les Templiers for our remaining three nights in Collioure. Les Templiers was a famous Collioure landmark, the choice of every celebrity who had ever passed through town. Many of them had been artists, and the walls of the hotel were said to be jammed with paintings that had been given to the hotel owners over the years.

That day we drove over to see Céret, a little village sixteen kilometers to the northwest where Picasso and his band often spent time in the years that Matisse and his friends were coming to Collioure. It felt good to be in the car again—just us, every card on the table. The route took us through lush cherry orchards. Behind them the mountains were blue-gray and misty like sculpted fog. Céret itself was a pretty little village with a winding main street already shaded by huge plane trees, even denuded as they still were; by summer it would be dark and cool on that street. But Céret didn't call to us, and we didn't stay long.

From there we drove to Banyuls-sur-Mer to see the Musée Maillol. Maillol and Matisse had met that summer of 1905 and had become great friends. In coming seasons the Matisses would take the train two stops from Collioure to Banyuls, and the Maillols would invite other area artists for long lunches whose main course was talk about art. Beth and I had a long lunch with almost no conversation. The unspoken subject was: *What are we going to do?*

Late that afternoon we checked into Les Templiers, which immediately felt like home—arty, laid-back, easily beautiful. We had a large room with red-and-white striped drapes, ultramarine shutters, and a view of the chateau and harbor. On every floor the corridors were hung carpet to ceiling with paintings and sketches, most inscribed "To René and Pauline Pous," the longtime hotel owners. Catalan, of course. In the art-filled bar—which wasn't so much a bar as it was an old-fashioned saloon—there was a photograph of René Pous and Pablo Picasso. The bar itself was made of dark wood and shaped like a boat with a pointed prow. It was the kind of place where you wanted the people to know your name.

The woman who worked at the desk—again a Véronique—spoke very good English, and we struck up a conversation with her. She was from Picardy, Matisse's home turf, and we asked if she could arrange for me to interview the present owner of Les Templiers. The next morning she told us we had a 2 P.M. meeting with Monsieur JoJo Pous, son of René and Pauline. He didn't speak much English, Véronique said. We implored her to sit in as our interpreter, and she said she would try.

Before the appointed time, however, we decided to take the plunge and talk with a Realtor if for no other reason than to confirm our good deal at Gerard's. Tessa had suggested a prominent local immobilier, whom we found around the harbor on Gerard's side of the village. A curly-haired piece of work in striped slacks and sharp-pointed Italian boots, she was busy with another couple, so we stood around the small room trying to make ourselves inconspicuous.

When it was our turn, we sat down across from her and started explaining—in tortured French—what had brought us to Collioure. Madame flicked her fingers like she was backhanding a fly. "Speak English," she said. It had the sound of a command.

Once she grasped that we wanted a place for the summer in which we both could work, she consulted her listings. "Hmmm," she said. "There is not much . . . though here's one that might be suitable."

It was the Moorish castle behind the church. I had already pointed it out to Beth and told her it was my favorite house in Collioure. Madame calmly read off the prices: 1100 euros *a week* in June and September, and 1300 euros *a week* in July and August.

"For the whole house?" I asked.

"No," Madame laughed. "Of course not for the whole house. Just a part of it."

Beth suggested, with great passion, that maybe the house's owner would love what we were doing and want to help us with—

She didn't even get to finish the sentence.

"Pardon me," Madame said, leaning forward and placing her chin on one bejeweled wrist for emphasis, *"but you are a dreamer."*

It was a stunning moment, funny and deeply disturbing at the same time. She had pierced Beth's soul with her damning use of the D-word. Not that it wasn't true—it was true about all artists. But in the wrong hands, the truth can always be used against you. "Of course we're dreamers," I said, trying to help. "That's why we're here."

Madame ignored me. "These people," she said, meaning the kings of the jungle who own big Moorish castles, "these people are not like you. They're in it for business. They want to make money!"

We all sat in silence for a few moments. Then she said, "Okay, tell me what you want to pay, and I will present it to the owner."

"We'll think about it and call you," we said, sliding back the chairs for our getaway. There was no way we were going to call back, and I just hoped Beth wouldn't blurt out a number and reveal how far apart we were. I didn't think I could bear the disdain.

But as we waved our rushed good-byes from the door, Madame did something totally unexpected. "I'm an artist too," she said, quietly. "Except with no talent."

JOJO POUS LOOKED like a Catalan John Updike—sharp face, prominent nose, small chin, great shock of gray hair. He was short and trim, wearing a gray worsted suit with a black shirt open at the collar. He didn't seem to know quite why Véronique was asking him to sit down with us rather than play his usual afternoon cards in the bar with his cronies, but he was old-world cordial just the same.

"I've stayed here in Collioure all my life," said Monsieur Pous, seventy-four. "The world has come to me." The world included Matisse, Dufy, Picasso, Pablo Casals, Edith Piaf, Maurice Chevalier, Roger Vadim. He explained that his *grand-mère* started a bar called Le Café des Sports on that very spot in 1895; in 1947, his father and mother, René and Pauline, opened a restaurant there; in 1955, they launched the hotel. Today Monsieur Pous is technically retired; his son, Jean-Michel, runs the hotel, and his daughter, Mané, runs the restaurant.

The many paintings weren't given in exchange for rooms, he said, clarifying a common misconception. "The pictures were for friendship. We have two thousand paintings, every one of them a piece of my life." In the unassuming way of small-town businesses, Les Templiers once hung very valuable pictures throughout the bar and hotel, attracting the world in a less benevolent way—twenty-five years ago, two Maillols, a Savage, and several Picasso drawings were stolen from the hotel walls. Since then, the Pouses have had to keep the originals under lock and key.

"Artists are very wonderful persons," said Monsieur Pous, looking to Véronique to make sure she was translating accurately about the book of personalized sketches, watercolors, paintings, and notes that the artist Willy Mucha had put together for the Pouses.

"Could we see it?" said Beth.

"Ah, *oui*," said Monsieur Pous, shrugging as though surprised we hadn't asked sooner.

The book, however, was stored elsewhere. If we could come back tomorrow, he said, Mané would bring it for us to look at. "Come back tomorrow?" I said. "Nous sommes à votre hotel!" Whether or not that made sense to him, he and Beth did the *triple*-cheek kiss, like longtime friends. I pumped his hand like I was running for office.

That night, exhilarated by visions of a summer by the sea, I drank too much. We had aperitifs at Les Templiers, wine with dinner at the tapas restaurant Pica Pica, and *digestifs* back at the hotel. The next morning I awoke with the predictable result—lamenting that I couldn't buy Excedrin in France.

But we had to phone Gerard to tell him the decision we had made over tapas the night before: *We would take the apartment.* I had two numbers for him and left messages at both. Beth later talked with Tessa, who said that Gerard was out of town. He and Pamela had left on Wednesday for his house in Mirepoix, about three hours away. Gerard was taking Pamela to catch her plane on Saturday morning.

We were slightly disturbed to learn that Gerard had left town, especially since we were leaving the next day. While Beth worked, I forced myself to get out my watercolors. We had a harbor view from both our bedroom and bathroom, and I sketched a scene of the sea framed by the chateau on one side and a village house on the other. Then I painted it, intending to apply just a light wash but eventually filling in every centimeter of white space like a second-grade dullard following instructions. "If there's no emotion, you shouldn't paint," Matisse advised. The only emotion I felt was for a nap, so I closed my paints and, soon after, my eyes.

At noon we went downstairs to meet Mané. A petite woman in jeans bearing a strong resemblance to her father, she was hugging to her chest two thick books about fourteen inches square. She led us into the dining room, laid the books on a corner table, and opened the first one to the handwritten title page:

Ce livre d'or
Édité par Willy Mucha pour
glorifier Collioure
dernier lieu des esprits librés,
poètes errants,
peintres assoiffés de
couleurs pures

There was more, but that captured the spirit of the "golden book"—
"Edited by Willy Mucha for the glorification of Collioure, last place
of free spirits, poets errant, painters thirsty for pure color." Mucha, a
longtime resident of Collioure, had over the years asked his many
friends to prepare something to be bound into the collection. It was
kind of an autograph book for artists. Now, as Beth snapped photos,
Mané slowly turned the pages. On some the sketches were very simple—a few smart lines making a picture of the harbor, say. On others
the entire space was filled with color—butterflies, the mountains
and the sea, brilliant village houses under the Mediterranean sun. I
didn't know many of the names, but the ones I did—Pierre Brune,
Salvador Dali, Raoul Dufy, Pablo Picasso, Henri Matisse—were
thrilling to see. In 1950, Matisse had penned a loose childish sketch
of sailboats in the bay and the ubiquitous tourist train that ran between Collioure and nearby villages. I touched the lines, tracing
them with my finger. I touched the signature.

In a few minutes Mané pointed to her watch and said she had
something to attend to, but that we were welcome to continue looking. She left us alone with those priceless books for nearly an hour.
"Man," said Beth. "I love this place! I want it to be my hangout!"

"Me too!"

That afternoon Beth worked in the room while I went to wash
clothes so we could pack for the next leg of the journey. It was one of
the duties of the road that I had taken on as mine. In fact, I enjoyed
doing the laundry. Sometimes I would read a book or magazine,
sometimes I would work on notes, sometimes I would sketch, sometimes I would simply sit and watch people. Whichever I did, it was a
nice time to be alone with my thoughts.

I found a coin-operated *laverie* on the street beyond the chateau leading to the Port D'Availl harbor. After I put my clothes in the washer, I stood on the sidewalk and looked down toward the water. There wasn't much going on yet, but give it a couple of months and kids would be playing on the swing sets and old men would be rolling their *boules*. Waiters wearing shorts would be crossing the street balancing trays of beer and pastis bound for seaside tables. Closer to where I stood, in the shade of a small park, workers were jackhammering a sidewalk and putting down new marble slabs, getting ready for summer. The house on the corner was being painted a color somewhere between ripe watermelon and neon terra-cotta, with shutters a deep blue and yet so translucent that I might've been seeing into heaven.

I read for a while that day. I'd been at the *laverie* nearly an hour and was loading the washed clothes into the dryer when my cell phone rang. Assuming it was Beth, I was slightly taken aback to hear the voice of Gerard on the line. "Yeah, so," he said, "I hear you've done your market research, umm?"

"That's right, and we've decided to take the apartment."

"Well," he said, "unfortunately I offered the second floor to someone else just last night. It's possible that he wants it for a year."

It was a perfectly nice conversation. We talked for a few minutes longer, and Gerard promised to get in touch if anything changed. After that there was nothing to do but laugh at my own doofusity. I wished I could manage it.

8.

Equilibrium

SEEING LIFE THE WAY a child does have its drawbacks. Our daughter Bret used to lie awake at night worrying that someone would scale the outside of the house, climb through her second-story window, and throw up on her. As a boy I saw Death cloaked in my bedroom curtains. The world viewed through a child's eyes is always menacing and a tad off kilter.

In the windy corridor between Perpignan and Narbonne, where

153

the A9 begins curving gently east following the edge of the sea, we occasionally saw big red-striped wind socks that put me in mind of the Cat in the Hat's cloche. Above the autoroute, automated signs advised motorists on the level of wind velocity. *"Vent violent,"* the sign said that day. *"Soyez prudent."* I instinctively gripped the wheel tighter.

A few minutes later we passed clusters of windmills lining the distant hills. They weren't old-fashioned windmills like the one in Collioure; these were sleek and white and tri-pronged, giant Mercedes-Benz symbols glinting in the Mediterranean sun. They reminded me of the pinwheels that we played with as children, which summoned images of state fairs, which evoked the indelible countenance of the smudge-eyed tart who tried to lure me into the fun house. Her twisted mouth was a slash of the same stuff the candied apples had been drowned in.

We had dearly loved Collioure and were leaving with a feeling that we had missed the first big opportunity of our new life. Our destination now was the Camargue, French cowboy country. Matisse had never been there as far as I knew (though as a young man he had liked to ride horses), but the Camargue happened to be on the way to Cassis, where Matisse had spent a month in the winter of 1909. Cassis was very near Marseille, where we planned to catch a flight to Tangier, Morocco, which had been pivotal in Matisse's art.

The very idea of French cowboys stirred a thousand silly notions in my head. Long before Hemingway and Matisse came along, my hero was Roy Rogers, and as I drove I amused myself with images of Beaujolais saloons, horses named Jean-Claude, and Maurice Chevalier as a sidekick. It was a cartoon world—funny on the surface, but a little disturbing in its ultimate tipability. As Gustave Moreau said to the legions of critics of Matisse's Belle-Île painting *The Dinner Table*, "Let it be; his decanters are solidly on the table and I could hang my hat on their stoppers." You can't hang your ten-gallon Stetson on a Beaujolais saloon.

For a long time I had considered Matisse's colorful canvases as delineations of serenity, a state I unabashedly aspire to and only occasionally—and temporarily—attain. To my eye, the paintings are mostly beautiful in their separate parts—rich and soothing in color, peaceful in subject matter, harmonious in line. But this has been the great criticism of Matisse, based in large part on a few Pollyannaish lines he wrote in his first essay, "Notes of a Painter," in 1908. "What I dream of is an art of balance, of purity and serenity, devoid of troubling or depressing subject matter . . . a soothing, calming influence on the mind, something like a good armchair that provides relaxation from fatigue."

Now, somewhere in the middle of my journey, seemingly from one day to the next, I was looking at Matisse with fresh eyes and finding his paintings to be a delineation of yearning. Some of it had to do with his penchant for viewing the world from a child's perspective. In *Le luxe (II)*, a scene of Collioure painted in 1907 or 1908, three naked yellow women are involved in a strange après-bathing ritual in which one dries another's foot while the third runs toward them from the sea carrying what may be a bouquet of seaweed. The woman whose foot is being dried looks searchingly into the middle distance. In *Music*, from 1909 or 1910, four naked orange people of questionable sex sit, and another stands, on a flat purple and green background while two of the five play musical instruments. The people seem a little *off*, like that bizarre little banjo picker in *Deliverance*, and the spaces between them are as empty as a wish.

Increasingly, from Matisse's early days in Collioure, his paintings convey an imbalance, an incompleteness. Eyes are as blank as a cat's. This coincides with the middle of Matisse's own journey. In time, a new portal—the mirror—helps facilitate the effect, as in *Interior with a Phonograph* from Nice in 1924. In a lush room a curtain is pulled back from the side, off center, to reveal the stark, staring face of the artist. It reminds me of the face my father painted in that singular, haunting bottle.

Even Matisse's last few easel paintings—some of my absolute favorites, done in the late 1940s, when he was an old man—convey a loneliness, a sadness, a nagging wistfulness. In beautiful rooms brimming with deep color, shadows and light tell a different story.

Having registered the feeling, I went looking for corroboration. "If Cézanne's painting offers *provisional* equilibrium," I found in

John Elderfield's introduction to *Henri Matisse: A Retrospective,* "Matisse's, then, offers *potential* unity. . . . This accords with his acknowledgment, toward the end of his life, that his researches could never be over. . . . Likewise, the journey of making a painting aims at something impossible to achieve. Hence the extraordinary amount of repetition in Matisse's art. He is constantly redoing the same subjects: returning to a given subject time and again. . . . Nothing is ever quite final, it seems. This evidences an endless cycle of hope of achieving unity, and disillusionment at not having discovered an ultimate unity."

It made Matisse modern, I thought, gliding the Peugeot off the exit at Montpellier. Matisse could've been created by Hemingway, except that he turned out so well.

APPROACHING THE SHORE feels the same everywhere. At Montpellier we turned south and soon were in the *Petite Camargue,* a flat marshy area of pines and scrub. The salty sea air told us that the beach was very near. For a while we drove along La Grande Motte, which had been swampland until the French government reclaimed it and made it into a summer playground. Travel writers look down on the Grande Motte's ersatz origins, but the French love it.

In time we arrived in the small seaside village of Saintes-Maries-de-la-Mer, where I was introduced to more of Jesus' relatives. Not being Catholic, I had known only the Nuclear Holy Family, but on a field trip in Brittany had seen the church built for Saint Anne of Auray, the Virgin Mary's mother. Saintes-Maries-de-la-Mer was named for Mary Magdalene, Mary Jacobea (the Virgin Mary's sister), and Mary Salome, mother of the apostles James and John. According to local lore, they were set adrift a few years after the Crucifixion and ended up washing ashore there at the southern edge of Provence. One of the Marys had brought along her black servant, Sarah, now known far and wide as the saint of the gypsies, who converged on Saintes-Maries-de-la-Mer every May to celebrate her life.

"I would *love* to be here then," Beth said. "Wouldn't you?"

"Sounds like fun," I said, feeling for my wallet.

Beyond the village we came to a strand of two-lane road with marsh on the left and shallow salt water on the right. In the water were scores of flamingos, striking pink birds with dramatic patches of black beneath their wings. Some simply stood on one leg, while others high-stepped in slow motion like Rockettes wading through molasses. In a few minutes the marsh gave way to hard-packed dirt. Corrals of white horses began to appear, and occasionally we saw a ranch hand leading a group of tourists on a trail ride. The white Camargue horses are descendants of prehistoric horses. They aren't born white, but their color changes around age seven.

At the sign for Le Cacharel, we turned right down a narrow gravel road to a ranch that could've been in Arizona. Except for the orange tile roofs, everything else in sight was as white as salt—the ground, the buildings, the sky. The nearby marsh smelled like rotted plants.

We checked in and a dark-haired woman told us, in English, "Don't leave *anything* in your car." We took her at her word. We needed to repack anyway. Fortunately, they had a large cart available, so I stacked all our bags and boxes on it and, in three loads, moved everything into what I had named "the bunkhouse." We were in number ten of the long building behind the handsome main hacienda where, one of the maids told me, the "Big Boss" lived.

Our room had admirable storage space, and we were still able to walk around despite the luggage. Through the back window we could see white horses in a pen. "Maybe we should go for a ride tomorrow," Beth said. I was surprised, since she had a pretty ambivalent relationship with horses; she'd once owned one who'd been prone to biting and bucking and running away with her. I personally liked the smell of horses better than the feel of sitting on them, but, once unpacked, we went to the reception area and booked a trail ride for the following afternoon. Then we took a walk on a clumpy path through the marsh. The flamingos were everywhere, weird and funny and exaggeratedly slow. I sketched a couple of them in my notebook, remembering a children's book about Matisse that showed three drawings he had made of a swan, each with less detail than the one before. The final picture was simply a series of elegant flowing lines, such as the one I drew of the curving necks of the flamingos.

Later, on our way into town for dinner, we saw a dozen flamingos standing in the water illuminated by an amazing golden light, their feathers almost orange, their reflections warm and shimmering on the dark blue pool beneath them. The birds' heads were underwater and their tails in the air. They reminded me of Matisse's painting *The Moroccans (Les Marocains)*, which shows several green-robed Muslims on their knees bent over at prayer. To me, they had always looked like Brussels sprouts. The wonder of truly seeing is that everything in life is a prism, filling your head with shards of complementary images. I made a note to come back the next day and draw the flamingos à la *Les Marocains*.

At the restaurant we ordered a *côte de taureau*—the steak of the black long-horned Camargue cattle—and drank a *pichet* of *vin rouge*. After dinner the wind had picked up, and I had to really fight the steering wheel to keep from being blown off the ghostly strip of pavement into the wet darkness. Back in the room at 10:30, we decided it was a good night to light the large candles from Lourdes we'd been carrying around for weeks. On our way south from Auray, we had stopped for an hour at that fabled mecca of the sick, the lame, and the helpless, and it had been a stunning experience.

Lourdes is a town of fifteen thousand inhabitants with 350 hotels. We passed through an archway to the wide esplanade leading to the Basilique du Rosaire, an imposing gray stone cathedral a hundred or more yards away. On Easter and during Holy Week, this mall would be jammed with pilgrims waiting to be healed or blessed. Flowers lined the esplanade, and flags and banners hung from posts along the route to the church.

Around the cathedral to the right was the grotto where in 1858 the young Bernadette Soubirous was first visited by a vision of the Immaculate Conception. Near the grotto was a wall lined with spigots tapping water from an underground spring that Bernadette uncovered with her own hands. We queued up with our fellow sufferers, many of whom were carrying bottles and jars to fill. When it was my turn at the water, I patted some on my left jaw for the Bell's palsy I had contracted in 1983, on the scar of the right parotid gland for the cancer surgery I'd undergone in 2000, and slapped a dab on my cheeks for the rosacea I had recently developed. Most of my afflictions over the years have been to the face and head—probably, as my mother says, because I "come from a long line of vain men."

"Put some on your head," Beth said. "Get rid of that negative thinking."

After taking the water, we had moved on to the candle lighting. In a line of metal sheds that might have housed contestants at a Texas barbecue cook-off, white burning candles of varying sizes were protected from the wind; some were as thick as small trees. I sat on a bench and made a few notes while Beth went to buy our candles. Not far away, a young black woman with dyed blond hair hugged a plane tree and sobbed. I watched her until Beth arrived loaded down with candles like a French woman carrying baguettes. Three of them were the same size—about a yard long and a couple of inches in circumference—but the other one was longer and thicker. "We're going to save these three for our personal use," Beth said. "This one we're going to light for all the people we love and for peace in the world." I stood behind her as she did the lighting, then we both observed a moment of silence. Finally Beth placed the candle in the holder. On the way out, we passed the blond black girl carrying three candles to light. I hoped they would help her. At the taps, I decided on a last-minute splash of healing water on my eyes to help me see better too, but something in it made my vision blurry.

Now, on a blustery night in the Camargue, we took out our three Lourdes candles and put them in their holders. One of them had snapped in the car from shifting luggage, but Beth retrieved a roll of Scotch tape from her BHV container and made the candle whole again. We turned off the lights, and Beth said a few words about Blair and Bret and her mother and brother and his family and my mother and my sons and their wives and our dog and cat and the rest of our loved ones, including her late brother, Brent. She's good at rituals and ceremonies, but they kind of embarrass me. I'm better at silent prayers. After she finished, we watched the flames for a while, then blew them out and tried to sleep.

Toward midnight the wind began to rage. The shutter outside our open window banged wildly, and I slipped on my jeans and went out and fumbled in the dark for a small stick to jam between the shutter and the metal hold. Even then I couldn't ignore the wind. It howled and moaned, throwing things in the night. Beth seemed to be sleeping through it, but I couldn't keep from tossing and turning, occasionally dozing but dreaming only on the surface. At one point I considered getting up to take a pill, but I looked at my watch and it was 4:15—too late. We would be riding horses soon and I didn't want to be drowsy and fall off into the marsh.

In the gray first light I looked over to see if Beth was awake. Though she was clinging to sleep, I detected a hint of eye movement. She could tell I was staring at her. "Did you hear that wind last night?" I said.

"Umh," she answered.

"I felt like it was going to blow the house down."

At 7:15 A.M. our cell phone rang. We scrambled out of sleep and Beth handed the phone to me. "Hello," I said.

It was Blair Arnold, Beth's brother. He asked if he could speak with Beth. His voice was strange. I gave Beth the phone and told her who it was. She took it and sat up slightly, listening. In about ten seconds she said, *"Oh no!"* Then she turned to me, her face distorted. "My mother died—can you believe it? *My mother is dead!"*

WE WOULDN'T KNOW for days what had actually happened, but apparently Bobbye hadn't felt well all day Saturday. In early evening she called her son and told him she had pressure in her head and was sweating profusely. "Do you want to go to the emergency room?" Blair Arnold asked, but Bobbye said no, she would take an aspirin. After Blair had showered, they talked again—we didn't know who called whom. Blair asked how she was feeling, and Bobbye said better. Then Blair heard her say something like, "Oh dear" or "Oh my," and the next sound was her falling. The doctors later said she was probably dead by the time she hit the floor. An aneurysm, most likely. Time of death was 8:15 P.M., Saturday, April 5, Batesville, Arkansas, time—and 3:15 A.M. Sunday where Beth and I were, in a salt marsh on the Mediterranean Sea hours from the nearest international airport.

Even as Beth talked to her brother, I lay there trying to wake myself from the horrible dream and at the same time starting to plan all that we needed to do. Beth later told me that the first thing I did was get out of bed and relight the candles. But the first act I remembered was going to the reception area and seeing a woman in a maid's uniform. She thought I wanted breakfast. "No, madame," I said. "La mère de ma femme est morte." The woman caught her breath and clutched her heart. Then I told her we needed to leave our luggage— *all of it*—at the hotel. The alternative, which wasn't an alternative, was to leave it in our car parked at the Marseille airport.

"No problem," the maid said immediately. She didn't consult a supervisor, didn't discuss it with her colleagues, she just made the decision herself, on the spot. I ordered coffee to be delivered to our room and went back to be with Beth. No more than five minutes later the maid knocked on our door. We were to store all our stuff in a spare room "in the Big Boss's house," she said. My face must have betrayed my anxiety, because she said, "Don't worry," and made a key turning motion to let me know that everything would be safe and secure. We weren't just discussing shoes and underwear; I would be leaving all my files and notes and books, my computer, and my five and a half first-draft chapters, which hadn't even been printed out.

"Merci, Madame," I said, and I think she had tears in her eyes. "Merci beaucoup."

The rest of our morning wasn't so encouraging. Having been exclusive Delta Airlines customers for some fifteen years, we held Delta SkyMiles return tickets for May 22, a date we had intended to change once we figured out our plans. Now Delta was refusing to free up seats on most of their flights because we held "award" tickets. One flight, which we couldn't possibly make, left Marseille for Paris in two hours. "The next available flight will be April 13," a Delta ticket agent told me. That was eight days away.

"Ma'am," I said, "my wife's mother has died. Can't you open some seats today so we can get there?"

"You're asking us to *give* you tickets," she said.

"No," I said, "we've already earned the tickets. I'm asking you to free some seats so we can take advantage of them."

That kind of thing went on for hours, during which we were often on hold listening to advertisements for Delta's Business Elite service. "If you don't like being pampered," the unctuous announcer said, *"stop listening right now."*

The bottom line was, after catching an Air France flight from Marseille that afternoon, there was one Delta flight and one flight only that would work for us. It would leave Paris at 10:45 on Monday with stops at New York and Cincinnati, and would arrive in Little Rock via prop airplane at 7:30 P.M.—eighteen hours after takeoff. "There are no other available flights," the Delta agent said. Unless we wanted to buy new tickets for fifteen hundred dollars each—in that case, we could get out immediately. The only good thing about the day was that we didn't have to worry about a hotel—we had a home in Paris. Whenever we phoned the Hôtel Saint-Germain to ask if they had room, either Wanda or Daniel said, "By all means." On that unreal Sunday morning, Wanda said not to worry—our room would be ready when we got there.

The two-hour drive to Marseille was made in shocked silence. Beth had reached her daughter Blair, but Bret hadn't answered. Beth looked out the window and sobbed most of the way to Marignane Airport. Both of us had thought that if we were to receive such a phone call, it would be about my ninety-three-year-old mother. Bobbye had been just seventy-four. She was busy and active. None of it made sense. I couldn't help feeling that our adventure had contributed somehow. Had our saddling her with Snapp and Cleo created the final, excessive stress? Bobbye had once told me that if she ever wrote a book it would be titled *I Never Got My Turn*. I'd thought she was joking, but she wasn't. Her husband had died in a diving accident at age forty-two leaving her alone with three teenagers. For years she had watched over her husband's mother, who lived until age 103, and had moved her own mother to Batesville for hands-on care that wasn't always appreciated. Even now, Bobbye's mother was ninety-five and still going strong. Where, I wondered, was the line between self-fulfillment and selfishness?

"You know," Beth said finally, "this means I'm an orphan now." It was life viewed by a child.

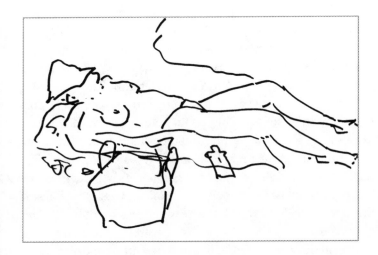

THE SKY IS ashy orange, the cloud dirty white descending to a leaden pink. The space in the center, either a low wall or a balcony floor, is a green of the drabbest hue. Sunshine enters on treads of gray. But inside the room, peering out the window at a world that appears to be erupting—it was, after all, 1918, and the world was at war—a young man in a khaki suit makes private music on a violin.

The painting is *Violinist at the Window,* which Matisse made in Nice in his second season there. This picture was on my mind as our plane made its descent into Marseille on Easter Sunday two weeks after we had left. We were deliriously happy to be coming back, to be re-burrowing into our private life. More and more, it was the message I took from Matisse—the gulf between the exterior and interior worlds, the surface and the subterranean. Balance—serenity—especially for an artist, was only possible if you kept the outer world at bay. Whether serenity was *probable* was an entirely different subject.

Recalling the tough Marseille of *The French Connection,* I had worried that we might find our silver Peugeot stripped and charred, but there it was parked perfectly intact in the April sun, shadowed by a date palm tree. From the airport Beth phoned Le Hôtel Mahogany in Cassis, where we had reservations for Monday night. Yes, they had a room available for Sunday, and we booked it on the spot. We had planned to drive directly from Marseille to the Camargue to pick up our things, but Le Cacharel had no availability and we didn't know where we might stay. This was better: Beth, especially, was exhausted. Cassis was only about thirty kilometers farther east. She could rest while I went back to Saintes-Maries-de-la-Mer.

Driving into Cassis on that Easter afternoon, we could understand why artists loved the place. Our hotel overlooked a small quiet bay a short walk from the village and port. A high chalky cliff grew out of the far left horizon, its spiny fingers forming *calanques,* or shallow fjordlike inlets the color of my cousin's big opal ring. Framing the view on the right stood a handsome two-terraced house that the hotel manager said had been featured in, ironically, *The French Connection.* Straight ahead—across the street—the Mediterranean rippled in short quick strokes of deep blue with a copper wash, an effect of the late-day sun on the cliffs beyond.

That night, jet-lagged and a little giddy, we ventured no farther than next door to a cozy restaurant. Modern travel moves the body faster than the mind can adjust. On Monday I went to retrieve our things. This time I realized, as I hadn't before, how close the Camargue was to Arles, where poor old Vincent van Gogh had tried in vain to establish the kind of art community that John Peter Russell later built in Belle-Île and Paul Signac had established in Saint-Tropez. The lessons of their lives weren't lost on Matisse, who increasingly sidestepped the notion of an artistic community and went straight to the ideal of a life built around the making of art. Van Gogh, whose unstable personality didn't mesh with mankind, had nevertheless had it right—art requires a private stand.

Beth and I loved van Gogh's work and in 1991 had even written a screenplay together called *Sunflowers,* about the theft of that famous painting. In the late 1980s, a Japanese billionaire had bought it for nearly $40 million—at that time the highest price ever paid for a single piece of art. Almost immediately, that record was eclipsed by van Gogh's *Portrait of Dr. Gachet,* which went, in 1990, for $82.5 million. When van Gogh painted *Sunflowers,* he was fasting and by necessity looking forward to receiving the fifty francs his brother Theo had promised to send. When he shot himself, at age thirty-six, he had sold only one painting. "Why don't you chase van Gogh?" a friend had asked, I think benignly, as though I had selected Matisse by throwing darts at names on a board.

"Too short a journey," I said. "I'm chasing Matisse so I don't have to chase Hemingway."

Driving through van Gogh country, I thought of an interview I had conducted the summer before with Townsend Wolfe, an artist in his own right who was then completing thirty-four years as curator of the Arkansas Arts Center. "What's the point of painting?" I had asked; it was the kind of surface question that most people would assume they knew the answer to, until they started drowning in the unfathomable depths of the obvious. Wolfe was a little taken aback. "It's a way to communicate, to someone else, emotions and intellect," he began. "Conflict and the resolving of conflict is what an artist deals with constantly. As soon as he puts that first colored mark on the white surface, he has corrupted that space. Then he has to *correct* that space, bringing order to it. It's that sort of back-and-forth involvement."

That said, Wolfe then moved into territory he later told me he had never really explored before: "The artist has total control," he said. "There is no editor. That's one of the reasons many artists do it. If a writer writes about a red barn, it's left to a reader's interpretation what color red it is. But if an artist paints it, it's the red he chooses. It's *that* red barn."

Control, I thought, as I exited the autoroute south of Arles. *What a joke.* Soon I turned onto a winding road down through the marsh to the sea. The white horses stood in their pens watching me pass. Tourists were out in force now, their packed minivans parked bumper to bumper along the shoulder by the corrals. On my left and right, plump holidaygoers in boat shoes held tight to the reins of horses walking in line behind cowboys. I was suddenly glad we had missed that adventure, though I was still in shock at the reason for it.

At Le Cacharel the owner, a man named Florian, was behind the counter at reception. Once I figured out who he was, I thanked him profusely. Waving away my words, he led me into his house to show me where to bring the cart. "We moved your things," he said. "It was

Easter. My cousin came; and we needed the bedroom." They had stacked everything behind a sofa in the big living and dining room. Needing to attend to his guests, he left me alone to come and go. I parked the cart by a side door across from the marsh and began carrying our luggage to it. This time the loading didn't feel onerous; I was glad to see my Matisse books, my French easel, my laptop. It was a reunion with old friends.

Before leaving, I stopped by reception to return Florian's key. The maid who had helped us that morning was standing there, and I took that opportunity to tell the Big Boss how helpful, how *comforting,* she had been. She smiled and blushed, and he seemed proud of her. I hoped he would promote her, or at least give her a raise. "We'll come back someday under happier circumstances," I said, and then I got in the car and drove off, past languid flamingos and staring white horses, doubling back toward the autoroute and the continuation of the journey.

BEFORE BOBBYE'S DEATH, we had planned to go directly from Le Cacharel to visit Anne Pierre-Humbert and see Pierre's southern studio in Saint-Laurent-la-Vernède when Anne was there before Easter. It was just up the road, as we say at home.

Pierre's painting continued to astonish me. In Auray I had propped up the Galerie Daniel Besseiche poster of his brick-red *Grenades et Anémones* so I could look at it while I wrote. I also pored over his catalogs for inspiration, and not just as a painter. What intrigued me was his absence of hard lines, rigid definitions, firm borders, like pictures of half-asleep prayer. In their amorphousness, his canvases seemed to capture the incomplete, elliptical nature of *real* real life. I wished desperately that Pierre-Humbert were still alive. His had been the only whisper I heard in the dark of a Paris winter. He knew what he was doing, and he knew why creating was a noble way to spend a life. Ultimately, what was more real—the surface life, or the life inside? Most of us wish for the latter and settle for the former, but it didn't have to be that way. I had the instinct, and sometimes the faith, but I needed someone like Pierre-Humbert to lead me through the paint. His replacement would be hard to find.

The white highway lines blurred past like so many sheep on a sleepless night, growing from dots to blocks and then disappearing in my wake. That day my frame of mind received the broken center line as the exquisite, timeless pattern of life and loss. How much art has been fashioned from such voids? Not just from the finality of death, but—as in Matisse's case—from the persistent, unbalancing loss of family. Estrangement from his father began early, but before Matisse's journey was over, his only consistently comforting blood bond was with his second son, Pierre. Of course, the other side of the question must also be asked: How many such voids have been fashioned from art?

Beth was in a different room when I got back to Cassis. The night before, we had stayed in a garden room; now we were on the front of the hotel with a balcony overlooking the bay. She had bought champagne, and we opened it outside where we could watch the cliffs and sea change colors. "People were swimming and sunbathing today," she said. "They lie out on those rocks like seals." We had yet to wear our swimsuits, but the time was near.

That night we walked into town and had an early dinner, then came back and went to bed. Cassis would be a rest stop. We needed it and this hotel provided it. It would've been a nice place to set up my easel and paint, but I didn't have the energy. I sketched the rocks, the bay, the villa, but after so much traveling, all I wanted to do was stare at the sea.

On Tuesday we put on our swimsuits and walked across the street to the little half-moon Plage de Bestouan, a rocky beach dotted by bright towels. The greased bodies made me think of oysters on the half shell, and quite a few were plump oysters. It didn't matter: Whether the women were young, old, thin, or fat, they took off their tops and let their breasts breathe free. The men all wore tiny triangles of shiny fabric, never mind the flesh cascading over the waistband. At 11 A.M. the beach was packed. We spread our hotel towels between a sleeping middle-aged woman with alizarine crimson hair and a young mother struggling to rein in two little boys.

We had on too many clothes, Beth in her one-piece and me in my baggy surfer trunks. I rubbed lotion on her upper back and shoulders, and then Beth addressed her part of the problem—she promptly peeled down her top and applied lotion to her breasts. *Lucky her.* She lay back and opened her book. I had planned to nap, but decided that this beach was probably as close as I would come to a life drawing class until we stopped traveling. Three feet to my left, the middle-aged woman dozed on her back, her face shaded by a canvas hat. She wore what appeared, from that angle, to be a thong. I opened my book and made a quick bold line without taking my eyes off the subject. "The hand is a tool and shouldn't have any input at all," Townsend Wolfe had said. "An artist sees both with his eyes and whatever soul he possesses."

I liked the drawing of the sleeping woman; it had the fluid movement of a tracing. Her breasts rested flat against her chest, the one in the foreground appearing fuller. I especially liked the way I captured the angle of her legs. Glancing around for another model, I met the eye of the young mother next to me. Her breasts were pink and firm, and I ordered my brain to keep my eyes steady. It was better for me to stick with sleeping or otherwise occupied subjects. *All these years later and I'm still hiding my pictures of breasts.*

Down by Beth's left foot a young blond woman in a red bikini bottom fiddled with her hair, twisting it through a black scrunchy into a tight ponytail. I dashed off a couple of drawings, one focusing on her body, knees raised, and the other on the way her eyes looked closed. After that I sketched a woman lying on her stomach reading, and then a young girl in sunglasses leaning over with a necklace dangling above her breasts. Turning to my last piece of drawing paper, I scanned the beach and settled on a buxom blonde sitting cross-legged fixing her hair. The final sketch was especially fast and a little crude, but, looking at it later, I felt that it caught a hint of Gallic nonchalance where the body was concerned. Judging from her pose, she might've been sitting on her bed after a bath. They were strange beings, the French: They erected walls around themselves and then went outside nearly naked.

"I would've drawn you, but I ran out of paper," I said to Beth.

"Promises, promises," she said, shifting her lovely bosoms to the sun.

We spent four nights in Cassis, most of it close to Le Mahogany. We did try to get out one afternoon. Sophie Maillard, the young hotel manager, had suggested we drive to the top of the cliff across the bay. From there, she said, we would be able to see down into gemstone coves of liquid light. Unfortunately, on the way we got stuck in a single-lane traffic jam on a hill. In a few minutes smoke obscured our windshield, but we thought it was pouring from the car in front of us; then we noticed people yelling and pointing in our direction. I pulled over as far as I could, increasing the congestion, and popped the hood. Billowing plumes, a veritable volcano on the verge of eruption.

We agreed that it was time to use our free Peugeot road service. Beth made the phone call, and then, while we were waiting, she spotted a puppy wandering alone near the busy intersection. She jumped out of the car and began chasing the dog, who thought it was a game and resolved not to be captured. Passing motorists didn't know which show to watch, Beth or me. Eventually she snagged the puppy, only to be caught red-handed by its owner, who seemed at first to think a dognapping was in progress. The two dramas resolved themselves at approximately the same time when the now-grateful puppy owner ordered her bewildered husband to inspect our smoking car just as the wrecker drove up. For the next few minutes the mechanic gave me a congenial lecture—in French—about riding the clutch. The clutch was fine, but my manhood was scorched. By the time the wrecker left, I had lost my heart for sightseeing. I drove back to the hotel, parked the car, and spent the rest of the day staring at the sea from the safety of our balcony.

Beth decided that the Mediterranean was bluer in Cassis than it had been in Collioure. I wondered if that was simply a coastal cliché— "the water's always bluer on the other side"—but she pointed to the big ships drifting just beyond the mouth of the bay and made the case that deeper water resulted in deeper color. One afternoon I asked Sophie, who was from Normandy, how it was to live in Cassis. She loved it. She liked to run and to ride bikes, and of course, being from the north, liked the sunshine. "How much are apartments here in the summer?" I asked.

"Ah," she said, in that suggestive French way, and then delivered the *coup de grâce:* "Three thousand euros a week." I mourned Collioure all the more.

Rest brought clarity, and clarity revealed the depth of my unease. We had been on a fast track, emotions on autopilot, acting without thinking. Now our job was to pick up the pieces and move on. But what pieces? Move where? Do what? Increasingly, I found home crowding my dreams. In one, my mother—whom I had visited while we were in the States—looked at me with her heartbreaking blue eyes. "What are you doing in France?" she said. When I told her I was researching a book, she promptly forgot and asked me the same question a few minutes later.

In another dream, Snapp and I were driving somewhere. "You don't love me anymore," he said.

"Of course I do."

He shook his head and looked out the window, and this time he didn't let his ears flap freely in the wind. "Not like you did two years ago," he said.

"Come on, Snapp Man," I said, pinching his little nub of a tail, and then I repeated the shocking statement that Henri Matisse had written, in the embattled year of 1941, to his son Pierre explaining his reasons for building a wall between art and family: "I have said that I love my family truly, dearly, and profoundly, but from a distance," I recited, watching Snapp to see if he was listening. "A hypersensitive organism like mine can find human contacts unendurable and deeply wounding, even if the heart remains tender."

In my dream, my dog's ears perked up and he cocked his head, but he didn't turn to look at me. "Human contacts?" Snapp said.

9.

The Veiled Eye

BLUE IS MY color, whether it's French blue, Havana blue, Prussian blue, Delft blue, cobalt blue, ultramarine, periwinkle. I don't know why I love blue so much. Goethe said that objects viewed through a blue glass look gloomy and melancholy, but to me they look soothing. Dr. Fairchild at the Rochester Institute of Technology says that statistics show more people choosing blue as a favorite color than any other, and though I hate being so ordinary, there's nothing I can do about it. Inevitably, blue compels my eye. I see blue shadows creeping across white walls in spring and blue grape leaves in green vineyards. Standing before the sea and sky, I read the mysteries of life as blue. "As we readily follow an agreeable object that flies from us," Goethe also wrote, "so we love to contemplate blue, not because it advances to us, but because it draws us after it."

I went to Morocco searching for blue, a blue like the one Matisse used for the walls of *Porte de la Casbah* from 1913. Blue called to him, as in the case of the blue butterfly, and I believe it was blue that lured him to Morocco. There he found an opera of arabesques and a blue as piercing as an aria. He also found a whole culture built around a rich, secret inner life.

His two trips to Tangier, from January to mid-April 1912 and from October 1912 to mid-February 1913, would forever change his art. In Morocco, decoration is part of everyday life, and Matisse reveled in the country's tiles, textiles, and tapestries. The pictures he made from his visits to Morocco are some of the most sumptuous of his entire career. By the time he arrived in Tangier for the first time, he had finally seen his paintings start to earn serious money. The works from Collioure had brought something approaching infamy from the Paris public, but also a few farsighted collectors. At the Salon des Indépendants in 1906, Matisse showed only one painting, the massive *Le Bonheur de Vivre*. A picture of nymphs lolling in a seaside nirvana of bright flat color, it represented to Matisse "my Arcadia," his ideal rustic paradise. In terms of technique, it was also a major breakthrough from the jarring dottedness of Divisionism. Except for its shouting colors, this painting was calm—almost serene. Signac hated it, and most of the rest of the art world mocked it. People who were there at the Salon recalled that all you had to do to find Matisse's personal vision of joy was to follow the hoots and jeers and screaming laughter.

But among the visitors to the Indépendants that year were two men destined to play huge roles in Matisse's life. One was Leo Stein, Gertrude's art-loving brother, who bought *Le Bonheur de Vivre* and hung it in his own home where it could be seen by all the writers, painters, intellectuals, and art collectors who frequented the Steins' salon. Another influential presence at the Indépendants was the Russian textile magnate Sergei Ivanovich Shchukin, who already owned a few early Matisses but who had never before been quite so convincingly smacked in the face by one. After seeing *Le Bonheur de Vivre*, he asked for a meeting with the painter, and that meeting resulted in many future commissions—including several from Morocco.

Matisse continued to paint often in Collioure, his colors gradually finding a more comforting decibel level, but increasingly he became obsessed with things African, such as masks and carved figures. In 1906, he made a two-week trip to French Algeria, where he found the sun too blindingly bright to do much work but, upon later reflection, discovered that certain images—such as goldfish in bowls—had lodged themselves deep in his unconscious. *Blue Nude: Memory of Biskra*, a 1907 painting sprung from his Algerian experience (and perhaps from Cézanne's rough nudes in *Three Bathers*), again confounded the Paris art world, including a young Pablo Picasso, who had met Matisse the year before at the Steins'. Picasso, who was eleven years younger, later claimed that he knew the instant he saw Matisse's work that it was "a two-man race." Their Tortoise and Hare would assume the trappings of the Professor and the Hustler. Matisse was earnest, Picasso was cavalier; Matisse was deliberate, Picasso was a quick study; Matisse strained to be understood, Picasso never explained. From their first meeting, Picasso eyed Matisse hungrily while Matisse regarded him warily from behind gold rims.

In the year before he left for Morocco, Matisse made a series of highly decorative paintings that were blatantly dismissive of any accepted Western rules of perspective. The relentless beautiful hues and patterns of *Interior with Aubergines,* painted in Collioure, dance along the edge of vertigo. *The Red Studio* evokes the drenched lushness of Persian miniatures. *The Painter's Family,* with its dizzying mosaic of rugs, textiles, and wallpaper, nearly swallows up the humans in the room the way tiles in Morocco can. No wonder, then, that as Matisse and Amélie steamed across the Mediterranean toward the Bay of Tangier, he could hardly contain his excitement. "On a slightly rough sea, but of the purest blue, the ship glides without rocking or pitching," he wrote to his daughter Margeurite in Paris. He approached Morocco thinking of blue, too.

Unfortunately for Matisse, the purest blue would soon give way to a "veritable deluge" that darkened the North African skies for weeks. Out of his mind with cabin fever, he nearly packed up and went home. Ninety-four years later, Beth and I were also met by rain when we arrived in Casablanca. But ours cleared the next morning, revealing not just the brilliant blue I had hoped for, but, set against the sky in a mass of mosaic tile, a sea-foam green such as I could never have imagined—a green that for a day or two made me almost forget blue.

THE MOROCCO THAT Matisse found in 1912 and 1913 no longer exists in Tangier. That mysterious international city, that alluring gateway to Africa that charmed so many Western writers and painters, is now a teeming metropolis of humanity washed there more or less permanently from distant ports. The operative image seems to have morphed from the boisterous exotic melting pot to the simmering cauldron of incendiary spices.

But we had to go anyway, no matter what. Beth had been to Morocco before, and for our anniversary in 1996, she gave me a book called *Matisse in Morocco*. "One of these days I'll take you to Morocco," she wrote in her inscription. "That's your future anniversary present." For Christmas one year we each gave the other—unknowingly—photo books of Morocco. Here was a land of pure jeweled color and sinfully sinuous pattern, a sensual paradise where even doors and walls were things of beauty. We didn't go to Morocco when we initially planned to, because of the Iraq war; nearly a year later, the timing felt right. From her earlier visit, Beth knew of a respected, reliable tour operator with the very welcome name of Olive Branch. It was Olive Branch's owner, Mr. Benachir, who suggested we get the feel of the country—Casablanca, Rabat, Fès, Meknes— before venturing into Tangier. Fortunately, we hired a guide, or we'd still be trying to find our way out of the Fès medina.

Our driver was a big pleasant man named Mr. Aziz. He had a

good sense of humor and a wide grin to punctuate his jokes. "That's the second American Embassy in Morocco," he said, as we approached a McDonald's in Casablanca. Big smile, pleased with himself. "There's the seven-stars hotel," he said, pointing out the Prefect of Police building—the jail—which was decorated with seven florets. We felt comfortable with Aziz immediately, though I soon discovered that the only problem with having a guide is that a guide's job is to *guide* you; we weren't ordinary tourists looking for just any treat we could feast our eyes on. I was in search of the Morocco that Matisse filtered through his soul onto his canvas. My discoveries began on our first day, with color.

In Casablanca, the sky was a wafer-thin blue, and below it the churning Atlantic was a rich dark carpet trimmed out in frothy white. Before we left for Rabat, Aziz asked if we wanted to see the new mosque erected in the early 1990s to honor King Hassan II, father of the present ruler. The true answer was "Not really," but instead Beth batted her eyes and said we'd love to. In Morocco, there seems to be a mosque every few blocks, its square minaret piercing the sky. Matisse drew several of them in his sketchbooks, and those were the ones I was after.

But there's a big difference between Matisse's crisp black-and-white drawings and Morocco in living color. The Hassan II mosque was a massive pale marble monument set on several acres of blinding marble plaza beside the ocean. Aziz took us to the center of the plaza and pointed up at the minaret. Decorated with intricate patterns of colored tile, it seemed to sway against the sky, as though the atmosphere was too fragile to contain such exquisite beauty. But about a third of the way down from the top the designer had wisely dedicated many consecutive square meters to a deep green that almost stopped my heart. It was the color of the blue sea viewed through the white froth of waves—almost a turquoise, but more green than blue. This stunning effect was multiplied when I viewed the green tiles against the blue of the sky, and that was the art of it—knowing how the colors would read from all angles. Matisse often said that nothing exists alone—not a line, not a color. Genius is being able to put them together so the viewer gets a glimpse of what you feel inside. In the case of the Hassan II minaret, the designer had used his sea-foam green and God's blue to celebrate the life of a king.

In Rabat we met up with a guide named Ahmed, who explained that because green was thought to have been the color of the prophet Mohammed's djellaba, it was green—a deeper, more leafy green than the one on the mosque—that became the color of Islam. Throughout Morocco the official buildings and holy places have tile roofs of that color. In fact, the country itself is color-coded: Rabat, because it's the capital, is the Green City, Casablanca is the White City, Marrakesh is the Red City, Fès is the Blue City, and Tangier is the Yellow City. Moroccans say things like, "I was in the Red City yesterday," and everyone knows what they mean.

It was late afternoon by the time we left Rabat for Fès. Beth sat in the front seat with Aziz and I sat in the back watching the countryside. This was the first time on our entire journey that I'd had the luxury of not driving. Just outside the city, blocky white apartment buildings sported so many satellite dishes that it looked like an army of Mouseketeers was storming the ramparts. Soon the apartments gave way to sprawling patches of green space that were neither parks nor pastures, but some combination of the two. The strange thing was the people—men in djellabas, women in head scarves, just sitting out in these grassy areas alone, or in groups of two or three. Sometimes they would be reclining slightly, but more often than not they squatted or sat with their legs drawn to their chests. Occasionally they grasped their knees in their hands. Their shadows were blue and long, and I felt that I had seen those people before. Fishing in my bag for my copy of *Matisse in Morocco,* I spotted them immediately. In the massive painting *Café Marocain,* they were lying and squatting against a Moorish arch, contemplating a pair of goldfish in a bowl. Matisse had seen the sitting people, too.

Up front, Aziz was telling Beth that he was a Berber, the ancient indigenous people of Morocco. All I knew about Berbers was that the carpet named after them at home was nubby, woolen, and expensive, and that I had bought my fair share of it. Now Aziz was talking about tribes and tattoos and language that couldn't be written down. When Berbers want to write, they use Arabic. Aziz understood Berber, but couldn't speak it. His Berber parents spoke to him in their language, and he answered in Arabic. It was the same with his wife, who was also his cousin. "For the first year of our marriage," he said, "she talked to me in Berber and I answered in Arabic. I spoke to her in Arabic and she answered in Berber." Listening to him tell his stories, I gathered that to be a Berber was to be a survivor—tough, untameable, resourceful. Whenever the invading hordes came, the Berbers simply retreated to the Atlas Mountains and the Sahara Desert and stayed there until the invaders gave up and moved on. Ahmed had been telling the same story in a different way when he explained why the minarets we were seeing were square instead of round like in the rest of the Arab world: "Morocco is the only Arab country not conquered by the Turks."

After a while we left the sitting people behind and moved through an area of red-dirt banks, like I remembered from Mississippi, into a terrain that was rolling but flat. Darkness was falling fast, and I watched men on donkeys going home from their fields, and shepherds marching their flocks in for the night. We had been told that everyone in Morocco had electricity, but Aziz drove at dusk past many houses in the country and not one had lights burning. A few did have satellite dishes, though, so I had to assume that the homeowners were simply outside hunkering in the dark.

Olive Branch had arranged for us to stay in a beautiful hotel in Fès, the Palais Jamai, whose deep bathtub was a welcome relief at the end of a long day. With only my eyes and nose above water, I studied the taupes of the tub tiles and tried to make sense of Morocco. In this third-world country, the most common car was a Mercedes-Benz, sheep grazed in urban construction zones, men in biblical dress talked on cell phones, and Western attitudes found surprising favor with a people who slaughtered a sheep a year—in apartment bath-tubs, on downtown terraces, in suburban garages—because of their religion. After drinks and dinner in the hotel, we returned to the room and got ready for bed. Our terrace looked out over the old city, which was built into a bowl surrounded by mountains. In the dark I could make out several jutting minarets.

I dreamed that night of that marvelous green. The sky was green, the sea was green, the mystery of life was tinted a deep and disturb-ing shade of sea foam. At some ungodly hour I awoke, startled, to the sound of loud agonized wailing from outside. "What the hell is that!" I asked Beth, who mumbled something about the *muezzin,* the people who go up in the minarets and call Muslims to worship five times a day. After the one began, others started. They seemed to be trying to outdo one another—hitting ever-higher notes, moaning with ever-more-pious-than-thou abandon. I lay in the dark dearly wishing that we had brought our white-noise machine. But in the interest of packing light—for once—we had left it in France. Unable to drift back to sleep, I got up and took *Matisse in Morocco* into the bathroom, where I sat on the edge of the tub looking for places where Matisse had used that green of my dreams. It makes the back-ground of *The Standing Riffian,* and there were hints of it, though a shade or so darker, in the street of *Le Maribout.* It bleeds through the walls of *Sur la Terrasse,* his beautiful portrait of the prostitute Zorah, and a delicate, washed-out tone of it fills the huge canvas of the fa-mous *Café Marocain.* But in none of Matisse's pictures does it have the same stunning impact that it has in that minaret against a blue Casablanca sky.

The White City, the Red City, the Blue City: I thought of the people sitting in the dusty fields and the Berbers with a tongue that couldn't be put to paper. No wonder Matisse loved Morocco—here, color was the first common language.

IN THE MORNING we met Rahou Omar, known to us as Mr. Omar, our guide for the next few days. He was a wiry man in a green djellaba, tasseled maroon Fès hat, white pointed Moroccan slippers, and argyle socks with his pants tucked into them. He addressed me as "Mr. Jim," which prompted acute discomfort and a vestigial thirst for mint juleps.

Omar had been a schoolteacher and a guide, but when the gov-ernment asked the citizens to give up all but one job so others could have work, he chose to be a full-time guide. He had worked with Aziz's late father, who had also been a driver. Aziz senior had died two months before at age sixty-one. At sixty-two, Omar considered himself very old.

Our lesson began at the sultan's palace, where he showed us the bronze doors and the intricate tile work. He explained that Islam forbids the depiction of any living thing, which puts the kibosh on heroic statues and commissioned portraits of founding fathers. But since a culture has to express itself artistically in order to *be* a culture, Islamic artists turn to a graceful geometry based on "arabesques." As Omar talked, I thought of Matisse, whose fluid lines reflect a deep understanding of how the eye perceives beauty. "The arabesque is musically organized," he said. "It has its own timbre. . . . It translates the totality of things with a sign. It makes all the phrases into a single phrase."

I tuned back in to Omar speaking the words "international Arab design" as he traced his finger around a graceful basket weave of tiles dotted with eight-pointed stars. "These are like the screens or windows we use so Arab women can see outside without being seen. That's what *moucharabie*—the name of this pattern—means: 'See without being seen.' "

It was a revelation, an epiphany, and I shivered to think how close I had come to daydreaming through it. After that, I saw moucharabie everywhere. The stars were the holes the women could look through. From the outside, all you saw was a pleasing crisscross design. Omar wanted us to see Fès from above, and while Aziz drove and Omar talked, I looked out the window. Moucharabie suddenly seemed the key to everything. Most of the women had on shawls covering their heads, and some still wore veils. The sultan's palace had been built in the Jewish section of Fès—as a wise, conciliatory example for the rest of the Arabs, Omar said—and the surrounding houses had balconies. But until very recently you would never have found balconies on Arab houses, because traditional Muslim women couldn't be seen by men other than the ones in their own family. Their houses were built around inner courtyards. And because traditional Muslim women couldn't go into the outside world, they spent their days inside making beautiful rugs or exotic tiles with designs that told stories of their hidden inner lives. This was a culture tailor-made for Henri Matisse.

Omar seemed able to tell when I wasn't paying attention. On a hill overlooking the city he asked Aziz to stop. "Come on, Mr. Jim," he said, helping me from the van. Spread below us, nestled in its cradle of mountains, was the dense sprawling beehive of the city whose buzzing I could hear from there. I had thought Fès, supposedly the most Moroccan of Moroccan cities, would be a small village, but instead it was home to some 1.5 million people. Omar waved his arm grandly over half of the beehive. "That's the medina, the old commercial and residential district. The medina in Fès is twelve hundred years old, the biggest and oldest in the Arab world. Twelve square miles of tiny winding streets wide enough for only a donkey to pass. Half a million people live in the medina. That's where we're going next."

It looked like my idea of hell.

In a few minutes Aziz had dropped us off and we were walking through the gate. "Here we go!" said Omar, striding ahead jauntily. He was entering his element. Beth followed Omar, and I brought up the rear. The first section of the medina, the outer ring, was where the artisans worked—the wool dyers, the metal hammerers, the pottery makers, the tin cutters, the wood carvers. The old stone street was soggy and slick and puddled with opaque water. "This is the dirtiest street in the medina," said Omar, stepping carefully to protect his argyles and explaining that the artisans needed to be by the outside wall so they could dispose of their wastewater. Beth looked over her shoulder at me and smiled. She had on her heavy black boots from Target, but I was wearing the sleek white Pumas I had bought in Corsica, something between a bicycle shoe and a ballet slipper. She sometimes called me "Pussy Boy" because I hated getting my hands messy eating barbecue and slogging through nasty medieval alleys in expensive shoes. In *The Pussy Boy's Guide to Life*, good shoes are a top priority. Not messing them up is a close second.

"Look out, Mr. Jim!" Omar called, and I glanced up to see a donkey and his handler bearing down on me. I jumped into a doorway and watched them pass. The animal's hide was gray and mottled and on his back he carried, besides flies, a massive load of garbage. This was the medina trash pickup. Over the donkey's rear was a kind of diaper arrangement, which apparently wasn't state of the art. In the beast's wake was a loose straw-encrusted *pomme de rue*. "Watch your step!" Omar sang out as he waited for me to skirt the obstacles and catch up with them. "Don't worry, Mr. Jim! They clean these streets three times a day!"

MOROCCAN MOSAICS MIGHT well be a tribute to the medina itself. The word *maze* pales at the fact of it. Omar led us through dark low tunnels, around narrow curves, beneath raffia roofs, then—suddenly, blessedly—into bright sunlight, and back into darkness again. I felt like I was in one of those science kits that takes you on a tour of the human body—blood vessels, veins, arteries—except that this particular body was ready for a nursing home. Snaggletoothed women held out gnarled hands, and Omar discreetly dropped coins in them. The streets were jammed with people. Everywhere we went, men in dusty djellabas and pointed shoes lurked in shadowed doorways, just sitting and waiting. Were they waiting for me? Beneath their hoods, their eyes seemed not to blink. We saw many cats, but few dogs. Like the men, the cats sat and waited and watched. Everyone—street people, lurking doorway men, even the cats—knew Omar. "Cats are the only animals we can touch and still pray after," Omar said, reaching down to stroke one. "If we touch a dog, we have to wash first."

After a half hour, he led us through a narrow portal and up steep stairs. On the way up, he reached into a box tucked into the wall and turned back to hand each of us sprigs of mint. "Are you ready for your surprise?" he said, smiling broadly.

"Is this where we mysteriously disappear?" I said, but Omar didn't hear and kept on climbing. At the top of the stairs we emerged into a warren of rooms lined with new leather bags. The deeper we penetrated, the stronger was the smell of something foul. Finally we came out onto a balcony looking over an inner courtyard filled with man-high clay vats brimming with dye. This was the famous tannery, whose photograph appears in every book about Morocco. If a picture is worth a thousand words, a sniff is worth a thousand pictures. The dye came in two rancid soupy flavors—anemic tomato and posthumous celery. Young barefoot men in shorts stepped from vat to vat, occasionally climbing inside and holding up a slimy dripping hide to check the progress of the dyeing. On a ledge across the way, hides lay drying in the sun.

"Those men make more money than teachers," Omar said, pointing at the barefoot men in shorts. "It's a dirty job, and they risk disease." I squeezed a mint leaf and inhaled. Omar handed us off to a salesman, who showed us bags and purses and pop-out ottomans, but we found little that interested us. Somehow, this didn't seem to be a smart way to sell leather goods.

But it might be a brilliant way to sell carpets. In a few minutes, Omar ushered us through a doorway into a darkened foyer. When he opened the inside door, the sight was breathtaking. We were in a former palace, in a two-story light-filled courtyard covered every inch in stunning mosaic tile: blues, greens—*that* green—yellows, ochres, creamy pale whites that looked like ivory. As disagreeable as all the outside had been, this rug store was every bit agreeable.

Omar introduced us to Yousef, our salesman—apparently we had an appointment—and we were ushered through a Moorish doorway to a side room with a soft silky banquette and lacquered tables in front. "Would you like mint tea?" Yousef asked, not surprisingly, and we of course said yes. It was my first mint tea in Morocco, and it was wonderful—sweet, aromatic, sensual, served in small fine glasses filled with beautiful firm mint leaves. Even without bourbon, mint can make a world of troubles disappear. I didn't care what was about to happen. I just wanted to stay on that luxurious banquette and inhale the clean healing essence of mint.

Actually, we were in the market for a rug—Beth actively, and I passively. I love rugs, and there was a time in my life when I thought that if I could only own an Oriental carpet, I would be a successful man. The biggest rugs in our house in Little Rock were ones I brought to the marriage—a huge red antique Sarouk in the living room, and a deep blue antique Chinese in the dining room. Now they and all the rest were rolled up and stored away. "Maybe we should buy a little one," Beth had said when the Morocco trip materialized. I was all for it, figuring that a couple of nomads ought to have a Berber rug to help cushion life's bumps.

But Beth was going to have to do the deal. I've never been a haggler. My preferred negotiating ploy is to ask whether they want my AmEx or my Visa. I grew up suspicious of bargains. My mother, long after she was widowed and living frugally in a small house in Mississippi, would turn away persistent phone solicitors with a line that inevitably stopped them cold.

"I'm not interested," she would say at first

"But, ma'am, I'm trying to save you money. Don't you want to save money?"

"No," she would say. "I have more money than I know what to do with."

Beth, on the other hand, grew up with a mother who taught her to look hard, and to fight harder, for bargains. I had great faith in Beth's bargaining ability, even against a Moroccan rug merchant.

"I'm going to leave you alone," Omar said, and from his djellaba he retrieved a folded copy of the morning paper's crossword puzzle. About half the boxes were filled with squiggly lines.

Yousef wasted no time getting the show on the road. He stood to the side laying down his patter while two young men rolled out carpet after carpet before us. The rugs were lovely, Berber, and old. On some, Yousef demonstrated how the old Berber rugs have a thicker winter side and a thinner summer side. "You buy just the winter side," he said with bada-bing timing: "We give you the summer side for free."

After about twenty minutes, we had narrowed the rugs down to a half dozen. "Maybe it's time to hear the prices," Beth said, and out of the corner of her mouth she whispered, "Brace yourself." Yousef inspected the tag on the one I liked best—a thick 6 x 9 burnt orange with Berber tattoo symbols. It had the same colors as the Pierre-Humbert painting I had loved in Paris. *Two thousand dollars,* I bet to myself. *Of course that would just be the starting place.*

Consulting his calculator, Yousef figured the exchange from dirhams to dollars and held up the machine for us to read. Having bet way low, I was stunned; Beth displayed not a hint of a response. "What about that one?" she said, pointing to her favorite, a busier blue 6 x 9 bearing every tattoo of every Berber tribesman in history. Yousef plugged in the numbers. Just as bad. I took a long slow sniff of mint.

"They're too high," Beth said, and inquired about another one. The lowest of the lot, a new turquoise rug, brought the figures down from exorbitant to unreasonable.

About that time Omar came in to see how things were going. He wanted to make sure we not only were enjoying ourselves, but that we knew never—*never*—to make an offer without consulting him. He could always get a better price.

"Remember the day Sidney Sheldon came in?" said Omar, plopping perkily on the far end of the banquette. Clearly, Yousef remembered, and no wonder. "He bought twenty-eight rugs!" Omar said, still marveling at the experience. "I was with Aziz's father that day. Look at this—" He handed over a creased photocopy of a letter from Sheldon, who waxed eloquent about what a successful trip he and his wife had had, thanks to Omar. "I have the original framed at home."

"Very nice," I said, and reflected privately on my own oblique brush with the prolific Sheldon at a Brentano's bookstore in a mall in Little Rock. I was manning a card table stacked high with copies of my house book, *If These Walls Had Ears*. I had sold one book all afternoon long. Finally a lady stopped at my table and surveyed the scene before her. "Are you the author or something?" she said.

"Yes, I am."

"Humph," she said, fingering a copy of my book. "You know what they really need to do is get Sidney Sheldon in here."

"Well, ma'am," I said, "I think the deal is, if you buy all my books, then Sidney Sheldon will come." She drifted away baffled, and I checked my watch to see how long until cocktail hour.

We continued looking at rugs—more rugs, other rugs, the same old rugs. Finally Omar glanced at his watch. "I'm going to go pray," he said, and it seemed like a good plan. While he was gone, Yousef gently pressed us to say which rugs we wanted to keep in the running, and which could be discarded. *Is this better than that? Is that better than this?* like at an eye exam. He had his men bring out black rugs, blue rugs, orange rugs, red rugs. They were beautiful and put me in mind of Gauguin's dictum that Matisse himself held dear: "O painters who are looking for a color technique, study rugs. You will find all the necessary knowledge there." Though there were many challengers, we still liked the two original ones best, along with a red-and-blue checkerboard Berber in the same price range as the others.

In time Omar returned, and by some vague clock inherent in the process itself, it was clearly time to talk money. "What would you offer for the three?" Yousef said, and I recoiled in horror at the number I heard Beth say. So did Yousef, who wanted not a penny less than twice that. It occurred to me that this must all be an elaborate joke—an example of Moroccan performance art.

"I don't want to even spend that much," Beth said. "In fact, I don't know if I even want to buy a rug at all."

Three hours after the match had started, we emerged into the medina the proud but slightly unsettled owners of three Berber rugs. Yousef, who had finally accepted *one third* of his asking price, looked a little punch-drunk when we left him, but Beth was dancing around like Muhammed Ali demonstrating the rope-a-dope. "If you're happy, I'm happy," said Omar, guiding us back into the netherworld in search of lunch.

OVER HIS LONG career as an artist, Henri Matisse formulated a theory of expression employing what he called "signs." Based on years of looking, years of internalizing, years of re-interpreting, this was what he meant when he talked about having to forget every rose ever painted or seeing as though for the first time. Take, for example, a tree. "I don't mean that, seeing the tree through my window, I work at copying it," he told the writer Louis Aragon in 1942. "The tree is also the sum total of its effects upon me. . . . I shan't get free of my emotion by copying the tree faithfully . . . But only after identifying

myself with it. I have to create an object that resembles the tree. The sign for the tree, and not the sign that other artists may have found for the tree."

I was thinking about Matisse's concept of signs as Aziz drove us through the Rif Mountains to Tangier. The designs on the Berber carpets were signs. The patterns on the Moroccan tiles were signs. Whole rugs, whole mosaic walls—they were signs made of signs. Paintings were the same. I thumbed through *Matisse in Morocco* and tried to figure out what of his perception of this strange country he had signed in his pictures. *Le Maribout,* the painting of the domed tomb of a saint, he had painted blue, even though maribouts are always white. That choice of color was a sign. Matisse obviously regarded Morocco as the essence of blue. So many of his paintings from his trips to Tangier are deeply, ravishingly blue.

Omar, who had traded his djellaba for a gray business suit for the journey to Tangier, was sitting next to me humming to the radio and tapping his hands on his knees like a teenager. He obviously loved music, and occasionally asked Aziz to turn it up. "This is the most popular chanteuse in Egypt," he said, and began to wail along with the singer. The music itself was a sign, a series of arabesques whose looping circles of sound conveyed the totality of lives lived closed to the outside. I had arrived at that conclusion the previous evening, when Beth and I had had dinner at the elegant Maison Bleue in Fès, a former palace whose interior was completely covered in mosaic tile. There were musicians playing, and their guttural, chanting, moaning songs filled the total space and mesmerized us in the process, just as the cocoon of tile did. It was all of a piece—the evocation, the celebration, the *re-creation* of a rich inner life. After we had bought the rugs, Omar had pointed out a run-down medina house to me: "Inside that house may be very grand, Mr. Jim. Here you can't tell about the inside from the outside."

Along the road were patches of vibrant wildflowers the color of the beautiful burnt orange of our Berber rug. "In another month, that whole meadow will be covered with blue flowers," said Omar. "That's where the blue dye comes from." It was also where the pigments for artists' paints grew. Painting was just organic recycling—no wonder it felt so elemental. Tile, too. In Fès, we had seen mounds of clay waiting to be soaked in water and shaped into thin bricks, which were then painted with color from flowers. The amazing part was that a painted tile appeared blank until it had been fired in the kiln. Young men shoveled crushed olive pits into the maw to make the fires white-hot. Only then did the tile show its color. Omar had snagged several small tiles for me, and I got them out of my bag and studied them. There was a yellow star, a sea-foam rectangle, and two squares of Matisse's Moroccan blue. They were shards of magic, those tiles, little handheld metaphors for creativity itself.

I showed Omar the painting of *Le Maribout* and told him I wanted to find that very one in Tangier. "We'll find one better," he said, missing the point. Omar didn't know Matisse, which surprised me, but then I found that no one in Morocco seemed to know Matisse. They knew Dustin Hoffman and Warren Beatty from their movie *Ishtar,* on which Omar had worked, and they knew Michael Douglas from *Jewel of the Nile*—also featuring the behind-the-scenes efforts of our man Omar. In a similar way they seemed to at least know *of* Picasso, who had made himself the world's sign for modern art. Picasso had expended as much energy creating himself in the outer world as Matisse had in his inner world. "By amusing myself with all these games, all this nonsense, all these picture puzzles, I became famous," Picasso once said. "I am only a public entertainer who has understood his time." Matisse was the antithesis of the public entertainer.

Back in Paris, Beth and I had had a conversation at the Hôtel Saint-Germain with Olivier Lorquin, the son of Dina Vierny, model to Aristide Maillol and founder of the eponymous foundation that operates Musée Maillol in Paris and Banyuls-sur-Mer. Dina Vierny also modeled for Matisse, Bonnard, and Dufy. We had hoped to interview her, but she wasn't up to it. Her son, who now runs Foundation Dina Vierny, cordially agreed to see us in her stead. He had grown up in the heady world of modern art. "Picasso was a monster," Lorquin said. "Matisse was the only painter Picasso respected—because he was himself, stayed to himself, stayed true to himself."

In 1907, Matisse and Picasso exchanged paintings, Matisse taking Picasso's still life *Pitcher, Bowl and Lemon,* and Picasso selecting Matisse's recent portrait of Margeurite, with her name printed across the top in the hand of a first-grader. Picasso's hangers-on howled at the disarming childishness of the picture, and even threw rubber-tip darts at it. Picasso, however, instantly understood the freshness of Matisse's vision.

But if Matisse respected Picasso for staying true to his own self, Matisse suffered no illusions about what that meant. This was in a 1946 letter to his son Pierre from Vence:

> Three or four days ago, Picasso came to see me with a very pretty young woman. He could not have been more friendly,

and he said he would come back and have a lot of things to tell me.

He hasn't come back. He saw what he wanted to see—my works in cut paper, my new paintings, the painted door, etc. That's all he wanted. He will put it all to good use in time. Picasso is not straightforward. Everyone has known that for the last forty years.

IN TANGIER, BETH and I were graciously welcomed at the classic El Minzah Hotel overlooking the bay. Back when the Matisses had steamed into these waters, they had been transported a few blocks away to the Hotel Villa de France, which occupied a high corner near the medina, with a view of the English Church and the port. The Villa de France, closed now, was owned by the company that owned the El Minzah. We asked if we could see Matisse's room, but the El Minzah desk man was vague about our prospects. In any case, it was "impossible" until Monday, and this was Friday.

Our room opened onto a wide terrace with nearly the same bay view that Matisse had enjoyed, except that the scenery had changed considerably in the ensuing century. Whereas Matisse had sketched a spare open waterfront with a neat jumble of houses rising behind the jetty, I stood on my terrace and surveyed dense development all the way to the sea. You have to select, of course, and maybe Matisse's sketch reflected his eye's fierce willingness to delete the extraneous. In my view, there was an L-shaped building with Moorish windows opening to a portico that my eye returned to time and again. The rest, until you reached the jetty with its constant parade of gleaming white ferries from Europe, was eminently deletable.

Omar and Aziz, who had stopped along the way to show us the cities of Ouezzane, Chefchaouen, and Tétouan, weren't nearly as confident of their knowledge of Tangier, and we could tell they were worried about our safety. "You should take your dinner in the hotel," Omar had advised as we settled on a 9 A.M. rendezvous in the El Minzah lobby.

"We'll be fine," we'd said. In fact we were unaccustomed to having guides with us constantly, and in Tangier we looked forward to having time on our own. I had noticed several nearby cafés as we drove into the city, and that evening we went to inspect them. By then it was dark, and from a distance the cafés looked like normal sidewalk cafés—Parisian, even—but the closer we got, the more we noticed one crucial difference: No one was in them but men. I thought of Matisse's *Café Marocain,* with its six gentle male figures leisurely—benignly—watching goldfish in a bowl. A small vase of flowers stood beside the fishbowl, and the whole café was open and airy like Hemingway's clean, well-lighted place.

The sidewalk cafés we saw in Tangier weren't like that. We didn't make it past the staring, glaring eyes of the men sitting outside sipping their teas and coffees. They reminded me of the shadowy figures in the medina in Fès. "Let's have dinner in the hotel," I said, and Beth readily agreed.

IF I COULD own any one painting by Henri Matisse, it would have to be *Porte de la Casbah.* Earlier I said that his interiors were my favorites, and that's generally true. But this picture of the old gate in Tangier has all the elements I require in a Matisse—color (especially blue), grace of line, and resonant mystery. To me, it's the last element that makes the painting great. Art—in any medium—is a celebration of the exquisite mystery of living. The works that haunt are those that pose questions, not answer them. We all know the questions, and we answer them in our separate ways. Answers in painting re-create the surface world and signify nothing. "You have to come down on the side of going with the mystery," Warren Criswell had told me, and I had thought he was ducking my interview. Now I got it. The questions were themselves the answer. Before I left Tangier, I wanted to stand in the very spot where *Porte de la Casbah* was painted.

On Saturday morning, Omar was waiting in the El Minzah lobby looking like a diplomat in his gray suit. He had to catch the bus home at noon, but he insisted on giving us a tour—his tour—of the medina. On the way over, I told him about our café experience of the night before. "The reason there are only men is that the women have so much to do," he said, and thought no more of the question. Beth gave me an amused look.

Matisse's hotel had overlooked the Grand Socco, the busy square outside the entrance to the medina. Beth and I searched for a deserted, down-and-out building in the area, but didn't see one. I studied the gate: Was this the one? It looked too ornate; the *porte* in Matisse's painting was relatively plain. "Here we go!" Omar said, but I was happy to discover that Tangier's medina held not a candle to the one in Fès. It was smaller, cleaner, lighter. For an ardent adventurer, that might be a drawback, but I considered it a high compliment.

Omar's tour was relatively painless. We wandered through the produce *souk*, saw the offices of the American Legation, admired the mosque where the king and his family had recently prayed, and emerged in a smaller square called the Petit Socco. There, sipping tea on a café terrace, was a man in a djellaba and a crocheted African hat who looked exactly like Henri Matisse. I had seen him earlier, and in fact had quickly sketched him. Now as I passed, following Omar, the man smiled and waved. It seemed like another kind of sign.

Aziz was waiting for us at the bus station. Once we had said our good-byes to Omar, we told Aziz to take the rest of the weekend off. "We'll see you on Monday," I said.

"Are you sure?" This wasn't what he was being paid for, though pleasing us was. I briefly considered even suggesting he drive back to Casablanca, where he lived with his wife, their three children, his mother, and his two sisters. I'm sure he missed them, and they him. The house they lived in had belonged to his father, but since his father's death, Aziz was the man of the house. He wouldn't have gone anyway.

"I'm sure. Take a load off. Go to a movie or something."

In the afternoon it rained, so we stayed in and I sketched and made a couple of very bad watercolors from our terrace. It was actually very nice to be inside and alone together for a change. Beth and I were fortunate in that we still enjoyed each other's company. We needed our separate spaces—more so, in fact, than we'd been able to manage in the past year—but basic compatibility and joint commitment to our journey made the tightness more than tolerable. I wondered how the Matisses had fared during those dreary weeks of rain that had marooned them together in a hotel room in Morocco. There were already indications that their marriage was in trouble.

That night we had dinner in our room. I read and reread *Matisse in Morocco,* trying to figure out how to find the places he had drawn and painted. Some locales, such as the English Church, were very specific, and if we could find that we could find his hotel. He had sketched the church from his window, and that view of it—called *Paysage Vu d'une Fenêtre,* or *Landscape Viewed from a Window*—made up the brilliant blue left panel of the so-called Moroccan Triptych, which he painted for I. A. Morosov, another wealthy Russian collector to whom Shchukin had introduced him. The center panel was *Sur la Terrasse,* the large picture of Zorah kneeling. The right panel was *Porte de la Casbah.* We were unlikely to find the site of the center one, since that was painted on the terrace of Zorah's bordello. Zorah was Matisse's favorite Moroccan model, and when he couldn't locate her again on his second trip to Tangier, Amélie helped track her down. Madame Matisse's appearance at the brothel reportedly caused quite a stir.

On Sunday morning the sun shone brightly, and, armed with my book of Matisse's pictures and a very unspecific tourist map from the El Minzah desk, we marched purposefully toward the Grand Socco. Vendors had set out their wares—everything from rugs to bicycles—and the crowds were milling. A snaking line of Mercedes taxis was queued up on the edge of the square. Sunday was apparently a big shopping and social day, so I was surprised to see a heavy-equipment crew blacktopping the medina's main street. But who was I to try to linearize the arabesques of Moroccan thinking? I opened my notebook and sketched the rare scene of men in robes stooping to scrape tar off their pointed slippers.

We studied our map, but couldn't locate the corresponding street signs on the streets themselves. In our usual way we just started walking. Soon Beth said, "There it is!" It was the English Church, or at least a sign for it affixed to a weathered stone wall whose iron gate was open. We wandered through the gate and found ourselves in a dense shaded garden with benches and a graveyard memorializing the many Brits who had adopted this country as their own. Beyond the wall Tangier was a teeming marketplace, but inside this small garden the spirit could buy a few moments of precious peace. While Beth read the gravestones, I sat on a bench and drew a picture of the church itself, a tile-roofed affair with a squared-off tower that looked like the proper British echo of a Moroccan minaret. Matisse had often painted in a private garden nearby. That's where he first saw acanthus—"magnificent" acanthus—growing from someplace besides the tops of Corinthian columns.

Through the trees we could see a stately old building rising on a nearby corner, entangled by overgrown brush and vines. It had to be the Hotel Villa de France. The windows were thick with dust, and some panes showed black voids where they had been broken out by tossed stones. Birds were nesting inside. *Window Viewed from a Landscape.* We were never going to see the opposite view. Matisse's window was probably one of the top ones, but it was clear that they weren't going to let us in. This would have to be inspection enough.

As for *Porte de la Casbah,* Omar had left us with a valuable piece of information. "Many people think the medina and the casbah are the same," he said. "But the medina is the commercial area, and a casbah is a military compound. Casbahs are usually on the highest available ground."

We entered the medina and tracked along the edge of the new blacktop until we could peel off onto a side street. From there we wandered deeper and deeper into the old city. Beth was trying to follow the map, but it wasn't precise enough. Finally we came to an intersection with steps ascending an incline. "Let's go to the high ground," she said. From then on, anytime we had an opportunity to climb higher, we took it.

After about fifteen minutes we rounded a turn and came upon steps curving gently toward a gate in a high wall. "This must be the casbah," I said, "but that gate doesn't look right." In the painting, a man sits in a kind of cubbyhole to the left of the gate. There was no such opening in the wall.

"Maybe there's another gate," Beth said.

As we passed through the opening we found ourselves in a small semi-enclosed area formed because the path didn't continue straight. If you stood outside the gate and looked in, you would see only a wall. But once you passed through the gate, you would see that the path angled left and then continued on through a portal at the end of the far wall. This was another trick of Moroccan architecture I remembered from a guidebook. The entrances were placed off center so those outside couldn't see in.

We stopped at the far wall and turned to study the gate from the inside. To its right the casbah wall was elaborately tiled, and to its left was a door. Just beyond the gate was a pattern of round stones, and then a low wall. "There's the door to the opening where the man sat," I said. "There's the round white thing in the picture. There's the low wall. There's even the house that had the trellis he drew so often." Casbah walls are often painted blue and white to symbolize the sea and sky; the one in Rabat had been that way, with beautiful blue doors throughout. Part of the Tangier casbah would be blue and white, but not where this gate was. Matisse had just placed those colors there, with that dramatic red as a rolled-out carpet into the imagination.

The scene itself wasn't the mystery; that came from Matisse's seeing. In the painting, that giant keyhole of a door draws your eye as surely as if you were a voyeur. What lies on the other side? To what secrets does that red path lead? Who is that shadow figure on the left, and what is he doing? Standing, finally, in Matisse's footprints, I discovered the most astounding thing: I had always seen that painting backward, as though he had been looking from the outside in— never mind that that fit neither the temperament nor the pattern of this most interior of painters.

For a while we wandered around the casbah, which had spectacular views of the city and the ocean. In no time we found the locales of many of Matisse's sketchbook drawings, and also for the painting *Le Maribout*. It made sense that Matisse would go up there to work. The medina was raw and loud and dirty; the casbah was Tangier's protected, private space, a whole city's *moucharabie*. I took out my book and sketched the maribout from straight on, but it wasn't a very good drawing. I couldn't seem to concentrate. All I could think about was *Porte de la Casbah,* my favorite Matisse, which I would never see the old way again. Forevermore it would be an interior, the way Matisse meant it to be.

Part III

THIS PERPETUAL DAZZLEMENT

10.

Exactitude Is Not Truth

THE PROMENADE DES ANGLAIS made a gentle sweeping curve around the Baie des Anges. Surf was lapping, palm trees were swaying, well-dressed couples were strolling arm in arm along the Mediterranean.

Actually, that was a sepia photo of Nice in the early part of the twentieth century. The surf still laps and the palms still sway, but now couples in gym clothes stroll with one eye on the sea and the other on looming rollerbladers and skateboarders. We drove in through urban sprawl and heavy traffic, and it would be a couple of days before we realized that Nice is a city best approached at twilight and from the air. Then the sky and the sea look like blues in a piece of cloisonné. Then the crescent glitters.

One afternoon, following the daily rain shower, an amazing rainbow appeared outside our hotel window. It was complete, well defined, arcing grandly from the sea to the blue hills above the city. In that joined band of light and color I think we actually saw what led Matisse to Nice. Back in Collioure, his friend Paul Soulier had praised the light of that area as "this perpetual dazzlement." But in the end, Matisse found his perpetual dazzlement on the Côte d' Azur. He first came, by himself, for the winter of 1917–18, taking a seaview room at the Hotel Beau Rivage at what is now number 107, quai des États-Unis. Nice was the sum of all the seaside sites he had tried over the years: more light, more color, more drama, more style. "When it became clear to me that I would see this light every morning," Matisse said, "I could not believe my bliss." Even though he kept a house and studio in the Paris suburb of Issy-les-Moulineaux until 1928, when Amélie came south to be with him, Nice or its immediate environs would from then on be Matisse's principal home.

He turned forty-nine years old that first season. He and Amélie had been married nearly two decades. Marguerite, who was as close to Amélie as if they had been biological daughter and mother, was twenty-four years old. The boys, Jean and Pierre, were nineteen and eighteen. With Henri and Amélie's extended working trips over the years, the children had grown up staying for long periods with both sets of grandparents, but photographs from Collioure, where Matisse had continued to spend most summers painting, show a family that enjoyed their time together. In Collioure they had spent the hot seasons swimming, picnicking, boating (Matisse was, strangely, a boat nut, a single sculler who in later life kept boats at the marina in Nice and haunted annual boat shows with the same discerning eye he trained on *salons d'art*), and both Amélie and Marguerite had posed for Henri, with and without clothes, indoors and out. For the latter canvases, they had risen early and gone up on a mountain above Collioure so Matisse could paint them without interference from too-interested onlookers, and before the southern sun became too hot to bear.

But between his Morocco years and the beginning of his time in Nice, he made some very strange paintings, such as *Goldfish and Palette* from 1914 and *Piano Lesson* from 1916. They're nearly abstract, and very disjointed. *Goldfish and Palette* relies heavily on a bold strip of black, the way the enigmatic *Porte-Fenêtre à Collioure*, painted the same year, did. Art historians have suggested that Matisse was reflecting, variously, the influences of Cubism and the anxieties of World War I. Knowing what happened in Nice, though, I think John Elderfield's comparison of two canvases, one from 1911 and the other from 1917, is worth bearing in mind:

> That summer [1917], Matisse gathered his family around him and painted them freely in quiet relaxation in a picture titled *Music Lesson,* utterly different from the cacophonous *Painter's Family* done six years before. This first image of familial contentment was, however, the last. . . . Mme. Matisse is expelled, and sits outside. And above her, dwarfing her, is an image so massive that it advances into the interior space: an enormously enlarged version of the 1907 sculpture whose pose had always signified *luxuria.* Before that year was out, Matisse had moved to Nice, where that image would be replicated in a multitude of forms for the remainder of his life.

The sculpture Elderfield describes is that of a nude woman reclining suggestively, exaggeratedly, her left hand propped on the back of her head like a 1930s movie star preening for a press photo. Something had happened to the Matisses between the years of those two paintings. And now, in addition to the kilometers separating them, Henri would very shortly embark on a personal journey into an exotic inner geography. His paintings of the 1920s would become elaborate postcards from a land inside his head.

WE HAD RESERVATIONS at Le Grimaldi, a four-star hotel in a quiet part of town a few blocks from the hubbub of the rue Masséna and a fifteen-minute walk from the Old City. Our room was big and beautifully decorated, with double doors that opened onto a balcony looking into a neighboring courtyard shaded by a big palm tree. A welcoming note from the hotel owner, Joanna Zedde, waited on the table, and while Beth was reading it a young woman knocked on the door and brought in a chilled open bottle of white wine. Such luxury. I poured us each a glass. "Here's to Madame Zedde," I said. "And to Lloyd, who receives the bills."

The celebration continued when Beth checked her e-mail and found a message from Tessa, in Collioure: Gerard's renter had reneged, and the apartment was available. "Yippppppeeeeeee!" wrote Tessa in her note. This time I immediately phoned Gerard and eagerly committed to taking the unfurnished apartment for the summer at a reduced price. We had been checking rental prices all through the South—they were sky-high. This was doable. Gerard and I agreed to talk more following his two-week walking tour of Robert Louis Stevenson country.

"Yeah, so," I said to Beth when we hung up. "We have an apartment in the South of France, umm?" We couldn't wait to phone the girls and tell them where they were going on their summer vacations.

Exhilarated by the news from Collioure, I had to force myself to focus on business in Nice—there was plenty to do. I got out my map. Over thirty-seven years, Matisse had lived in several residences in the area, and I was still a little confused about which was which. I especially wanted to see the Beau Rivage, where he had made the sumptuous *Interior with a Violin,* in which the blue velvet of the violin's inner case almost freezes the eye. His very first pictures in Nice, at the Beau Rivage and the Hôtel de la Méditerrannée are free of the elaborate fantasy that would come later. These early depictions of hotel rooms open to the sea and sun come across as the personal musings of a man deliriously happy with his simple life inside these clean, pretty, simple rooms.

I also wanted to see Villa "Le Rêve" in Vence, where he made his last great easel paintings and his cutouts for the book *Jazz.* As for the others—the address 1, place Charles-Félix in Nice and the Hôtel Régina in Cimiez—they were private residences and would probably be difficult, if not impossible, to get into. The Hôtel de la Méditerrannée had long since been torn down, though a snazzy new Vegas-like incarnation was rising at the same locale.

Our first evening in town we walked three blocks to the rue Masséna, a pedestrian street full of restaurants. Black men in caftans hawked gold bangles and knockoff designer purses. A young man played guitar and sang Beatles songs. Clowns and mimes occupied their specified spots. The mime with the best location, the intersection of rue Masséna and rue Jaubert, was decked out in a *Mutiny on the Bounty* captain's costume and performed with a pair of trained cats. They would climb up his arms and wave to the crowds, all the while regarding us blankly, the way cats do. "Can you imagine Cleo doing that?" Beth said. It was a rhetorical question.

In the Vieille Ville (Old City), the warren of gritty little streets that felt Italian and once had been, we ambled for a long time, not knowing or caring where we were, but certain that around the next corner was something beautiful. Light and color had led us to this city, too, and in a way that was beyond my feeble attempts at painting. Following the essence of seeing, we had chanced to open our eyes to the world's perpetual dazzlement. How could we ever close them again?

After a while we emerged on the Cours Seleya, another pedestrian street but much wider than Masséna. In the mornings the market took place there, and in the evenings the space was filled with tables and umbrellas and waiters uncorking bottles of wine. We sat in the front row at a café and ordered Nicoise salads and the local ravioli stuffed with *daube,* meat or fowl stewed in a rich wine broth. During the meal, Beth noticed an ornate building at the east end of the street. "What a fabulous house," she said. I turned and looked. The building, a deep yellow, was so luminous that it appeared to shimmer, like a TV image viewed through another TV.

Maybe that was its magnetic field we were feeling, because the house seemed to pull us to it. Studying it closer after dinner, we counted four stories, the top one surrounded by a terrace. Above many windows were bas-reliefs. Beside the massive door was the number 1. A sign on a nearby building said "Place Charles-Félix."

"This is Matisse's house!" I said. Of course it was—it was the most beautiful in town. He hadn't owned it; in 1921 he moved into an apartment on the third floor. Six years later, he took the top floor—keeping, for a time, his space on the third as well. From the fourth floor, he could gaze out at the calm Baie des Anges or the excitement of the morning market. He lived in that building from 1921 until 1938.

We crossed under the archway separating the Cours Seleya from the quai des États-Unis and stood by the sea looking back at the yellow house. From there we could see the cobalt sky above the city lights. Against that blue, Matisse's house shone like gold bullion. On the top floor was a big square window with five vertical panels and one horizontal panel at the top. "That was his studio," I said. "I have a picture of it in a book."

In that studio, during most of the 1920s, Henri Matisse traveled to the Orient of his imagination. Now the distant disjointed abstracts gave way to a tactile, nubile, incredibly *interior* universe whose inhabitants were mostly half-naked women lounging in silk harem pants on recamiers layered with lush fabrics. Intricate Moorish screens evoked every beautiful mystery there ever was. The classic nude, Matisse felt, was inherently artificial, so he turned to fantasy to make it real. "I do Odalisques in order to do nudes," he told the editor Tériade in 1929. "How does one do the nude without it being artificial? . . . I know that [odalisques] exist. I was in Morocco. I have seen them."

These paintings were too beautiful for the avant-garde, who dismissed Matisse's strange turn toward decoration. Matisse didn't seem to care. In his gilded palace he was Kublai Khan, and his ripe courtesans lay in luxury waiting for his call. The earliest of these paintings are loose, jewel-toned, sensuous, even natural in their way. *Odalisque with Red Culottes* lolls dreamily in a room resplendent in red, gold, and blue. The porcelain-pale model of *The Hindu Pose* sits cross-legged on a blue-checked chair next to a vase of beautiful lilacs. In the richest one of all, *Odalisque with Magnolias,* the bed fabric is so lustrous that you can feel it touching the woman's skin, just as you can smell the sexy sweetness of the magnolia blossom.

The odalisque has her eyes closed and there's the hint of a smile on her face. Is she anticipating, or remembering?

Matisse's travels in this inner world continued for most of the decade, but his courtesans became increasingly wooden, as though he could no longer summon up his belief in them. Probably, real life was intruding too insistently. In the spring of 1928, Amélie left Paris and moved to Nice to be with her husband. That summer, he painted the lovely but simple *Still Life on a Green Sideboard,* in which ripeness was restricted to the oranges.

Back at the Hôtel Le Grimaldi, Beth and I pored over photographs in *Henri Matisse: A Retrospective.* In his fifties in the pictures of 1, place Charles-Félix, he wore elegant suits and looked more like a banker than a painter. Amélie liked him to dress that way. In one shot, from 1929, Monsieur and Madame Matisse pose together in their dining room. A beautiful flower arrangement graces the table, which is laden with a fine tablecloth set with elegant china and silver. There's an open bottle of wine, and Matisse's curving pipe. Behind Henri and Amélie is a wall of his paintings. Finally, at Matisse's feet is a dog bed, just like the ones you can buy today at Wal-Mart. In the cushioned basket the family dog lies snoozing.

"But dogs know when something's wrong," I said, and I thought back to that bizarre painting from 1919 called *Tea in the Garden.* Two women are sitting in a sun-dappled copse in Issy having a nice spot of tea, and the picture shows them interrupted suddenly, as though a photographer had asked them to look his way. All is beauty, calm, serenity, except for the real focal point of the painting, the wrong detail that no one dares mention but which can't really be ignored: The family dog, who lies on the pathway in the midst of licking himself, his hind leg straight up and his business fully exposed.

THE MUSÉE MATISSE in Cimiez is Mecca for Matisse lovers. Anne Pierre-Humbert said that she and Pierre used to travel there once a year, such was Pierre's fascination with the master. I had looked forward to our own pilgrimage ever since Arkansas, and now, finally, it was upon us. On a sunny Sunday we made the easy drive up a winding road bordered by stately homes and shaded by old trees. Situated on the site of a former Roman territorial seat, Cimiez was now a gracious residential area with spectacular views of Nice and the sea.

Near the top of the hill, the road appeared to be heading straight into an ornate building that looked like a huge white wedding cake. Then suddenly we curved right and missed hitting the Hôtel Régina. I couldn't believe our good fortune. "I thought we were going to have to *search* for Matisse here," I said. "Instead, we keep running into him." The Régina was where the Matisses moved, in 1938, when they gave up their lease at 1, place Charles-Félix. I had known it was in Cimiez, but had no idea that it was so close to the museum.

Half a block away we parked and went down some steps into a grove of olive trees with white gravel walkways. The paths were marked with street signs bearing the names of American jazz musicians—Duke Ellington, Miles Davis, Louis Armstrong. "Wow," said Beth, "this must be where they have the Nice Jazz Festival." Another sign soon confirmed it. "What a great place to hear music!" It was at the same time both *intime* and grand, like some Roman god's hilltop drawing room. On the other side of the olive grove, standing out against the sky, was a brilliant brick-red mansion with yellow trim— the Musée Matisse.

As we got closer, Beth said, "Look at the windows."

They were tall and elegant, with pale green shutters outlined in buttery yellow wood. A couple of the shutters were open. "They're beautiful," I said.

"They're fake."

I looked again: She was right. The windows, the shutters, the moldings, even the balusters of a lower terrace—all of it was *faux,* a brilliant trick of *trompe l'œil.* "Fool the eye," it literally means. In one way, I could read this as disturbing: *The windows in the museum dedicated to the painter who loved windows were . . . artificial?* On the other hand, it was a vivid celebration of the magic of painting. The illusion of reality, the reality of illusion. Just another mansion in the fantasyland of Matisse's mind.

"It's probably a perfectly nice building for a museum," I said finally. "Plenty of wall space, not all chopped up." In time we found out that the house, which dated from 1670, had been built that way. Like all houses, it had a history, but over its various permutations the three constants were its magnificent location, its Genoese style, and its illusive decoration. Trompe l'œil was a favorite diversion of the Nicoise.

It's possible that Beth and I weren't your typical pilgrims. We had seen a lot of Matisses over the past few months, from Le Cateau–Cambrésis to Paris to Nantes to Saint-Tropez to Collioure. I had spent untold hours looking at his paintings in books. Surely that explains why we found the outside of the Musée Matisse more compelling than the inside. There just weren't a lot of pictures—not nearly as many, or so it seemed, as at the museum in Le Cateau–Cambrésis.

What the Matisse Mecca did have was his furniture—the rocaille armchair, the marble and wrought-iron table, the red-striped easy chair that had figured in so many of the paintings I loved. The little white-and-blue pitcher from *Still Life on a Green Sideboard* was there, and so, even, was the huge fingerlike green plant that makes the background of *Music*. These were the mere artifacts that he turned into archetypes.

Seeing them made me think again how different painting was from writing. In my office/studio in Little Rock was a strange Middle Eastern chair that I found myself drawing and painting again and again. It was made of intricately carved wood and studded with pearl inlay, the largest of which was in the shape of a six-pointed star. The chair's gold paint was very old, so that what once might have gleamed had long since taken on a burnished patina. Connecting the arms to the seat on either side were five carved "ribs," which continued on beneath the seat, undulated slightly, then crisscrossed to form a saddle-shaped base. I had owned the chair for years before I realized that it actually folded down. Since then, I've always thought of it as the traveling seat of some Bedouin nomad, who rode across vast deserts in it atop his camel.

How many times could I write about that chair? How many ways could I describe it? Maybe if I wrote fiction I could imagine tales of distant lands and exotic faces that would cause readers to see that chair freshly over and over, beyond the limits of my pure description. But a painter could paint that chair many times, and each picture would evoke a different mood, a different attitude, a different understanding. Paint is closer to feelings than words are. And paint pulls the viewer's emotions into the picture, his own unspeakable aches and regrets and hopes and desires. The word *blue* takes time to assimilate, but the color blue is immediate. "A certain blue enters your soul," said Matisse. "A certain red has an effect on your blood pressure." On days when the world feels out of balance, I would rather go to an art museum than to a library.

After the Musée, we went next door to the Franciscan monastery and walked in the manicured garden. Matisse used to spend time there in his old age. It was a place of beauty and calm, the way he hoped his paintings could be. Flowers formed designs in the grass and turned arbors into secret passageways. To the south the sea was sparkling, the light still winter-clear. A sunlit hill overlooking all of nature's creation, Cimiez seemed to us a kind of paradise. No wonder Matisse decided to move there. In Cimiez, he had what he loved in Nice, the sun and the sea, but remained above the fray—and far enough from it that the unpleasant details of everyday life blurred into a brilliant mosaic. The view reduced the real world to Matissean signs—the green flip of the palm fronds, the undulating orange of the rooftops, the mottled blue of the sea. Serenity may be a synonym for distance.

ON MONDAY, I had an appointment at the Office de Tourisme, supposedly a twenty-minute walk from our hotel. But Nice is too wonderful a walking city—the trip took me twice as long. I had to stop and look at every shop window, every statue, every beautiful park, every piece of stunning architecture. And of course there were all the savory scents that I had to track to their delicious source. We had an article from *Gourmet* by Calvin Trillin, who had run wild in Nice for a few days looking for the best *socca*, *pain bagnat*, and something unfortunately called *blette*. When we had time, we wanted to chase Trillin, too. In the meantime, I was to keep my eye out for any good places to eat.

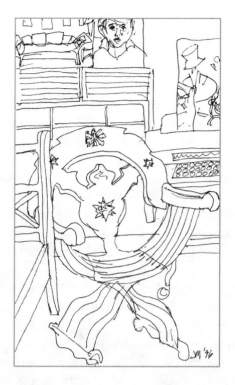

I walked up the rue du Maréchel Joffre to the avenue Jean Médecin, then turned left on the rue Gioffredo as far as the rue Désiré Niel. On that short street I noticed an art gallery, L'Atelier Soardi, that didn't look like the usual tourist place. I jotted myself a note to take Beth and go back. We had looked at art in galleries all over France—a lot of it bad. What did Nice have to offer?

In a few minutes I was sitting in the office of Sandra Jurinic, a woman who the French Tourist Network's Louise O'Brien had suggested could help me with my search. Louise had just sent the terrific news that we could visit Villa "Le Rêve" in Vence, so my questions for Madame Jurinic were about getting into Matisse residences in Nice. We would be staying one night at the Beau Rivage, she said, though the part where Matisse painted had long since been sold off for private apartments. Place Charles-Félix was a private residence, and she couldn't call the owners. That left the Hôtel Régina.

"Well," she said, "I did escort a journalist to Matisse's apartment there two years ago. I think the same woman owns it." She looked in her book and gave me the name and number.

"Does she speak English?"

"Oh, I should think so. The Madame is young, so . . ."

She loaded me up with brochures, press kits, and maps, and as she walked me to the elevator, she said, "You should also go to the gallery where Matisse painted the large *Dance* mural. It's called L'Atelier Soardi, on rue Désiré Niel."

Outside in the sun, I marveled at how Matisse's world was opening for me in Nice. Paris had been hard, but of course I was new at it then and shell-shocked to boot. Paris would have been different in better weather, and so would I. The gray skies had blurred my vision.

At L'Atelier Soardi, the woman that Madame Jurinic had suggested I see wasn't there, and the only other person in the shop was busy with frame customers. But there were brochures about Matisse and the famous mural. In Paris, I had walked three hours one day to the Musée d'Art Moderne to see the painting in person—actually version one of it. Commissioned in 1930 for the Barnes Foundation in Merion, Pennsylvania, the mural was to be enormous—about seventeen feet high and forty-five feet wide. There was no way Matisse could paint it in his home studio at 1, place Charles-Félix, so he'd gone looking for another space. He found it in a vacant warehouse on the rue Désiré Niel.

As soon as I walked into the rear gallery, I recognized it. I had seen it many times in a famous photograph of Matisse wearing a black suit and beret and standing on a bench sketching high with a long extender. He looked like a high school history teacher writing a test on the blackboard. Clearly he wasn't a math teacher—he ended up miscalculating the dimensions of this mural that had to fit precisely in three alcoves over a doorway, and had to paint it twice. Version two is the one now installed in Pennsylvania.

La Danse opened the door to another passage in Matisse's life. It was this painting that brought Lydia Delectorskaya to him. A Russian émigré, she had moved to Nice and was looking for work; he was looking for someone to help him with the large mural project. "At the end of six months, with *La Danse* completed, he resumed easel painting and no longer needed my help," Delectorskaya writes in *With Apparent Ease,* her book about her time with Matisse. "But four or five months after that, Mme. Matisse, in very delicate health for many years, found that she had to replace the young girl who had been her sitter as well as companion. They thought of me. . . ."

Back at the Grimaldi I phoned Madame Claude Malaussena, the owner of Matisse's apartment at Hôtel Régina. *"Bonjour, Madame, Parlez-vous anglais?"* She shot back a barrage of very fast French, which I didn't understand, but the tone sounded friendly enough. Somehow I managed to convey to Madame that my phone call concerned Henri Matisse and that I would call back. Then I ran downstairs and asked Françoise, the head of reception, to ring her up and do a sales job on my behalf. Françoise seemed able to handle anything. To my astonishment, that included landing me interviews: Madame Malaussena agreed to see me two days later at 2 P.M. "She says the apartment is for sale," said Françoise.

That night Beth and I celebrated my *coup de Régina* by dressing up and strolling along the Promenade des Anglais. We began with a drink at the famous Hôtel Negresco. Built in 1912 by a onetime gypsy violin serenader, the place was New Money's vision of Old Money, starting with a 16,000-crystal Baccarat chandelier in the *salon royale.* Before we went in, Beth snapped my photo outside near the spot where Isadora Duncan got her scarf caught in the spokes of a Bugatti in 1927 and her companion drove off at breakneck speed. She had been staying at the Negresco.

But it wasn't our style—too fussy, too stuffy, too dull. We sipped gin fizzes on a sofa in a paneled bar listening to proper British ladies and gentlemen whispering to one another. Perhaps they were gossiping about the couple on the banquette across from us, who were making out to the point of serious concern. We left before seltzer had to be sprayed in their direction.

On the promenade, young men were playing bongos and flutes. Beth danced as we passed them, and they laughed and applauded. The sun was gone but it wasn't dark yet. Far ahead in the gentle turn of the bay the citadel was lit up dramatically, but where we were everything was deep blue, as though some unseen hand had laid on a lapis wash along the shore. Down on the beach the lines of white chaises glowed. We passed the large sculptures of steel circles and soon could see the window of Matisse's studio at 1, place Charles-Félix.

"What was the matter with Madame Matisse?" Beth said.

"I don't know for sure. I've seen it called 'acute and cumulative nervous anxiety.' "

I told her how Lydia described the beginning of her relationship with Matisse. For the whole first year that she lived in his house, he paid absolutely no attention to her. He was obsessed with his art. All day he worked in his studio at the back of the apartment, breaking only occasionally to look in on Amélie, who spent most of her time in bed. Lydia, being the nurse, stayed in the room while they chatted, but she could tell that Matisse's head wasn't in the moment. He was back in the studio, lost in his work.

"Then," I said, "one day Lydia noticed him looking at her differently. He sketched her with her head down on her arms, which were crossed on the back of a chair. After that, she started posing for him every day as soon as she finished with Madame Matisse."

"How old was Lydia then?"

"Early twenties. Matisse was early sixties. Lydia said he used to place his easel almost right on top of his model. He told her, 'A cake seen through a store window doesn't make your mouth water as much as when you enter and it's right under your nose.' "

"What a line," Beth said.

We wanted to climb the stairs to the top of the citadel, but the gate was locked. Nearby was the elegant Hôtel La Pérouse. "Let's go have a drink there," said Beth. When we mentioned to the desk man that we had hoped to climb the citadel, he invited us to see the city from the hotel's rooftop terrace.

A bellman had to lead us—up in one elevator, down a series of hallways, into another elevator. In one of the halls we passed a print of one of Raoul Dufy's scenes of Nice at night, which was obviously painted from a room in La Pérouse. It showed two pairs of open French doors. Through one, you could see the palm trees and the curve of the bay right outside the hotel; through the other, you could see far down the promenade into the blue we had just strolled through. The artist's easel was reflected in a mirror in the center. We weren't chasing Dufy, but it was always exciting to see where art was made. I had liked Dufy ever since someone who probably didn't know better told me that I painted like him. My appreciation for his work had only increased since we'd been in France.

The bellman showed us the terrace and left us alone. We were the only ones there, and couldn't imagine why. It was probably the best view of Nice from anywhere in the city. Near the shore, the rich old Italian buildings huddled close and spoke of timeless secrets. The new city rose gleaming behind them, and lamps sparkled from the dark of distant hills. Laid out at the city's feet, the Mediterranean looked like a Persian rug whose colors changed constantly with the light.

We had a drink in the hotel's enchanted garden, then lingered over a long dinner in a small *place* with a church and a fountain. Heading home near midnight, we emerged from the maze of the Old City and found ourselves in a park whose sidewalks passed under white wrought-iron arbors weighted down with wisteria. The iron curved gracefully at the bottom and then rose to form a tunnel of purple flowers.

I DIDN'T PAINT much in Nice, though I did go out a couple of afternoons with my pen and sketchpad while Beth was in the room working. One day I wandered over to the Old City and sketched the little square where we'd had dinner a few nights before. Another day I climbed the steps to the citadel, but the view was too breathtaking for me to attempt. Instead I stood at the rail looking down at the orange tile roofs and the whitewashed walls against the blue of the sea. I could never get enough of that.

From the citadel I could also see Matisse's house at 1, place Charles-Félix, where he made wonderful pictures once the odalisques had been banished to whatever region of the psyche they had danced in from. Beginning even before Lydia started modeling for him, his paintings of the 1930s were clear and fresh and alive again. I remembered seeing *Interior with a Dog/The Magnolia Branch* from 1934 in the Cone Collection in Baltimore. It is huge, much bigger than I had expected from looking at it in books, and its colors and patterns have great energy. Then, below the table, was that calm still point, the family dog asleep in his bed again. *Dogs are a good influence.* How many times had Snapp pulled me out of myself? Matisse had included dogs in his paintings at least as far back as *The Red Studio,* in 1911, but for him to give the dog so prominent a position in so large a painting was a good sign about his mental state.

The Lydia pictures would never end, not until Matisse did. She became his muse in a way that no one had before, whether she was posing for his sinuous India ink nudes or for the throbbing color puzzle *Woman in a Purple Robe with Ranunculi.* She would show up in some of his finest easel paintings from Vence, and in his last great cutouts.

That day when I got home, Beth was on the telephone talking to a friend at home. I sat at the table and made a sketch of the far side of the room using my bold felt-tip, drawing the easy chair by the bed, then adding my sign for side table. It was three-legged, like the actual table we'd had in the Geranium Room at 501 Holly, except this one was round. On top of the table was a quick blip of a vase with a few flowers in it. I put two pictures on the wall, the pictures that were actually there—framed decorator prints of fruit. Then, looking at my reflection in the foyer mirror, I drew myself drawing the scene. It was a surprisingly good picture. Even in the moment, I knew there was something more there than an empty chair and a spy in the corner looking at it.

After that I continued my reading of Lydia's book about Matisse. No one else could have given so detailed, so nuanced a picture of how he worked. A bundle of nerves, this seeker of serenity cursed so as he painted that she once told him she was going to impose a fine for each oath. "But the very first time after that, having counted twenty-one offensive exclamations, I realized it was I who would have to redirect my thinking."

Covering the years of their collaboration at 1, place Charles-Félix, she describes how he would have her photograph a painting after each session so that he had a record of the way it looked; he also dictated notes on the colors used in each part of the painting as well as of the changes at every stage. Then the next day, he would tackle it all over again, sometimes revamping the picture almost entirely from the session before:

January 25.

NU MI-COUCHÉ (begun on 1–22)

Worked on the flow of the pelvis and legs in relation to that of the shoulders, arms and head.

Lightened the color of the figure with some White and Cadmium Red Light.

The background was not touched.

The Red of the materials was reduced with some Ivory Black.

But the most striking changes he never even mentioned—the face of the model. From one day to the next, she looks like a different person. The majority of the pictures in Lydia's book are of her. She had an oval face and a prominent nose, and she usually wore her hair parted in the middle so that each half made an arabesque like dueling waves on a rolling sea. In Matisse's hands her hair changed constantly and her face was sometimes long and thin and other times nearly round. The only way you can be sure it's Lydia is the nose—he always captured her classic nose.

This was the old joke about Matisse from as far back as Bohain: *He can't paint a picture that looks like the subject.* "Exactitude is not truth," Matisse countered, quoting Delacroix. "When I paint a portrait, I come back again and again to my study and every time it is a new portrait that I am painting . . . , not one that I am improving, but a quite different one that I begin over again, and every time I extract from the person a different being."

He even justified pictures—not portraits—without faces, asserting that too much detail can inhibit a viewer's imagination. "If you put in eyes, nose, mouth, it doesn't serve for much; on the contrary, doing so paralyzes the imagination of the spectator and obliges him to see a specific person, a certain resemblance. . . . Whereas if you paint lines, values, forces, the spectator's soul becomes involved in the maze of these multiple elements . . . and so, his imagination is freed from all limits."

It was a revelation. Beth got off the phone and I closed the book. "I think I'm ready to paint your picture," I said.

11.

The Silence Living in Houses

FOR THE LAST fifteen years of his life, Henri Matisse made his homes in personal casbahs, as though he could actually keep the troubles of the world at bay. "We live way above the fogs," he wrote in early January 1939 to his son Pierre, announcing that he and Amélie were finally ensconced in their new digs at the Hôtel Régina, "and we are both well. Let us hope that this will continue." But this was the case of a father putting the best face on a very bad situation.

Amid the threat of imminent war, the Matisses had moved to Cimiez in the autumn of 1938. Amélie was falling apart. First, she was nervous about *la guerre;* on top of that the apartment wasn't ready, so they had to live in a nearby hotel for a month. She felt like a gypsy. But when they finally got in, she got no better. She was suspicious of nearly everyone. The workmen, her servants, her husband—all were co-conspirators in a fiendish plot against her. By now, she saw Henri only during meals, which were taken in total silence. The unspoken word was Lydia.

You never know what's going on in someone's house, I thought, pulling up in front of the Régina for my appointment with Madame Malaussena. *What sad song is that violinist playing at the window?*

As Madame buzzed me in, I realized that I had garbled the directions she had given Françoise. I had written down the words "lobby" and "left bank of elevators," but nowhere was there a notation of which floor. I entered the sunny tiled loggia where Matisse used to walk his exercise laps, then passed into the white-columned lobby. The parquet floors were the color of honey, and the marble columns reflected in the deep clear wood like birch trees on a pond. It was a far cry from the *Studio under the Eaves.*

Built in 1897 as a palace for England's Queen Victoria, the Régina is a huge place, and from the center of the lobby I could see a bank of elevators some thirty yards down a dim paneled hall. Nodding to a man watering plants on the marble staircase landing, I walked to the elevators and pressed 5—top floor.

At the most there were three apartments to a floor in that section, so I tiptoed across the marble looking at the names by each door. She wasn't there. Then I went to the fourth floor, and on to the third. Madame Malaussena's apartment was the center one on *étage troisième,* facing south. I rang the bell two minutes late.

When she opened the door I was nearly blinded by light. *Heaven,* I thought, but it was more the musing of the light sensitive than the sycophant. Madame was tall and trim and probably in her forties, with short bleached blond hair. As she welcomed me into the expansive living room, a fluffy gray cat with piercing blue eyes came and rubbed against my leg. Squatting to pet the cat, I asked Madame how long she had lived there. Twelve years, she said. She had bought the apartment from "fils de Pierre Matisse."

I recognized, from photographs, the wooden floors, parquet in a large /\/\/\ pattern. At the front of the room was a center alcove with a huge bay window from floor to ceiling, and on either end were French doors leading to balconies. Beyond that were the hills and trees of Cimiez, and in the far distance the sea. In Matisse's day, that space was jammed with props and divided into sections according to whichever paintings he was working on, and part of the floor—the dining room—was black-and-white tile on a diagonal.

Madame Malaussena wanted me to see the marble mantel, which had been there in Matisse's time. I opened my book and showed her a photo of him sitting by that mantel painting Lydia for *Dancer and Rocaille Armchair on a Black Background*. Then I showed her the painting, in which he had made white crisscrosses against black to indicate the tile floor.

I wondered what room Amélie barricaded herself in while Henri was painting Lydia. How could he work? Amélie's tirades raised his blood pressure and gave him nosebleeds. Soon it was decided that Lydia would no longer be his live-in secretary but would come and go like any other employee. Amélie wasn't mollified; she wanted Lydia gone completely, but Henri refused to terminate her. "At my age, and given the poetical nature of my work," he wrote to Pierre, "she is essential to me." The result was inevitable: In March 1939 Amélie returned to Paris, and Henri rehired Lydia.

I followed Madame Malaussena down the hall to see the other rooms. On the way she stopped to point out a dark space where he had stored his paintings. "*Noir*," she said, and I understood that he had painted that storage area black. The room immediately east of the dining room was now Madame's workout area, and the room beyond that was her bedroom. Again, I had seen photos of Matisse and Lydia working together in that space, with Lydia posed next to what was now Madame Malaussena's balcony overlooking the sea.

Did they talk about Amélie while they worked? Henri was soon hearing from her lawyers requesting valuations on every bank account, every piece of furniture, and every drawing and painting.

"Your mother thinks only of revenge," he wrote to Pierre. "If she ruins me, she ruins you and ruins herself as well." To console himself, he returned—for the first time in years—to the desire of the line. Listening to Beethoven on a phonograph, he worked in bed on an elaborate series of seventeen groups of drawings that would be published, in 1943, as the magnificent *Dessins: Thèmes et Variations*.

I COULDN'T HELP thinking of Jeannie Michels as I walked through those rooms. A former model for Matisse, she had entered our lives during our time in Honfleur. The stories she had told then now came fully to life.

At age eighty-two, Madame Michels was still a striking woman—tiny, with flaming red hair and a band tied stylishly around it. Her eyes were lively beneath long lashes, and her lips were red and full. The day we met her she wore white jodhpurs, tall black boots, and a heavy sweater with pearls. On an easel in her living room was a poster from 1941 announcing a show of drawings by Henri Matisse. The woman in the poster drawing was Jeannie Michels.

In 1941, when she met Matisse, she was living in Cannes and he at the Régina. Though a non-activist in the war, Matisse had felt strongly that French artists and celebrities like himself should remain in France as a show of solidarity with the French people. For that reason, he turned down an offer to become a visiting professor at Mills College in California. He had spoken about the need for courage in a couple of radio speeches, and one of the people who heard him was a pretty young girl living in Cannes.

"His message make me happy," Madame Michels had said. "So I went to the Hôtel Régina to meet him. Lydia Delectorskaya opened the door. 'He will see nobody,' she told me. Then she called after me and asked for my telephone number. Matisse rang me the next day. He asked me to come have a talk."

Jeannie, an aspiring painter, had studied at the Belgian Academy. Her progress as an artist was part of their early dialogues. "Forget everything you learned at the academy," he told her. He especially preached against traditional ideas of perspective. "You have to see, first, your construction, like an architect," he said. "On your paper, things have to be put in the right place. Then comes color. Color takes the place of perspective."

Madame Michels opened an art book and pointed to a 1941 Matisse painting called *Jeune Fille à Robe Blanche.* "That is me," she said. "I posed for Matisse for several years—but never nude." Once she began modeling for him, she would take the bus from Cannes to Cimiez two or three times a week. He began drawing her in charcoal, then switched to sketches with a pen. At first, she was nervous and stiff. "I was posing with a flower, and I didn't want to move. Finally, I had to. I said, 'Oof,' and relaxed. *Then* he began making good drawings. I was surprised, because he did it very quickly. He made hundreds of drawings with the same expression."

That reminded me of something Matisse had written: "When I take a new model, it is from the unselfconscious attitudes she takes when she rests that I intuit the pose that will best suit her, and then I become the slave of that pose. I often keep those girls several years, until my interest is exhausted."

To my mind, his last sentence turns the artist-model relationship a notch toward the dark side. So much need, in both parties. So much intimacy. So much pressure to please. Such emptiness when it's over. "He knew how to take possession of people and make them believe they were indispensable," Lydia Delectorskaya told Hilary Spurling. "It was like that for me, and it was like that for Mme. Matisse."

"He liked to have his models in his hands," Madame Michels said, and by that I understood that while the fascination was still there, he wanted her at his beck and call. "He would have Lydia give me a ring, and he would ask me to come to this or come to that. From 1940 until he died, in 1954, I saw him in Paris, Vence, Nice. I always follow him, everywhere."

I asked if Matisse seemed happy while he was creating. "He was very concentrated," she said, "until he got what his emotion told him. An artist is only happy when his emotion is what he gets."

Feeling that we had perhaps overstayed our welcome, I made a motion toward leaving. But Madame Michels didn't want us to go. She had one more memento that she wanted to show us, and disappeared up the stairs. In a few minutes she came back lugging a huge published portfolio in a gray case. This was a first edition of Matisse's *Thèmes et Variations*. It smelled musty, and she explained that water had once gotten in and soaked some of the pages.

She wasn't depicted in this volume, but in 1948 Matisse had inscribed it to her: "À mademoiselle Jenie Michels, en homage. H.M."

THE REST OF the Régina apartment included a small computer room, a sitting room that was once Matisse's bedroom, a large new kitchen, and, in what was now the breakfast room, an old sink and counter where food was prepared. After the tour, Madame Malaussena led me back into the living room. Walking over to the bay window, she stood in the alcove and pointed to the floor. Today, that small section was covered in black-and-white tile. But when she moved in, it was wood. "Paint all over," she said in halting English. "Matisse—rouge, azure, rose."

We stood for a moment looking out from that spot where Matisse had painted. A purple cloud trimmed in pure light had invaded the sky, turning the sea a greenish gray. Apologizing for the appearance of the Mediterranean, Madame lightly touched the petals of a delicate blue flower in a vase on the dining room table. "Le couleur est *ça*," she said, or something close to it. The sea was usually blue like the flower because the sky was usually blue like the sea, and all of it bathed in a quicksilver light.

Afterward, I stood outside sketching an ornate corner of the Régina. While I drew I thought about Matisse and the pressures on him when he lived in this house. There was a marked change in his appearance between the mid-1930s and the early 1940s. Lydia snapped a photo of him in 1935, the year after she began posing for him, which, had I been Madame Matisse's attorney, I might have labeled "Exhibit A." He sits outside among spindly trees wearing a suit and tie and a jaunty straw hat, and there's the hint—the lascivious hint, I have to say—of a smile on his face. His shadowed eyes appear to twinkle. Though Matisse was sixty-five when that picture was taken, he exudes the *joie de vivre* of someone much younger.

But in photos taken in his studio in 1941, he looks like a fat, bald old man. By then, he had been worn down by the legal separation from Madame Matisse, and in early 1941 he had undergone surgery for duodenal cancer—his age-old intestinal problems taken to the extreme. The operation weakened his stomach muscles and would make him a semi-invalid for the rest of his life. Still, he was happy to be alive, happy for the privilege of continuing his life's work. He even found a *noirish* humor in his unenviable condition: An acquaintance had undergone surgery to be fitted with an artificial anus, and, "Between you and me, I, too, have one now," Matisse wrote Pierre during his long recuperation. "Not everyone who has drawn that particular ticket in the lottery likes to talk about it, though a surprising number of people make a discreet use of the ornament in question."

When I first read that, I imagined the same thing happening to Hemingway: *Oh, Jake, what a rotten business. Our nada who art in nada . . .*

But Matisse rededicated himself to creating. Beginning in 1943, when Nice came under threat of Allied bombing, he and Lydia were forced to leave the Hôtel Régina and move to a handsome villa in the hills of Vence. Villa "Le Rêve," it was called—"The Dream." There Matisse dreamed up his last, and some of his most beautiful, paintings.

And it was there, to the Villa Le Rêve, that Beth and I were headed on that very day.

THE DRIVE TO Vence took no more than twenty minutes. East of the airport we crossed a dry rocky riverbed and soon exited the autoroute into a dense commercial zone. In time, we began climbing a winding wooded road with grand views across the hills toward the sea. As I drove, I wondered what we would find at Villa Le Rêve. When Louise O'Brien had e-mailed saying we could stay there, I was surprised. Was it a hotel? A bed and breakfast? A private residence? All I knew was that we were booked there for three nights, were due at four o'clock, and that the villa was "just across the street" from the Matisse-designed Chapel of the Rosary.

Downtown Vence was a construction zone, jackhammers

pounding, but even in the confusion the chapel would have been hard to miss. It was white and modern on a street of old homes. On the side with the chapel the houses backed up to a wide valley. On the opposite side they had been built on higher ground for the view. I looked across the street for a house that resembled the picture in my Matisse book; nothing fit. The chapel was closed, but we could see a woman at a desk inside the adjacent nunnery. I went to the gate and pressed the buzzer, and she waved and came out. She was wearing jeans. Nuns scared me when I was a child, but if this was a nun she was totally nonthreatening. I asked where Villa Le Rêve was. She couldn't have been more helpful. "*Là*," she said, smiling broadly. "The yellow house." She pointed down the street on the other side. All I could see was a terra-cotta roof and the tops of some palm trees.

The front gate to the house was locked, and the steps that rose from it were overgrown with brambles. After a couple of passes, we figured out that the entrance was up a hilly winding driveway reached by crossing the opposite lane on a perilous blind curve. Once there, though, we simply followed the drive to the first gate on the right, which opened to the villa in my picture. I pulled the Peugeot through and parked in the gravel driveway. Ours was the only car there.

The hair on my arms tingled as we got out. What a day it had been: For once there were no velvet ropes, no metal detectors, no monitors in chairs watching the looking. It was just Beth, myself, and Matisse—or at least his spirit—in the two homes that had marked the culmination of his long journey. In these houses, he had made his final stand. "I'll bet that was his studio," I said, pointing to a large terrace on what was the main floor but was upstairs from the driveway where we were standing.

On a ground-floor door I found a sign marked "Office," but no one answered my knock. From the gravel where we stood, wide stone steps descended between tall palms to a big front garden that needed mowing. A couple of benches, carefully placed for peaceful contemplation, were in danger of becoming entangled in vines. The house itself wasn't in much better shape. Its cracked and peeling stucco wasn't yellow—it was more of a beige terra-cotta, and it looked rosy in the afternoon sun. The shutters were the same hue and in great need of paint—but first they required the stripping of about a hundred years of cumulative coats. In spite of all that, Villa Le Rêve was imposing—not grand in the way of so many faded French manses, but solid, sturdy, bearing the dignity of good bones.

The house was built into a hill. You reached its front door by ascending worn stone steps on the left side. There appeared to be two floors of living space, the top with narrow balconies outside the windows and the bottom with that wide terrace stretching to accommodate three windows and a pair of French doors. Below the terrace was what probably used to be the basement or garage. Now it was the office, and perhaps an apartment. A white plastic table and chairs were set up in the gravel overlooking the front garden, and a small blue trampoline was sheltered by the terrace above. Next to the trampoline, a porch swing hung from thick beams. Someone had taken great care to cultivate flowers in terra-cotta pots, and also on a trellis. Roses climbed up and over the short wall of the wide terrace, becoming interlaced with the arabesques of the rusted wrought iron.

As we took seats at a long table in the side yard, I found myself straining to comprehend what was happening. Soon I went to the car for some books and thumbed through them looking for photographs of Matisse in the villa—real evidence, a reality beyond dreams. I found a picture of an old sick man posing on a nice day outside a nearby window holding a cat. Most of the pictures were inside. As I was showing Beth the photographs, a small maroon car pulled through the gate and parked next to ours. A pretty woman with short dark hair got out and waved. She was wearing a loose blue jumper and flip-flops. "I'm Joelle Audry," she said. She was the house's caretaker. "Sorry I'm late. I had to take my daughter to dance class."

She unlocked the front door and we followed her into a small entryway tiled in black and white. To the left was a staircase, and straight ahead was a narrow hall. The doors on the right were numbered, and Joelle stopped and unlocked number two. "This is your room," she said. "It was Matisse's studio."

Matisse's terrace,
Villa Le Rêve
JM '03

Dazed, I stepped through the door and immediately recognized the window with the palm tree outside: *Interior with an Egyptian Curtain. Nature Morte aux Grenades. Petit Intérieur Bleu.* The palm was taller now, but the scene was essentially the same. Precious little else was, however. When Matisse lived here, rooms one and two were one large room. This end was the studio, the other was his bedroom. "In the 1960s," said Joelle, "a woman from Paris bought this house and turned it into a girls' school. She chopped it up into small rooms, installed a dormitory-style bathroom, put shower stalls in each room." I could see that she had also carpeted over the black-and-white tile and lowered the ceilings with squares of acoustical tile. "There used to be fireplaces in every room," said Joelle. "She ripped them out."

"Who owns the house now?" Beth said.

"The city of Vence. Now they have a project to fix it up."

"Why don't you advertise? Matisse's villa Le Rêve—lots of people would love to come."

She explained that they couldn't advertise using Matisse's name without paying to license it. "But I've gotten word out on the internet that this was the house he lived in, and now we have groups of painters in many weeks of the year. Come on, I'll show you the studios." We followed her upstairs. The rooms with the balconies had been fitted out with inexpensive easels and a table and chair. Then she took us back down and showed us the community bathroom. All along the halls were small rooms, maybe 20 in all. The center of the house had been partitioned off into a dark dining room, a storage area, and a kitchen.

"I've got to go get my daughter," said Joelle. "We live downstairs. You're the only ones here. Please lock up whenever you go out." And with that, she handed two dreamers the keys to Matisse's house of dreams.

The room was sparely furnished—double bed, an extra single, a small freestanding wardrobe closet, an easy chair, a desk chair, and a table beneath the window. There was no telephone or TV. The French doors opened from our room, and after we put things away we went out and sat on the terrace. There was a plastic table with a faded green tablecloth, and two plastic chairs. The terrace was chipped red tile decorated with pigeon shit, especially heavy in a line corresponding to the edge of the roof. But the roses and the wrought iron were pretty, and in time the light became golden on the palm fronds. Then the sky turned a deep purplish blue, the color of wine. I thought about how wonderfully strange life could be if you let it.

That night I couldn't sleep. Lying in bed in the dark, I found that the window had a curious power, and I kept opening my eyes and looking at the moonlight on the palm. Had Matisse painted any one window more than that one? Probably not. And it was the window he looked through with the wisdom of age. I turned my head and watched the palm fronds swaying lightly. Somehow, that window framed all I needed to know about the world.

ON SATURDAY WE woke up not wanting to budge from our room. The day was hot, the light white and dazzling. But inside, the shadows were cool and dark. "I can't stand to leave here," Beth said. I couldn't either. The space felt magical, and all I had to do was turn my head and look at the window to summon up the many brilliant paintings Matisse had made in that room. He was nearly eighty then, operating on faith and instinct. His *Jazz* cutouts had decorated the wall by the door, and the light from that very window illuminated his handwritten and very personal text: *"In art, truth and reality begin when you no longer understand anything you do or know . . ."*

The window was the key. In those final easel paintings of his life he embraced the mystery of light with all its implications. The window, with that palm tree exploding just beyond, became a constant presence in the kinds of ordinary rooms we all inhabit. *The Silence Living in Houses,* he called one of his paintings from 1947. In it, the sun is bright and the walls of the room inside the window are black. Two ghostly bluish figures, a man and a woman, pore over a book on a table set with flowers. That's what life in houses can become, but by then he was too old to run from it. This was no doubt the room where his daughter Margeurite told him the astonishing news of her and Amélie's arrest and Margeurite's imprisonment during the German occupation. Amélie, the nervous one, had been active in the French Resistance. Matisse was furious at the chances they had taken.

But now, being there, I understood that he used black not to signify darkness, but to extol light. This southern light that Matisse first saw in Corsica a half century before was so pure and so strong outside the window that it seemed to roar, drowning out all sound. In one sense it felt like a little thing, that insight. And I had traveled a long way for it. But maybe that was what it was like to see the world for the first time.

We finally roused ourselves in time for Joelle to serve us a breakfast of coffee and croissants in the dining room. She was very down to earth, and we liked her very much. She had a funny mannerism that I had noticed right away. Talking about the cost of fixing up the house, she rolled her eyes and made a *pfhew* sound with her mouth.

She would do that a lot while we were there, about everything from money to politics to her estranged husband, and I would come to interpret it as a deep mixture of cynicism, humor, and resignation.

We told her that we were going to see the Matisse chapel that afternoon, and Beth was even thinking we might go to Mass there on Sunday, which was Mother's Day.

"They lock you in at Mass," Joelle said. "And if you're not Catholic, well, *pfhew*."

While we were eating, she brought her daughter up to meet us. "This is Sourya," Joelle said. "Her father is from Africa." She was eight and very pretty—*café au lait* skin, with big brown eyes, long wavy hair, and a sly smile. *Sourya,* Joelle explained, is the Hindu word for *Sun.* I held out my hand to shake Sourya's, but instead she kissed each of us on both cheeks.

"Oh," said Joelle, "I meant to tell you. The man next door knew Matisse. He's been ill, but I'll see if he's up to talking. He said Matisse was the most narcissistic person he ever met." She chuckled.

Back in the room, Beth worked on her diary while I took out my sketchbook and drew a picture of the open doors to Matisse's terrace, with the palms rustling gently in the evening breeze. Soon I set up my easel and began brushing in the outline of the drawing I had made. My idea was to try to capture something of Matisse's sensibility of the light in that room, and on the foreground door I painted the back—the inside—black. For the open door, with the light hitting hard from outside, I laid down a mix of pinkish beige and then slathered on a little Cadmium Red Light. Through the glass door panes was an inside corner where two walls met, and I painted them dark blue and black. The octagonal terrace tiles were red outlined in black, the sky was light blue, the palm fronds were yellow and green.

Suddenly I had a *déjà-vu* of being in Mademoiselle Gauthier's atelier. This time the presence behind me was Beth, who had stopped tapping on her laptop. She was staring at my easel. "What?" I said.

"You're painting Halloween colors again," she said.

"Dammit, that happens to be the way I *see* it."

"Really." And as she started typing again, I thought I heard her say "*Pfhew.*"

THE MATISSE CHAPEL opened at 2 and wouldn't be open to tourists again for days. At 2 on the dot we walked across the street, and I noticed a detail I hadn't seen the day before: The chapel's roof tiles were white except at the front, where they became gentle waves of ultramarine. Inside, a young nun was waiting to accept our euros. Then we passed through the simple door into the chapel. It was already crowded, and very small—so small, in fact, that once Matisse was able to move from Le Rêve back to the Régina, the two front rooms of his apartment were exactly the dimensions of the chapel, enabling him to work on his designs at life size.

Beth and I took seats and listened to a nun explain, in French, all about the design of the famous yellow, green, and blue stained-glass windows, the ceramic tiles indicating the Stations of the Cross, and the lectern. Not understanding what she was saying, I let my mind wander. Matisse considered the *Chapel of the Rosary* his culmination as an artist, his life's masterpiece. One of his models in Nice had subsequently become a nun and persuaded him to take on the project, which offered him free rein over the design and decoration of the space both inside and out, and also of the vestments, crosses, cups, candlesticks, and other liturgical accoutrements. How could he resist? "My only religion," Matisse said after the chapel was consecrated in 1951, "is the love of the work to be created, the love of creation, and great sincerity. I did the chapel with the sole intention of expressing myself *totally.*"

I was contemplating the bottle green of the windows when Beth leaned over and whispered, *"This place is a torture chamber!"* She had a slight problem with claustrophobia, and Matisse's masterpiece seemed to have triggered it. As soon as the nun stopped talking we made our exit, and for once we didn't linger at the gift shop.

FOR MOTHER'S DAY, we enjoyed a long Provençal lunch as the guest of a friend of a friend. Later we stopped at a phone booth in town and phoned our daughters and my mother. Beth had been fine until then, happily distracted. Trying to regain that, we went to a small park and watched some children perform folk dances, and then we drove back to Le Rêve.

"Monsieur will see you at 6," Joelle said. "I'll go with you."

On the way across the alley, she explained that he didn't want his name used. He was an aristocrat, a member of a famous French family. In his nineties now, he had lived in that house all his life. His wife had died several years ago, and now he was alone except for his servants and his dog. He painted in an upstairs studio, but no one had ever seen his pictures. When the elderly Matisse moved to Le Rêve, Monsieur had been a very young man living with his young wife in the family home.

Now he seemed like a soothsayer. His weathered gate was sheltered by a canopy of thick twisted vines, and his old stone house on the hill had watched over Vence for nearly four centuries. We knocked on the door and he poked his head out an upstairs window to say he would be right down. When he appeared, he was the picture of the country gentleman—brown corduroys, French blue shirt, beige V-neck sweater, beige cardigan, paisley ascot. He was thin but spry, and his eyes sparkled. He welcomed us in and led the way to a second-story room lined with books. As I placed my tape recorder near his chair, he said, in perfect English, "I will understand your questions, but I won't always know how to give the answers in English."

Then for the next hour he held forth with humor, grace, and unwavering charm. Matisse and Lydia had come in May or June of 1943, he said. They had knocked on his front door and announced that they wanted to be good friendly neighbors. "I think he was attracted by the house," said Monsieur. Lydia became a good friend of Monsieur's wife, who was close to her age. Matisse was very ill and couldn't move around much. He had a day nurse and a night nurse, but he worked all the time. Models came and went constantly. Matisse always showed Monsieur his new work, such as the *Jazz* cutouts, but Monsieur never saw Matisse actually working.

"What kinds of things did you talk about?" Beth asked. Monsieur laughed and began speaking very fast in French to Joelle. I caught the words "*narcissisme extraordinaire.*"

"He had a reputation among Bonnard, Marquet, Picasso," explained Joelle. "Nice, but very narcissistic."

"Did he have a sense of humor?" I said.

"Ouiii," said Monsieur. "He made many jokes. He could laugh about Picasso, but not about himself!"

Monsieur told about the day Picasso came to the front door thinking that this was Matisse's house. Monsieur had opened the door and recognized Picasso immediately—his eyes were like coals. Picasso had brought along his pretty young girlfriend, Françoise Gilot, for Matisse to meet. "Where is my good friend Matisse!" Picasso said, and Monsieur had escorted them across the alley to the house next door.

"Lydia, who was big and strong, looked like a giant next to Picasso," said Monsieur. "Matisse looked like a sultan from Baghdad"—fat, in flowing clothes, always sitting on sofas. Monsieur thought it was hilarious that when the famous photographer Henri Cartier-Bresson came to Le Rêve to take pictures, Matisse wore a turban.

They exchanged books often, and Matisse was especially interested in books about Japanese and Chinese art. He wanted nothing to do with the war. "In the last days of the German occupation, shells from artillery and destroyers hit Vence. One landed in Villa Le Rêve. Matisse and Lydia spent days in a bomb shelter in the front yard."

"Did you get the sense that Matisse was a hard person to live with?" I asked. Monsieur pondered that, and mentioned Matisse's illness and infirmity. Then he said that Lydia had once told his wife, "There are two persons you never mention in front of The Boss." One was a former servant he had in Paris. "And the other was Raoul Dufy."

"Why Dufy?" I said, but Monsieur had no idea.

"What about Lydia," Beth said. "What was she like?"

"She was devoted to him," Monsieur said. "When he died, she left immediately." Lydia was not invited to Matisse's funeral. "The last time I was in Paris, I called and asked her to lunch. We had a *rendezvous*—and then, at the last minute, she called and cancelled. She killed herself a couple of years ago."

After Monsieur had told all his stories, Joelle invited Beth and me for *pastis*. We sat at the table in the gravel and Sourya brought out her three new kittens for us to see. I told her that Matisse had had a cat and a dog while he was at Le Rêve. He also had birds, several cages of rare species stacked by the window in our room. The famous picture that Monsieur had laughed about, with Matisse wearing a turban, showed him sketching one of his rare white pigeons.

While Sourya jumped rope and did everything she could to keep our eyes on her, Joelle watered her plants and told us about her extensive travels in India, a country she loved. That was where she'd learned her excellent English. We talked about the places we had seen and the new life we wanted to make for ourselves. It was a lovely evening, and we felt comfortable and natural being there. Tomorrow we would have to leave. "Why?" said Joelle. "No one's coming till next weekend. I have an art group. Until then, the house is yours." She poured us another *pastis*. Beth and I looked at each other and decided without a word.

"One more night," I said, but I was underestimating Le Rêve's pull. We ended up extending two more times, and even then we had to force ourselves to leave.

OUR FINAL DAY was lazy and luxurious. We didn't go anywhere. We slept late, ate peanut butter and crackers for lunch, and in the afternoon Beth worked on her diary while I reconsidered my painting. I moved my easel to the terrace for a clearer view. It *was* pretty garish. One problem was that it was me trying to do Matisse instead of myself. The roses entwining the wrought iron reminded me of what I needed to forget.

I repainted the open doors, lightening them with white and gray and beige. The corner walls became brighter, and the outlined terrace tiles were scrapped for a flat dark red. The sky took on a deeper blue, and I began to see the picture as a scene of evening. Drooping palm fronds gathered yellow light from some unseen source. More light flooded up from behind the scrolled iron railing, as though the terrace were a stage. For the final touch, I opened a tube of Cadmium Barium Red Light oil and made a triangle on the floor between the doors—a slice of brilliant light from Le Rêve going out into the darkness.

Beth looked up as I brought the picture in and propped it on a chair. "What do you think?" I said.

"Much better. It looks real. You could walk through those doors."

I studied the painting for a few minutes. The palm tree still wasn't right. "The fronds are too long," I said. "And I screwed up the trunk by hiding it behind the door." I picked up the picture and took it back to the easel.

"It's really good," Beth said. "Aren't you afraid you'll mess it up?"

It was true—I might. But what choice did I have? "Matisse said you have to risk ruining everything to make it better," I said, and I set to work with my wide square brush dipped in blue.

WE LEFT THE next morning to take care of unfinished business. Backtracking down the wooded hill, we passed again through the commercial zone and picked up the autoroute across the dry rocky riverbed. Soon there was the airport, and before long the Promenade des Anglais. In time we caught the turn to Cimiez and made our way up the gentle winding hill with the big houses and shady trees.

At the Hôtel Régina, I pointed out Matisse's apartment to Beth. After leaving Le Rêve, he'd had five more productive years in his aerie overlooking the sea. There he had finished plans for his chapel and made bright bold cutouts with such titles as *The Swimming Pool, Acrobats, Blue Nude, Zulma*. He called it "drawing with scissors." I hadn't fully appreciated the cutouts until I saw *Zulma* at the Matisse-Picasso show in Paris. An Amazon as tall as the gallery wall, she exuded sexual energy.

"Great love is needed," Matisse wrote in an essay the year before he died, "to inspire and sustain this continuous striving towards truth, this concurrent generosity and profound laying bare that accompany the birth of any work of art. But isn't love at the origin of all creation?"

Matisse never stopped believing that, and in one of my books there's a picture of him sitting in a wheelchair, barefoot and in pajamas, wielding a huge pair of scissors as he adds to the jumble of paper cuttings on the floor. On the very last night of his life he made four sketches of Lydia. She had washed her hair and had it wrapped with a towel, like a turban. "When he had finished, he gave me the sheets of paper and the pen. Then he asked to see the last of the four drawings once again. He held it before him, not quite at arm's length. He looked it over, severely. Then he said, 'It's good.' "

Matisse died on November 3, 1954. A month later, Hemingway accepted the Nobel Prize for Literature.

We curved around the Régina and drove a couple of blocks to the Franciscan monastery. Monsieur had told us that Matisse was buried in a plot not in the cemetery itself but near it, on a piece of ground donated by the city of Nice. For ten minutes we looked for it, and then Beth asked an old couple sitting on a bench. "Où est Matisse?" she said, and they arched their arms in unison, pointing up and over the monastery and the graveyard beyond. "Là!" they said.

The only way in on that side of the building was through the cemetery. Just inside the entrance, a life-size angel prayed over the tomb of someone's lost loved one. "Look at that," Beth said, and I realized she wasn't indicating the angel; it was a sign to the grave of Raoul Dufy.

"Fancy meeting him here," I said, and we continued around to the right, through the main cemetery and along the edge of the hill. Dufy's grave is in a plot of ground between the cemetery proper and the monastery gardens. If he could raise up a bit and crane his neck a couple of notches, he would be able to see the Mediterranean. He died the year before Matisse.

Following some steps down to a lower part of the cemetery, we finally came upon a sign with an arrow. Henri Matisse's final resting place is a massive light-gray tomb on a grassy terrace surrounded by flower beds, rose bushes, and olive trees. The grave looks east to the mountains and the observatory, though unfortunately a railroad line and a truck depot have inserted themselves prominently in the middle distance. "Dufy has a better view," I said. "I bet Matisse hates that."

Matisse was buried with Amélie, which pleased Beth. "Well, he used her up and threw her out. You know it's true. At least she's the one who ended up here."

I was happy enough that they could continue their journey together into eternity, but I also harbored a secret empathy for Lydia. She had given herself to Matisse just as Amélie had. Both had been devoted to him. Both had believed, supported, sacrificed for him and his art. Were his pictures worth their pain? I wouldn't touch that one with Raoul Dufy's brush. It was just one more part of the larger mystery. Beth snapped some photos and then picked a rose and laid it on the tomb. "For Bobbye," she said.

I felt a little sad going on without him, but Beth said to get over it. She was right, of course. "You have only one idea," Matisse said, "you are born with it, and all your life you develop your fixed idea, you make it breathe." The chase had always been, and would always remain, essentially the same. Only the scenery really changed.

We looked out from the heights of Cimiez to the sea. It was sparkling, and very blue. Beth put the camera back in its bag. "So where do we go from here?"

I shaded my eyes and glanced at the sun. It was high in the sky, and the only shadow I could see was beneath the rose where it curved on the glaring gray of Matisse's tomb.

"Home to Collioure?" I said, and the strange words flew into the air like birds.

12.

The World As It Isn't

HENRI MATISSE DIDN'T just make paintings, he created his own world out of line and color and light. The still life became a prop in the unreal life, which is to say the fantasy life. Models played the roles of dreamers. Color acted out their dreams. Light beamed like a guest star. For Matisse the ultimate open door was his own canvas, and he disappeared through it to live among his arabesques.

It's a great life, fantasy. But why does it have to be fantasy? "I am always doing things I can't do," said that cocky Picasso. "That's how I get to do them." If life is too red, paint it blue. If it's too blue, make it green. If there's not enough beauty around you, sketch in a vase of flowers. Matisse was always with me that summer in Collioure—not because I was writing about him, but because I was living in a dream world. *Read, write, paint, think, travel:* Finally my surface life and my subterranean life had meshed in perfect harmony.

The architecture of dream worlds depends upon the dreamer. Mine forms its foundation from the exquisite unreality of being a writer. Having spent most of my adult life in corporate offices, I cherish beyond measure the luxury of thinking for myself, and whenever possible I choose to spend my days imagining the world as it isn't instead of fighting the world as it is. In my world, everything is possible. There are no walls, only free-floating floor-to-ceiling windows made of brilliant color. The roof is lightly tiled with clouds.

We saw the sea every day in Collioure. We took our coffee by it, took our walks by it, took our wine by it. We watched it change from gray to green to blue to turquoise. In the evenings the yellow lights from the chateau danced long across the harbor, and the dome of the *église* was pink against the cobalt sky.

Our apartment was forty-five seconds from the water—a minute if we had trouble locking the door. In the end, we didn't move into the second-floor flat; Gerard wasn't quite finished with it, and he suggested we take the top floor at the same price. That's how we happened to have a balcony overlooking a castle in the Pyrenees, and a skylight framing a windmill lit golden every night.

The Berber rugs softened our tread and made the rooms ours. Beth found exotic Indian fabrics to throw over the sofa and bed, and from the light in the living room she suspended a delicate flying goddess from Indonesia. We had Matisse posters framed and hung all over the house. I set up my easel out of the way beneath the slope of the roof. We bought platters and a compote made locally, and in Céret we rounded up a dozen clay bishops whose miters could hold place cards for dinner parties. We bought a DVD player so we could see movies in English. Beth planted geraniums and lavender in terra-cotta pots on the balcony and named it the Bobbye Arnold Memorial Garden.

The weather turned hot as if on cue, and the tourists began pouring in. Most came by car, but quite a few sailed into the harbor on their own boats. A big white catamaran with blue stripes was anchored straight out from Copacabana for most of the summer.

A couple of weeks after we arrived, a work crew erected a bandstand in the Place du 18 Juin, in the center of the village. At the end of May the first big seasonal festival got under way—a three-day celebration of Catalan, Basque, and Corsican cultures. Beth and I were there that first evening as a local orchestra, starring Jean-Michel Pous on an instrument that sounded like an oboe, filled the air with haunting Catalan melodies while circles of men and women held hands and performed the *sardane,* the folk dance that had inspired one of Matisse's most famous paintings. Matisse's red naked dancing figures look like madmen compared to the people we watched, and yet those dancers, men and women of all ages, wearing espadrilles that wrapped around and tied above their ankles, appeared transported as they stepped slowly, broodingly, toe in, toe out, leg crossed, leg uncrossed, arms up, eyes skyward while the oboe's notes caressed red-and-yellow Catalan pennants hanging high in the leaves of an old plane tree.

The bandstand stayed up all summer, becoming the focal point for concerts, art shows, dances, wine tastings. We heard Corsican chants in the church, watched flamenco under the stars. There was always music in the village. People danced in groups large and small. I saw a couple rise from their lunch at a sidewalk café, twirl a couple of times, then sit back down and continue eating.

I set up my desk in the bedroom beside the bed. Occasionally I took breaks to change the music or to refill my coffee cup. It was hard passing up that view toward the Pyrenees, so I usually spent a few moments on the balcony watching the world—*Violinist at the Window on his Coffee Break.* "You are still in a great hurry in your country," Matisse told an American interviewer in 1933, just as he was about to crate up the *Danse* mural for shipment to Dr. Barnes in Pennsylvania, "and for art leisure is necessary."

The same is true of seeing, and in that wonderful Collioure summer I felt like I finally had time. Everything was new—even the old.

I often watched a blind man, who lived nearby, as he passed beneath the trees below, tapping out his path with his cane. Every day he went out to buy his bread, and on market days he carried a bag for more serious shopping. He had a small dog, a blond poodle, that he walked on a leash as he raked his cane along the edge of the curb. From the other direction came a little old lady who reminded me of my mother. "So she's pretty," my mother said when I told her. She was also stooped and used a walking stick, and was never any less than impeccably dressed, even though it was usually the same dress. Her hair was gray and her eyes, which stayed riveted on the ground in front of her, were a steely blue. Sometimes she would pass while I was outside emptying the trash, and I wanted to speak to her, to say, "Bonjour, Madame," but I was afraid I might throw her off her gait. I worried about the blind man and the little lady, and every day when I saw them pass, I felt relieved.

For our morning walks, Beth and I often took the vineyard trail past the house where Patrick O'Brian wrote all his sea stories. The grapes were green and no larger than BB's at first; later they would turn dusty red and have an obvious heft. The men tending the vines had propped up dragging branches with thick rocks picked from the shale all over the ground. Sometimes we climbed up to the castle and the fort. Following the crest of the mountain, I scouted out locations for painting landscapes like the ones Matisse did in Collioure. In one spot where the road starts winding back down toward the village, there was a stand of cork oaks that seemed to bend in the same graceful pattern as the trees in *Le Bonheur de Vivre*. One day I took my watercolors there and made a couple of quick reference sketches to explore later in oils.

Other mornings we walked in the village, and soon we knew all the local characters. There was the Blue Man, who was tattooed so densely from neck to toe that his skin was blue; the Sailor, a man with a denim fisherman's cap, bushy muttonchop sideburns, and a single crutch; Madame de *Plein Air,* who owned a house but preferred to sleep outside; Cyclops, a young man who wore his slouch cap low over the lost eye that ended his brilliant career as a long-distance runner; Scarface, who sat by the church accepting coins from tourists who thought they had to pay to get in; and the Hippie Boys, who dressed like Matisse's *Smoker at the Window* and stood by the chateau playing American jazz better than most we had ever heard at home.

Beth, deeply engrossed in true tales of the kings, knights, crusades, and conquests that had happened all around us, soon had mapped out a long list of day and weekend trips for us to take—blanketing the Languedoc, dipping into Provence, shooting across to the Basque country, spiraling into Spain. It sounded fantastic, but in fact it was eminently possible. All we had to do was get in the car and go.

One of our first excursions outside Collioure was to Toulouse, the city in which Amélie and Henri had awaited the birth of their son Jean in 1899. Toulouse looked different from other French cities. Instead of marble and limestone, its buildings were mostly made of an orangeish brick whose sleekness made the city look Italian. We parked in a garage and emerged in the cavernous Place du Capitole, where the morning market was just breaking up. A lot of black men had been selling African masks, something I hadn't noticed in French markets before. At café tables, dark-eyed mustachioed men wearing crocheted skullcaps sipped coffee and talked intensely.

I headed east from Place du Capitole toward the boulevard Lazare Carnot. At rue de Metz the boulevard broke into two wide, tree-lined one-way thoroughfares. Down on the left before the Grand Rond was rue des Abeilles, where Amélie and Henri lived with her grandparents during those months in 1899. I walked down the street looking for number 14, which I found at the very end of the block where Abeilles intersects with rue des Poitiers; a nice building, three-story orange brick with white shutters and a Havana blue door. I made a sketch of the door.

From this house Matisse would take his paints to the nearby Canal du Midi, the man-made waterway across southwestern France linking the Mediterranean to the Atlantic. Today the shady paved path along the canal is a favorite of walkers, runners, and bike riders, some of whom almost ran me down as I ambled along studying the docked barges. One had been converted into a gaudy Chinese restaurant. Nearby, two others were floating slums with debris on their decks. On another, four young men sat around a café table with so many longneck beer bottles on it that it looked like a birthday cake with candles. But the barges were colorful—bright blues, orange with green, whites and reds. I made a quick drawing just for reference.

At Place Wilson, a small park with lovely plantings, people sat on benches turning their faces to the sun. They looked like sunflowers. In France—at any time of day or night—you could see perfectly respectable people just sitting outside *being*. As the sun sank ever lower, the light caused the bricks of Toulouse to change color minute by minute. Sometimes they were golden, other times rust, still other times pink with a copper wash. It was as though they—the bricks— were themselves infused with life in all its mystery.

ONE AFTERNOON AS Beth sat reading on the sofa, I sketched a picture of her in my notebook. It came out surprisingly severe, emphasizing her short bangs and high cheekbones. I tried to soften it by drawing in the Indian fabric draped on the couch and the striped curtains over the archway in the background.

As I flipped the pad to another page, she said, "Let me see it." I held it up and watched her face. She studied it for a few moments. "I like it."

"It doesn't really look like you," I said. She was pretty. This wasn't a pretty picture, but it had a certain imposing strength.

"I see the resemblance," she said.

"You really like it?"

"What did I say?"

When I painted her portrait, I placed her on a seat that you couldn't really see. She sits in color. It is blue, with a green cushion, and the blue climbs past her on the left, around a clear vase of yellow flowers sitting on something—I don't know what—to the wall. The rest of the background is a burnt-orange shutter that echoes the color of her hair. It's a beautiful color, full of fire and drama. She wears pearls and a black short-sleeve top, and she rests her head against her hand. I never did paint in her eyes. I meant to, but then I began to like the painting the way it was. Unable to decide whether the picture was unfinished or perfect, I chose perfect. In either case, it was a beginning.

Our daughter Blair came to visit in June. She and Beth drove up into the mountains to see Peyrepertuse and Quéribus, some of the last great castles of the Cathars, the liberal Christian sect that so threatened the Catholic Church. The citadels were built on cliffs so high and so steep that the poor inhabitants must've felt they were already in heaven. Soon they would be, thanks to the Pope's Crusaders. Another day, the three of us had lunch outside in a tiny mountain village, and then climbed part way up Le Canigou—highest peak of the eastern Pyrenees—on a switchback trail. Late that afternoon, we visited a monastery perched on a ridge over a green valley. The view was a prayer in itself.

Our big outing was a long-weekend trip to *Le Côte Basque.* In Saint-Jean-de-Luz we bought a book of photographs by the famous photographer Jacques Henri Lartigue. It was about the Basque country in general, but its focus was on the elegance of the famous seaside resorts—Biarritz, Saint-Jean-de-Luz, Ciboure, Hendaye. From 1905 to 1939, Lartigue had photographed this stretch of heaven as though he were documenting the life of a world-famous fashion model: She was slim and tan and dark-eyed and elegant, and everyone in her circle drove convertibles, wore white linen, sunbathed on white sands shaded by striped tents, and spent Saturdays at bullfights and Sundays by the pool.

In 1940 the photographs change. Young shirtless German men in white gym shorts now jog in formation through the streets of Biarritz. The beach where the beautiful people played is now used for maneuvers by *l'armée d'occupation.* The year 1940 was when Matisse and Lydia came to Ciboure, across the bay from Saint-Jean-de-Luz. Having left Paris in advance of the German army, they had stopped first in Bordeaux, then moved farther south. They were trying to make their way back to Nice, but the trains weren't yet running. "And now, my dear Pierre, what do you think of the collective madness that is ravaging both the Old World and the new one?" Matisse wrote to his son. "Do you feel, as I do, that there is something foredoomed about it, and that the whole world is bent on destruction? I think the forgotten cities of Moslem civilization in Iraq—ancient cities whose monuments are as fragile as they are precious. . . .These are some of the oldest monuments in the world. It will take just one bomb to reduce them to dust. And I think how troopships laden with soldiers are being hunted down to be sunk with all hands. It's simply horrible—and for what?"

Saint-Jean-de-Luz's seafront has a modern look, with boxy hotels and swathes of glass, while Ciboure's features Basque houses hugging a hill above the harbor. I liked the drawings I did there. Instead of an ink pen or pencil, I used a black felt tip. Working quickly and with little detail, I sketched the fort, the Basque houses, the plane trees, the church and fishing boats. "I have a room that has windows with verandas, in the Basque manner," Henri Matisse wrote to his son. "It's just a few yards from the channel that leads out towards the sea from the harbor of Saint-Jean-de-Luz. When I look out, I can see the little steamboats that come and go. They are all painted a pure ultramarine blue with a little chimney that is painted pure vermilion. They bring back sardines, anchovies, and mackeral."

On Sunday we drove to Hemingway's Spain for lunch. From Saint-Jean-de-Luz to San Sebastián is only twenty-six kilometers, and if you take the small road you can drive through green hilly farm country with sheep grazing and white Basque houses everywhere and the foothills of the Pyrenees rising in the background. There's no border anymore. Coming back later on the big highway we would see the remnants of a border station, but the gendarmes stood around talking and waved us through "like greeters at Wal-Mart," as Beth put it.

The San Sebastián I had read about in *The Sun Also Rises* seemed like a small village, so I was surprised to find a charming city of large stucco houses, elaborate arches, tile roofs. At the waterfront the ancient ritual was in full swing—couples, families, singles, all dressed

in their Sunday best, were promenading in a rigidly choreographed pattern that took them along the harbor, then right onto the flowered Alameda del Boulevard, past the big gazebo where the black-clad orchestra was playing, down one side of the wide shady boulevard, then back up the other side and to the waterfront again.

Occasionally they would stop to talk to one another, resting for a few moments on one of the many benches along the route. The Spanish are a beautiful people. I saw many elegant old men with silver slicked-back hair and sharp handsome faces, and many pretty women, though not as many pretty older ones. A young boy, maybe seventeen, sat on a bench with a winsome blond girl of the same age or younger. They smiled nervously. He leaned over and kissed her. She glowed. She looked around to see who saw, but she positively glowed. I thought of a wonderful *New Yorker* piece by Peter Schjeldahl that I had clipped for my files. Writing about Vermeer, he says, "The play of sunlight on the collar and cowl of the girl in *Young*

Woman with a Water Pitcher also jolts—it could be the secret of life." I had just glimpsed one of those moments.

We found a café on the boulevard and took an outside table on the front row in the sun. The waiter brought a sampling of tapas— anchovies, Roquefort, crab, eggs, ham, and some potato and cheese balls that were fried like dumplings. After lunch, we wandered through the small streets, eventually finding ourselves in a large sunny square with shady arches on three sides. An accordion trio was playing jazz to an appreciative café crowd, and I managed a quick good sketch of the musicians. Jazz accordion sounded amazingly cool. Maybe I was learning to hear as well as see.

TESSA HAD A new boyfriend, so we didn't see much of her. But Gerard came up a lot over the summer, sometimes just for late-afternoon tea or wine, but quite often for meals. He seemed to like having us in his house, and we enjoyed having a neighbor again. Beth teased him about his girlfriends, and he chuckled and made wry jokes. Having been many places in his life, he knew a lot of things. His stories were funny and self-deprecating, whether about his business trips to China or his motorcycle jaunts into the Sahara. He owned four motorcycles, and at his other house in Mirepoix he had built a small walled-in gazebo where, as he told us, "My biker buddies can sleep and not disturb me with their snoring, umm?" He kept at least the same number of bicycles. On many days he had pedaled sixty kilometers before Beth or I even rode the elevator down to check the mail.

In July our major topic of conversation was the Tour de France, the three-week bicycle race in which Germany's Jan Ullrich was bearing down on the U.S.'s Lance Armstrong. As the duel progressed leg by leg from Paris south over the Alps through Provence and into the Languedoc, Gerard seemed philosophical about it all. I thought I couldn't stand it if Armstrong didn't win. When Bret came for her visit, we decided to go see the Tour in person.

We selected one of the dramatic climbing legs in the Pyrenees, and on a glorious Saturday we exited the A64 west of Toulouse onto a winding two-lane south following the mighty Garonne into the mountains. The countryside was almost unbearably green, with fat cattle grazing in pastures anchored by stone farmhouses. Our destination was Luchon, a revered spa town.

I had a personal interest in seeing Luchon. On January 21, 1944, three days before I was born, my uncle Archie Roland Barlow Jr., a gunner on a B-24 shot down over northern France, parachuted into a village whose citizens hid him until the French Underground could take over. By that time other downed flyers, including some of Roland's crewmates, were in the same situation. Eventually they were transported to Paris, where they waited several weeks in safe houses before being transferred by train—riding among German soldiers—to Toulouse to rendezvous with the guides who were to escort them into the Pyrenees.

A day later they caught the train to just north of Foix, where they jumped off and hid in tall grass before hiking into the mountains. There the initial guides turned them over to the Basque mercenaries who would lead them over the Pyrenees into Andorra and on into Spain. Roland got sick on that first mountain trek and they had to leave him behind. Alone but with help from many French citizens, he made his way back to Foix, Toulouse, and then to Paris, where he searched out the safe house. After resting several weeks, he was ready for another run at the mountains. This time he was successful, and the village that served as his launchpad to freedom was Luchon. It's an amazing story that Uncle Roland told compellingly in a self-published book called *Pursuit in the Pyrenees*. Now, looking at those snowcapped peaks glinting in the sunlight, I wondered what it would take to make me climb them.

Our hotel was on the town's main tree-lined boulevard. On Sunday morning early we set up our beach chairs across the street on the curb where the road started curving in a double dogleg around a pretty park. Beth and Bret went to do some sightseeing, but I stayed in my seat and watched the crowd for a while. It was still several hours until the racers were due to come through. Two little girls in a third-floor window waved to me and giggled, and I waved back, causing them to giggle all the more. That kept up all day. Lots of would-be Tour de Francers were in town wearing snazzy biking clothes. Occasionally a pack of them would zip by my post and lean dramatically into the turn, as though acting out a fantasy. As I sketched them, I thought of all the times as a kid that I came home from a war movie and played army, or watched a football game and immediately dressed out in the Grid Champ uniform I had gotten for Christmas.

In a way, that was the subject of the book I had brought along with me, the critic John Berger's complicated *Ways of Seeing.* "We never look at just one thing," Berger writes. "We are always looking at the relation between things and ourselves." Struggling to absorb the ramifications of that sentence, I had begun to suspect that I wouldn't truly see without distortion until I could see myself differently—as more neutral, perhaps. Berger seemed to be getting at the "unthinking" I had prescribed for myself in Paris. "The way we see things is affected by what we know or what we believe," he says. I did feel different now in France, so cut off from my usual element. Back at home, even assumptions carried the weight of knowledge or belief. I could drive through the American South and see a couple of strangers sipping iced tea on a clean white porch, and I would say to myself, *I know those people.* At that point the damage was done. Here, everything was new, for the moment, anyway. The trick—a very, very hard trick—was to become new myself.

About an hour before the racers arrived, the prerace parade began. Cars and floats emblazoned with advertisers' logos rolled through with horns honking and young pretty people tossing out T-shirts and keychains and beads like at Mardi Gras in New Orleans. One gleaming black truck featured a blow-up of Arnold Schwarzenegger, whose latest *Terminator* was about to open in Europe. We collected our goodies and put on our yellow Tour de France T-shirts and ball caps. Then, while we waited to hear that the racers were coming, I put the finishing touches on a stars-and-stripes poster proclaiming "Arkies *pour* Armstrong."

It was over in no time. They flew past so fast that all we could see were colored blurs. I did grip the camera and try to shoot Bret and Lance as he whizzed by an inch away from her. We wouldn't know for months, until she sent us a framed picture, that I had snapped his yellow jersey just as he brushed past hers.

WE WENT TO Spain to see Salvador Dali's weird house, held our breath as we skirted the Costa Brava's cliffs, and sat with Gerard in the hot stands of the Collioure arena one Saturday evening watching brave matadors hide behind steel shields anytime the *taureau* looked their way. After the picadors had ridden in for the kill on horses outfitted like prehistoric shelled beasts, the splendidly dressed matadors strutted the circumference of the arena with their sphincters so tight that their toes turned out. We watched five kills before calling it a night. So much for Hemingway's fabled bullshit detector.

Bret flew home from Montpellier early one morning, and when she was gone Beth and I drove up to see Anne Pierre-Humbert in Saint-Laurent-la-Vernède, northwest of Avignon. We found her standing in the street waving her arms. Behind her was a high wall with a big door. I loved this house already, before I had even seen inside. The French spend much of their time behind stone walls, closed shutters, high hedges—the protective outer barrier that preserves the sanctity of the inner life. As Anne opened the door and led us in, I found myself thinking back to a train ride that Beth and I had taken from Paris to Auray one evening in the beginning of spring. It was for me one of the most indelible episodes of our entire journey. The light had been warm and golden, and as Beth napped I watched the countryside go by. Cows ambled home and laundry swayed from clotheslines. In time the sky turned a lovely cobalt blue. Clumps of mistletoe were silhouetted in the tree branches. Sometimes I spotted a lamp in a window of one of the big *mas,* but very seldom did I catch a glimpse of people. Eventually the sky went from blue to black, and then all I could see was my own face in the window.

Anne's house was actually two houses connected by a small open courtyard, where she served us tea at a table beneath a shade tree. As we talked, I asked her which door had been the inspiration for Pierre's doorway paintings that I had admired at the Galerie Besseiche in Paris. "Là," she said, pointing to the one we had entered through. I got up and opened it slightly. A ribbon of light cut across the courtyard. "Yes, now I see it."

After tea she showed us the house, which had the feeling of a small mas. An old stone staircase led up to the structure on the left, which had a sunny living room, a bedroom, kitchen, and a bathroom whose window looked out over a tiled terrace. The structure on the right had a ground-floor kitchen/dining room, and maybe a bedroom in the back. "Let's go upstairs," Anne said, and we followed her up the narrow steps. To the right at the landing was the guest room. "One more flight," she said.

At the top of the stairs she opened the door to Pierre's studio. It wasn't as large as his space in Paris, but it was a very comfortable place to paint—high in his light-filled room overlooking his cozy courtyard: within walls within walls. His easel still stood by the window. Across the room, small canvases were stacked like coffee-table books on a low shelf. Anne took them out and showed us—landscapes, figure studies, birds and fish, still lifes. Even small, they had a power. More than that, they had a mystery. In their fluidity, they were no less than portraits of time passing. They captured something elemental about the impermanence of life, which, depending on your point of view, could either be exhilarating or heartbreaking.

"I want you to choose one," Anne said.

We protested, but she insisted. "Pierre means so much to you." She was right about that. I would've loved to hear him tell what he saw when he looked at the world. In any case, he made mutability beautiful.

The picture we picked was of a reclining nude on a blue background. She rested her head on a red pillow, and there was a slash of emerald green beneath her feet. That night we took Anne to dinner in Uzès. After we dropped her back at home, we carried our very first Pierre-Humbert into the hotel room and propped it on the mantel like a jewel-toned night-light.

IN AUGUST IT seemed as if all of Europe had congregated in Collioure. The Feast of the Assumption in mid-month marked the summer's fever pitch. Music rang from every corner of the village. Entranced *sardaners* circled and enthralled twosomes tangoed. Beaches were breast to breast. Boats in the harbor hosted floating parties. On shore, café seats were at a premium. From early morning till late at night, laughter and song rode high on the sea breeze, while the Catalan pennants crackled overhead.

I stayed inside and painted. One picture was of bicycle racers curving in a pack through a colorful French village with the Mediterranean in the background. Another was a scene of my studio in our apartment. It looked from the big main room through the arched, blue-and-white-curtained doorway into the bedroom, where the skylight turned all but the rug white. The front room where my easel stood was darker, but a river of light washed in from the far room. At the top center I showed a hint of the brown overhead beam, and just to the right of that I indicated the slant of the ceiling. I called the painting *My Studio Under the Eaves.*

I wrestled with it most of the month, especially with a rectangle of light on the floor where the sun shone through one of the skylights. I painted it yellow, then white, then light brown. Just as I thought I had it nailed, I would walk through the room and glance at the canvas and see not sunlight, but an obvious rectangle of oil paint. A former art director of mine, the now-famous, fabulously successful outdoor artist Terry Redlin, used to refer to such blemishes as "buckeye," I suppose because your eye could never pass over it without bucking. That's the way this rectangle of light affected me. I could hardly write for thinking about it, and occasionally, in the middle of a chapter, I would slip on my Celebrity Bartender apron and start messing with it again. Two hours later I would go back to writing while a new shade of buckeye rectangle lay on the floor like a welcome mat.

The summer wrapped up with me struggling to sustain this illusion. When September came, the change was again right on cue: overcast skies, cooler temperatures, choppy seas, occasional heavy rain. The tourists disappeared overnight, and café tables were stacked and chained. The blue-striped catamaran sailed out of the harbor for ports unknown, and Beth and I drove to Paris to fly to Arkansas and deal with her mother's estate.

WE WERE GONE three and a half months, more than twice the length of time we expected. It was a very hard, very painful, very emotional process. When it became clear that the business was going to drag into December, we decided to stay in the States through the holidays. Every month on the 19th I wired Gerard money for the rent.

We flew back to France in early January, bringing Snapp with us. He had just turned twelve, but that first night in Paris he sniffed the ground like a bloodhound and leaped like a puppy. He marked a considerable portion of the Left Bank for his own. Over the next couple of days, he would add other firsts to his first airplane flight: First trip to a department store. First visit to a boulangerie. First time to go with us to a café.

We reached Collioure at night in a pounding rain. During our descent from the highway into the village, the church tower rose from the black harbor like memory's ghost. Having stopped off in Perpignan to buy supplies, we now muled the groceries from the car to the elevator while Snapp shook water all over the basement. We were glad to be back, but Beth and I both noticed that it felt different—not as exotic somehow. At a service station on the way down, I'd watched three jake-leg rounders standing outside the store laughing and smoking, beer guts oozing over their jeans. *Rouge necks,* I thought. At the supermarket I was surprised at the number of fat ugly people pushing carts loaded down with bread and cheese. Had they always been there? Hadn't I seen those same wide butts waddling through Wal-Marts from Arkansas to Minnesota?

Gerard was a little surprised to see Snapp, but he was a good sport about it. "Did you have a good shit, umm?" he said, patting Snapp's head as we came in from a walk. Back in the apartment, I became reacquainted with all the niggling nuances that make daily life in France a trial. The French have succeeded brilliantly at solving major life problems such as edging your car too close to the stoplight so you can't tell when the light changes (they post a miniature version of the light low on a nearby pole), and not being able to find a grocery cart because they've all been abandoned on curbs in the parking lot (they charge a euro to unchain a cart from the stack, and you get your money back when you rechain it). But they have no understanding of the concept of *ice,* which means that not only can't you buy bags of it, the French ice trays are designed so that (a) when you stack them, the one on top displaces the water in the one below, and (b) when you try to get ice to pop out of a tray, the tray breaks in two. Similarly, they seem to have no use for tongs, which we couldn't find anywhere. The clingability of their plastic wrap is also challengeable.

Besides the indigenous problems, it quickly became obvious to us that I had not trained Snapp to be a French dog. French dogs trot docilely beside their masters on leashes. Having lived his entire life wandering at will in our Little Rock neighborhood, Snapp hates his leash. When I put him on it he balks, and then I'm faced with giving in and unhooking it or dragging him down the sidewalk like an abusive parent while cliques of disapproving French dog lovers stand by and condemn me—as they should. Beth says the problem is me. Her theory is that I'm projecting some deep-seated power struggle that he's picking up on, and it's true that he doesn't balk as much with her. I'm trying to do better, but in the meantime there's a little white-haired lady in the village whose dog has the same hairdo she does. Every time I let Snapp off his leash, we seem to round a corner and run smack into Madame and her dog, whom Snapp proceeds to sniff while Madame berates me for not keeping *mon chien* on a leash.

Then there's the bathroom situation. Having a dog in a third-floor apartment is a different proposition than having a dog in a single-family house. At home when Snapp wanted to go out early, I simply stumbled to the door, let him out, and wished him well. Now, after enduring a period of his needing a bathroom break at 5 a.m., I found myself lying awake in the wee hours mentally designing a step-stool platform contraption that would fit over our commode. Surely, he could be trained to climb up and use it. I even came up with a brand name: "Here, Spot!"

AND YET: AT a certain stage of life, sunrises become more precious than sunsets. Thanks to Snapp, I've seen more sunrises lately than I've seen in years. They're especially beautiful over the Collioure harbor, the sky an inferno of red and orange and pink and purple while the sea reflects it all as just so much rolling gold. Whatever washes our way, we are back, we are here. And we're looking forward, not backward: There always needs to be a next project. Failure isn't in not selling; failure is in not creating.

This is a year of momentous birthdays for us—Beth's fiftieth, my sixtieth. On my birthday I painted a self-portrait, after Matisse, of myself sitting in his suit at his easel in his room at the Beau Rivage. For Matisse, that picture, which he made his first season in Nice, marked a major turning point. Mine does too, I believe. Matisse got us this far, but now Beth and I continue on. We've made our bargain with the world—we keep our eyes open, and the world shows us fabulous things. Though my technical skills as a painter haven't improved as much as I might have hoped, I know I've made a great leap in understanding paint's purpose and potential: Being alive itself, paint confronts the mystery even when words hang back. In my birthday portrait, the paint took it upon itself to describe me as I probably wouldn't have dared in writing: not just white-bearded and blotchy from age, but wary, walled, questioning.

"Demands to be taken seriously," said Beth, walking through the room where I had my painting propped up to look at while I wrote. "Makes jokes about others, but can't take them about himself."

"Wait a minute, you're cheating," I said. "You didn't just read that from the paint."

"Has a wild side he's afraid to let loose," she said, blowing me a kiss over her shoulder.

For Beth's big birthday, I bought her a compass. It was sterling silver, ordered from Tiffany, and I had her initials engraved on the case. What else do you give a woman hell-bent to wander the world with style? She surprised me with a classic leather club chair from the 1930s. I'm not sure how the two gifts will work together, but this chair, whose burnished brown hide reveals a lifetime of cuts and scratches, is surely the very one Matisse had in mind when he likened his art of balance, purity, and serenity to a good armchair.

Isn't it pretty to think so? said Hemingway's hopeless hero Jake Barnes, and it's true that not everything worked out quite as Matisse had wanted. Does it for anyone? But he didn't give up his search. He kept painting, growing, changing, probing, *seeing*. And in continuing to make his art against all odds, he proved that learning to see is as vital to the art of a life as to the life of an artist.

We placed the comfortable old chair in the bedroom, its rakish Deco slant angled just so beneath the skylight by the bed. In the mornings, the depth of its patina reminds me of the rich caramel cakes my Aunt May always made whenever she heard I was coming. In the afternoons, I look at that *brûlé* leather and think of the Sugar Daddies I loved to lick through long Saturday matinees at the movies in Mississippi. In early evening, the color shifts more toward bourbon. It's the color of sustenance, maybe even of serenity. I find it's a good place to sit on those rare days when art isn't enough.

A Note on Sources

IT'S NO EXAGGERATION to say that this book couldn't have been written had Hilary Spurling not paved my way with her groundbreaking biography *The Unknown Matisse: A Life of Henri Matisse: The Early Years, 1869–1908* (New York: Alfred A. Knopf, 1998). In the following paragraphs I've included a list of written sources, but Spurling's work requires singling out as indispensable to *Chasing Matisse* from inception to completion. The other dog-eared veteran of my own personal journey is *Henri Matisse: A Retrospective,* by John Elderfield (New York: Museum of Modern Art, 1992). How many hours have I spent engrossed in its unparalleled display spanning all the periods of Matisse's art?

In addition to those two stalwarts, Jack Flam's *Matisse on Art* (Berkeley: University of California Press, 1995) lent me the benefit of the painter's own analyses of his work. In a similar vein, John Russell's *Matisse: Father & Son* (New York: Harry N. Abrams, 1999) provided a priceless glimpse into the mind (and family) of the artist through letters between Henri and son Pierre. James Elkins's brilliant *What Painting Is* (New York: Routledge, 2000) offered a whole new way to view the insanity of painting. And when it came to the difficult business of seeing like an artist, John Berger's classic *Ways of Seeing* (London: Penguin Books, 1972), Rudolf Arnheim's *Art and Visual Perception: A Psychology of the Creative Eye* (Berkeley: University of California Press, 1954, 1974), and Gyorgy Kepes's *Language of Vision* (Mineola, N.Y.: Dover Publications, 1995) opened my eyes to just how far I had to go.

Other very helpful volumes included *Matisse in Morocco: The Paintings and Drawings, 1912–1913* (Washington, D.C.: National Gallery of Art, 1990), especially the essays by Jack Cowart, Pierre Schneider, and John Elderfield; *Henri Matisse: With Apparent Ease* by Lydia Delectorskaya (Paris: Adrien Maeght Editeur, 1988); and

The Artist in His Studio by Alexander Liberman (New York: Random House, 1988).

Among the scores of articles I drew upon, I especially want to acknowledge Stanley Meisler's "Points of View," about Paul Signac, in *Smithsonian;* Peter Schjeldahl's "The Sphinx," about Johannes Vermeer, in the *New Yorker;* and Hilary Spurling's "Matisse on Belle Île" in the *Burlington Magazine.*

Acknowledgments

AN UNDERTAKING OF the magnitude of *Chasing Matisse* requires so much support that I hardly know where to begin. My agents, Michelle Tessler and Michael Carlisle, championed the idea even when it was still half-baked, and Michelle forced me to continue defining the proposal until she thought it was ready to go. She then delivered me into the capable hands of editor Leslie Meredith of Free Press, who forced me to continue defining the manuscript until *she* thought *it* was ready to go. I'm especially proud of this book, which always was a labor of love, and I'm grateful to both Michelle and Leslie for their vision and persistence. I also want to single out Eric Fuentecilla for coming up with the book's dynamic cover design, and my able copy editor, Tom Pitoniak, for his meticulous work, which included correcting more than *un peu* of incorrect French.

Launching and sustaining Beth and me on this grand adventure took an international coalition. In the United States, Mims Wright donated many hours of his valuable time advising us on everything from Web site to travel logistics to financial planning. Matt Olson and his team at Matmon Inc. made www.chasingmatisse.com one of the best-looking places on the Internet (special thanks to Thaddeus James, who created the site's look, and to Jason Miller, who made the look work). Congressman Vic Snyder of Arkansas, with special input from his assistant Devon Cockrell, helped get us off on the right foot, as did Cynthia Edwards and Rod Sweetman of Senator Blanche Lincoln's office. Keith Bellows, editor of *National Geographic Traveler,* provided financial assistance early on. Alfred Celentano of Europe By Car did everything possible to make our series of leased and rented automobiles affordable. ("We're all envious," he said. "We want to help.")

Lloyd Cobb, our great friend and accountant, made sure Celentano (and all the others) got paid and that we worried as little as possible about money. John Gaynor and John Uragami showed admirable good humor in making sense of income-tax records cobbled together on the road. Betsy Otwell, Mary Busby, and Cheryl Case helped smooth over the thorny issue of insurance, and Dr. Stephen Tucker often consulted by long distance regarding medicines and prescriptions. Patti Kymer found a much-appreciated renter for our house and car, and then, when the house finally sold, used her precious days off from her job as an anesthesiologist to oversee the final packing, making sure that plates and boxes and furniture went where they were supposed to go (a very special thank-you to Patti's husband, B. J. Davis, who must have cursed me every time he hauled a load of our stuff up the three flights to his attic). Dianne Cobb stood in as on-the-spot surrogate mother to our girls whenever needed. And many, many friends supported us with a steady stream of encouraging e-mails— notably Thom Hall, Lynda Dixon, Ginger Snapp, Trish McAlister, Susan May, Susan Gregory, Elizabeth Evans, Steve Wright, Bill Allen, David Sanders, Todd Bagwell, and Buddy Slate.

Based in New York, the stalwart and indefatigable Louise O'Brien, of the French Tourist Network, smoothed our path in France, making calls on our behalf and getting us into places where Matisse once lived. Jacques Misery of Paris Welcome Service was the first Frenchman we met, and he's since driven us and our family and friends back and forth between Paris and the *aeroport,* as well as on other missions. Michel Tessel of French Home Rentals donated his Marais apartment for three weeks at the beginning (additional thanks for that to FHR's very supportive representative in Oregon, Randall Vemer). Ruben Milogis befriended us and introduced us to *his* friends. Alice Pennington-Mellor became more commonly known to Beth and me as Saint Alice of Auray, for her extraordinary good deeds on our behalf. Because of Alice, we're able to thank Anne Pierre-Humbert for her instant and lasting generosity, Mike and Denise Cornall for their astonishing hospitality, Jean-Pierre and Véronique Leger for their warm *Breton* welcome, and Guy Vignais for his friendship both to us and to our dog, Snapp, for whom Guy became Veterinarian-at-Large once we brought Snapp to France. When we began the driving part of our journey, Michel Malric at the wonderful Hôtel Saint-Germain at 88, rue du Bac, offered us "a home in Paris," and for some seventeen months thereafter he and his staff stored our bags, received our mail, and welcomed us home whenever we needed to visit. I want to thank them by name: at the desk, Daniel Peraffan and Vassanda Rettiname (Wanda), ably backed up by Dany, Ram, Boby, Prasana, Manil, Rangi, Rohana, Sena, and Siri. A warm *merci* also to Madame Malric. I hope all the buyers of this book will make the Hôtel Saint-Germain *their* home in Paris whenever they're visiting.

During our months on the road, we encountered many people— *business* people—whose imaginations were movingly stirred by our wanderings. In Etretat, the staff at the Dormy House made their priceless view available at a great price. At Saint-Jean-de-Luz's luxurious Hotel Hélianthal, Jean-Christophe Dambreville supported us with a special rate, personal help in making further reservations, and beyond-the-call-of-duty restructuring of those plans when Beth's mother died and we couldn't keep our schedule. I've already written about Le Cacharel, in the Camargue, and how the owner and his staff unflinchingly took charge of all our things while we flew home for the funeral. I also want to thank an employee from Air France— Fatisa B., said the name on her blouse—who, hearing why we were traveling, got us on an earlier Air France/Delta flight that Delta reps hadn't even told us about. Not only that, but she accomplished it during a terminal-clearing bomb threat that she ignored until she got us booked on the plane.

In Collioure, the Pous family extended us a warm Catalan welcome at their legendary artists' enclave, the Hotel des Templiers, where Véronique Crepin attended to all our needs, including translation. At the Hôtel Grimaldi in Nice, Joanna and Yann Zedde and their friendly crew made our ten-day stay seem too short. At the Villa Le Rêve in Vence, Joelle Audry became not just our host, but our friend. In Saint-Tropez, the staff at the elegant Hotel Le Yaca treated two budget guests like movie stars. And in Aix-en-Provence, Ricardo at the Grand Hôtel Negre Coste extended us a special welcome even though Aix wasn't part of the story. All of this, I feel compelled to point out, was while our friends at home were being told that the French hate Americans.

In Morocco, we owe special thanks to Benachir Akli and his colleague Adel Mzil of Olive Branch Tours in Casablanca. They threw their considerable resources into providing us a safe and productive trip, and through their contacts in the travel industry arranged extraordinarily generous lodging in extraordinarily beautiful hotels. We're especially grateful to Omar Azizi for the hospitality he and his staff showed us at the Palais Jamai in Fès, and to Sanae Bakkali Kasmi and her team at the El Minzah in Tangier. Thanks, too, to the fine staff of the Royal d'Anfa in Casablanca.

Many, many others helped in ways so numerous that it's impossible to mention all their kindnesses here, so I'll just list their names and trust that they know how much we appreciate their help: Chris Ashcraft, Stephanie and Jerry Atchley, David Bailin, Bev Best, Julia Bethay, Liz and Bruce Cochran, Warren Criswell, Augusta Day, Monique Diderich and Robert Bonet, Kit Frick, Tom Gray, all the staff at Hillcrest Animal Hospital, especially Lorie Mabry who coordinated preparations for Snapp's trip abroad; Connie and Fritz Hollenberg, Kathleen Hooker Jones, Ellen Kennon, Madame Claude Malaussena, Dureen and Jim Massey, Mary Kay Mitchell, Rachel Mollenkopf, Veronique and Eric Monsel, Gemma and Kevin O'Toole, Jim Ritchie, Jeffrey Robinson, Reverend Betsy Singleton, Dr. James Suen, and William Whitworth.

Finally, I want to thank my family—my mother, Pat; my brother, Philip; my sons, David and Matthew, and their wives, Erin and Samantha—for their constant support. To my late mother-in-law, Bobbye Arnold, I owe a debt that can never be repaid. As for my stepdaughters, Blair and Bret, noone sacrificed more for someone else's dream. At least they get to come to France on holidays! First, last, and foremost, however, I thank my wife, Beth. She saw this book before I did, and she made it a gift to me, knowing it was the idea I was trying to summon up. To make it a reality, she worked tirelessly and selflessly, putting her own work on hold for more than two years, to serve this project as strategist, travel agent, Webmaster, marketing manager, diarist, photographer, concierge, navigator, supply sergeant, drill sergeant, office manager, hostess, model, art critic, cheerleader, and Big Whine suppressor. Compared to Beth's, my job seemed almost easy.

Index

About the Author

A former magazine editor, JAMES MORGAN is the author of *The Distance to the Moon: A Road Trip into the American Dream,* which the *New York Times Book Review* named one of the "notable books" of 1999. He is also author of *If These Walls Had Ears: The Biography of a House,* which became a selection of the Quality Paperback Book Club. In 1994 Morgan collaborated with Virginia Kelley, President Clinton's mother, on her best-selling, critically acclaimed autobiography, *Leading with My Heart.* Most recently, Morgan collaborated on *Stronger in the Broken Places: Nine Lessons for Turning Crisis into Triumph* by James Lee Witt, former director of the Federal Emergency Management Agency.

Morgan's articles and essays have appeared in publications such as the *New Yorker,* the *Atlantic Monthly,* the *Washington Post Magazine, Preservation, Men's Journal,* and *National Geographic Traveler,* and he has written a screenplay, *Hot Springs,* for Paramount Pictures.

James Morgan currently lives in Paris, France. He can be contacted by clicking on www.ChasingMatisse.com.